An Introduction to Constitutional Interpretation

AN INTRODUCTION TO
CONSTITUTIONAL
INTERPRETATION

Cases in Law and Religion

Lief Carter

University of Georgia

Longman
New York & London

An Introduction to Constitutional Interpretation: Cases in Law and Religion

Longman, 95 Church Street, White Plains, N.Y. 10601

Associated companies:
Longman Group Ltd., London
Longman Cheshire Pty., Melbourne
Longman Paul Pty., Auckland
Copp Clark Pitman, Toronto
Addison-Wesley Publishing Company, Inc.

Senior editor: David J. Estrin
Cover design: Anne M. Pompeo
Production supervisor: Anne P. Armeny

Library of Congress Cataloging-in-Publication Data

Carter, Lief H.
    An introduction to constitutional interpretation : cases in law
    and religion / Lief H. Carter
        p.   cm.
    Includes bibliographical references and index.
    ISBN 0-8013-0316-8
    1. Freedom of religion—United States—Cases.   2. Church and
state—United States—Cases.   I. Title.
KF4783.A7C37   1991
342.73′0852—dc20
[347.302852]
                                        90-43846
                                        CIP
ABCDEFGHIJ-MU-99   98   97   96   95   94   93   92   91   90

For John and Rachel Carter
and
Betsy Carter

Contents

Preface   *xi*

1 INTRODUCTION   1

The Problem of Constitutional Interpretation ————————   1
Constitutional Interpretation and Politics ————————————   2
Interpretation as a Form of Power ——————————————————   3
Two Cases about Law and Religion ——————————————————   5
Audience ———————————————————————————————————   6
Bibliographic Notes ———————————————————————————   8

2 FREE EXERCISE OF RELIGION:
The Case of the Captain's Yarmulke   10

The Case ———————————————————————————————————   11
Postscript ———————————————————————————————————   24
The Constitutional Law of Free Exercise ————————————   25
Precedents in *Goldman*: A Dialogue ——————————————   27
Conclusion —————————————————————————————————   33
Bibliographic Notes ———————————————————————————   34

3 ESTABLISHMENT LAW:
Genesis v. *Charles Darwin*   35

"We Are a Religious People" ————————————————————   36
Thomas Jefferson's "Wall of Separation" ————————————   39

The Case _____ 42
Postscript _____ 68
Another Dialogue _____ 69
Conclusion _____ 71
Bibliographic Notes _____ 71

4 THE HISTORY OF CHURCH AND STATE:
Two Lectures   73

Lecture I: The Historical Basis of Liberal Individualism: Keynote
Address to the 1990 Annual Meeting of the National Bar
Association _____ 74
Lecture II: On the Need for Communitarian Values: Keynote Address
to the 1991 Annual Meeting of the National Bar Association _____ 84
Conclusion _____ 92
Bibliographic Notes _____ 92

5 FROM CORRESPONDENCE TO COHERENCE:
Trends in Natural Philosophy   94

Classical Philosophy: Truth as Correspondence with Nature _____ 95
The Modern Scientific Revolution: Truth as Coherence _____ 96
The Professor and the Reverend _____ 99
The Morality of Science and Religion _____ 102
Bibliographic Notes _____ 106

6 RELIGION AND CONSTITUTIONAL INTERPRETATION 108

Religion and Right Answers _____ 109
The Bible as Narrative _____ 110
What Biblical Stories Teach _____ 111
Conclusion _____ 113
Bibliographic Notes _____ 113

7 GOOD LAW   115

Where Are We? _____ 115
Narrative and Conversation in Law and Religion _____ 117
Coherence, Trust, and Justice _____ 119
Evaluating Goldman and Edwards _____ 120

''To Enter into the Conversation Is the Point of Education'' ———— 123

The Last Case ————————————————————————— 124

Bibliographic Notes ————————————————————— 149

Bibliography   *151*

Index   *155*

Preface

The task of constitutional theory . . . should be to contribute to a political movement that may bring about a society in which civic virtue may flourish.
—Mark Tushnet

This argument suggests not that the university has *a civic mission, but that the university* is *a civic mission, is civility itself, defined as the rules and conventions that permit a community to facilitate conversation and the kinds of discourse upon which all knowledge depends. On this model, learning is a social activity that can take place only within a discursive community bringing together reflection and experience. On this model, knowledge is an evolving communal construction whose legitimacy rests directly on the character of the social process. On this model, education is everywhere and always an ineluctably communal enterprise.*
—Benjamin Barber

This book explores contemporary approaches to constitutional interpretation. Its academic roots lie in critical theory, in the Rortyean "new pragmatism," in the work of Stanley Fish, and in the law and language movement in legal theory. However, these theories themselves reject the notion that one must learn interpretive theories in order to understand the political practice of constitutional interpretation. So, this book speaks to a general student audience and presumes no prior digging among these academic roots. For the student or lay reader, this book begins with the observation that, at least in our day, people don't seem to agree about much of anything. They certainly don't agree about interpretive theory. But we can converse and disagree in ways that connect us to each other. This book suggests how we, or any modern pluralist culture, can talk in ways that preserve respect for constitutional decision making even when we disagree. It does so by examining rather closely two recent First Amendment decisions, the free exercise case of *Goldman* v. *Weinberger* and the establishment case of *Edwards* v. *Aguillard*.

My approach to constitutional interpretation may strike some academics as curious. This book does not analyze in any detail the many modes, approaches, and techniques of interpretation. It says virtually nothing about modern hermeneutics, critical theory, the new pragmatism, Richard Rorty, James Boyd White, or Stanley Fish. Instead it assumes that the best way to learn these perspectives is to practice them. Contemporary theory confirms law's inherently discursive, experiential, aesthetic, and political character. At a deeper level, however, this same theory urges us to learn about law, or about any social activity, in the same discursive ways. A book will not teach the political reality of law-doing if it reviews the various theories of legal reasoning and constitutional interpretation and points out all the flaws in each. Such descriptions and analyses represent a scholastic activity whose structure, whose audience of professionals and graduate students, and therefore whose politics, differ greatly from the political activity of deciding cases. It might teach what professors do, but it won't teach what lawyers and judges do.

Hence this book strives to convey to a general audience the discursive politics of appellate court lawmaking by modeling discourse rather than by analyzing discourse to death. My experience teaching constitutional law by using Murphy, Fleming, and Harris's *American Constitutional Interpretation* (1986) has motivated this book. That work, a superb extension of the familiar constitutional casebook genre, elaborates all major approaches, modes, and techniques of constitutional interpretation, from literalism and the intent of the framers to Charles Black's structuralism to Sotirios Barber's aspirational approach. Partway through my course, however, I play a game with my students. We put the Murphy, Fleming, and Harris interpretive approaches, modes, and techniques in three hats. A student chooses any case the course has covered. We then pull a slip from each hat and justify the case outcome, and often the dissenting position, in the terms we drew from the hats. We have yet to fail to construct coherent justifications for any case outcome this way. Students soon see that judges and cases mix the methods up, and there is no necessary connection between any constitutional issue and any interpretive method.

This nestling of these theories in the rich cases only emphasizes how tenuous are the connections between interpretive theories and what judges do. The experience teaches Holmes's truth that general propositions do not decide concrete cases. To limit the meaning of these cases to these indeterminate interpretive forms has the same effect on our appreciation of law as it would if we reduced analysis of a painting to the colors the artist used. Picasso's "Girl before the Mirror" describes for me that moment when we first sense the finitude of our lives and the inevitability of our aging. It may mean something quite different to another viewer. But it doesn't help either of us much to note that Picasso paints the girl's mirror image as an older woman in darker, cooler colors than those representing the girl before the mirror. This fact may contribute to the overall coherence we find in the work. However, this one fact about Picasso's creation hardly captures the essence of the work. Its essence, for me, lies in the coherence we experience in the work as a whole. The same truth applies to appellate court decisions.

The "awful task of judging," as Felix Frankfurter once called it, does not at its core "interpret" through these conventional categories any more than the core act of painting "uses color." Interpretations, like colors, or musical pitches, lead to many different but equally satisfactory results. Judging has something to do with achieving justice. Constitutional judging tries, though often badly, to "bring about a society in which civic virtue may flourish." It tries to weave interpretive methods together with many other elements in our lives in order to confirm that we can act justly. In my view, justice is something we experience through the quality of the communion we have with the decider and the work she creates. It is not something we can know only by academic analysis. Some of us experience it sometimes, others at other times. This experience of political connectedness in some ways parallels religious experiences; it is partly for this reason that this book uses religion cases to make its points. This book uses a dialogue format at several points in the hope that it will help enhance that experience. I hope readers will find that I have created a coherent position and that in doing so I become a member of a community readers can trust living with. That, I think, is the best that law and religion can do for any of us.

To put it another way, the tradition of teaching law Socratically rests on the truth that law, at least the Anglo-American common law heritage, is fundamentally discursive. This perhaps too familiar dialogue may illustrate:

STUDENT TO PROFESSOR: So what's the answer?

PROFESSOR: There isn't any one answer. This material is complicated. Answers depend on perspectives, and all I want is for you to answer in terms of a perspective you can defend.

STUDENT: I know that's the *real* answer. I just want to know what you're looking for on the test. My career depends on my GPA.

PROFESSOR: If that's your perspective, then you do not care to enter into community with me, to converse with me about what it means for you and me to belong to the same community.

I make no effort to be comprehensive here. Comprehensiveness, itself a scholastic exercise, would require an encyclopedia. Coherence requires a frame. This book's audience, lay students of constitutional law, sets its frame. Democratic practice must not disenfranchise the layperson from evaluating judicial opinions. My reviews of medieval history, philosophy of science, theology, political philosophy, and so on are samples of ways an educated layperson might frame a coherent reaction to these cases. I do not offer them as "the truth." Measured by the standards of a scholarly treatise, my argument will seem incomplete and often superficial. It simplifies and fictionalizes. But that is exactly what judicial opinions do. And so do scholarly treatises, only in different ways.

Thus I hope this book takes a small step toward restoring the spirit of the liberal arts. Doing so requires broad thinking, integrative thinking, not technical thinking. Roger Sale, writing in Herbert Costner's *New Perspectives on Liberal Education* (1989), says

> The task may be the simple but elusive one of living decently and well; it may be that of listening to music, watching a movie or ballet, with intelligent pleasure; it may be that of striving for an intelligent, or even an intelligible, body politic; it may be that of exploring what currently are the frontiers of medicine or philosophy.

This book encourages the layperson to engage the legal process with intelligent pleasure, not technical correctness.

ACKNOWLEDGMENTS

Many sources have helped me put these ideas together. Besides Murphy, Fleming, and Harris, I'm especially grateful to Frank Alexander and John Witte of Emory University for giving me copies of their extensive and exhaustive photo-copied law school readings, to the Hon. John Noonan for his book, *The Believer and the Powers That Are* (1987), to Sandy Levinson, whose book *Constitutional Faith* (1988) and whose personal encouragement I especially value, and above all to Milner Ball, my friend, teacher, and gadfly. For a variety of reasons, I studied this past year in the lay program in theology called "Education for Ministry" created by the School of Theology at the University of the South. I have benefited immensely from Charles Winters, William Griffin, and Richard Dietrich's *Education for Ministry: Year One, Hebrew Scriptures*, and even more from Dr. Cecil Hudson and the members of the weekly EFM study group. I suspect all these sources would disagree with much in this book, and they have no responsibility for its imperfections. I trust only that we share the belief that we are redeemed from our sins, or, in secular language, that when we make fools of ourselves, we don't do a permanent job.

I deeply appreciate the smooth and accommodating work of the Longman staff and associates, particularly David Estrin, Shelley Flannery, Halley Gatenby, Victoria Mifsud, and Janice Wiggins. Finally, my special thanks go to Susan Austin and Diane Wahlers of Athens, who far exceeded the call of duty in helping me meet my last-minute deadlines.

AN INTRODUCTION TO

CONSTITUTIONAL INTERPRETATION

CHAPTER 1

Introduction

The more you press in towards the heart of a narrowly bounded historical problem, the more likely you are to encounter in the problem itself a pressure which drives you outward beyond those bounds.

—Arthur O. Lovejoy

THE PROBLEM OF CONSTITUTIONAL INTERPRETATION

The United States Constitution in Article VI describes itself as "the supreme law of the land." Article III gives the Supreme Court jurisdiction to decide cases and controversies arising under this supreme law. In 1803, in *Marbury v. Madison,* the Court interpreted this language to give itself the power to strike down acts of government inconsistent with the Constitution. The Court has done so with increasing frequency, especially in this century. Many of these decisions provoke intense controversy. In 1989, for example, *Texas v. Johnson* struck down by a 5–4 vote a conviction for burning an American flag in public because the statute punishing desecration of the flag violated the constitutional protection of freedom of speech. The President immediately proposed a constitutional amendment to protect the flag. Congress responded by passing the Flag Protection Act of 1989, which the Supreme Court, by the same vote, struck down in June of 1990 in *U.S. v. Eichman.* Later that month a proposed constitutional amendment to protect the flag failed to receive the two-thirds vote required to pass in the House of Representatives.

How can we tell whether the Court interprets the Constitution well or whether we should amend the document itself? How can we tell whether the Constitution gives courts the power of judicial review, or protects flag-burning? This is the problem of constitutional interpretation. Interpretation is a political problem just now because neither lawyers nor scholars have agreed about how to answer these questions. We have no agreement about how to decide what the Constitution means. In *Marbury*, Chief Justice Marshall did not demonstrate that the courts have a power to interpret the Constitution *superior* to the interpretive power of other branches of government. Four of the nine justices in the flag-burning cases dissented. How shall we resolve this deep and persistent disagreement over fundamental questions about who we are and what we stand for? This book proposes a way to structure and clarify arguments about how good the Court's constitutional interpretations are, in spite of the prospect that we will never agree on one best way to interpret.

CONSTITUTIONAL INTERPRETATION AND POLITICS

The problem of interpretation is not merely a failure of ivory tower professors to agree on a theory. The Supreme Court plays a political role comparable to that of Congress, the Executive branch, and state and local governments. When it interprets the Constitution, it tells other branches of government what they may and may not do. It governs the government. In our common law system, a decision by the Supreme Court (and by all federal and state appellate courts) creates a precedent which speaks authoritatively for the future. Just as elections and legislation do, these precedents create policies that reallocate resources among citizens and promote public values that some people approve and others reject.

Interpretation changes people's wealth and lives. When an interpretation concludes that the Constitution permits the death penalty, it kills. The Supreme Court decides hundreds of constitutional issues each year. Since the Court does not possess power of purse or power of sword, these decisions depend on public acceptance. Some, like the recent flag-burning decisions, the 1954 school desegregation decision, and the school prayer decisions in the early 1960s, make headlines around the country. Constitutional interpretation itself has become politicized. President Reagan nominated Robert Bork to the Supreme Court in 1987 because Bork advocated an approach to constitutional interpretation that Reagan endorsed. The Senate Judiciary Committee disagreed with that approach and rejected the Bork nomination. Hence this book examines not just academic theories of interpretation but a political phenomenon in the raw.

Robert Bork (1990) advocated interpreting the Constitution by discovering the principles that guided the men who wrote it and applying them the same way now. Other theories of constitutional interpretation include the following:

1. Enforcing the document only as far as a literal reading of its words allows.
2. Enforcing the document only to solve the historical problems faced by those who wrote it.

3. Determining its meaning over time through the development of a consistent body of Supreme Court precedents.

4. Discovering the eternal principles of natural law that underlie all efforts to promote human justice.

5. Treating the Constitution as an incomplete statement of a theory of good government and filling in the constitutional blanks and ambiguities consistently with that theory.

6. Following whatever contemporary popular opinions think the document ought to mean.

This book will touch on each of these ways of interpreting the Constitution, but a warning is in order. Not only have scholars, judges, lawyers, and politicians failed to agree among themselves, let alone with each other, about how to interpret the Constitution, but the Supreme Court has never consistently practiced any of these theories. We have no more reason to expect the Court to settle the problem of interpretation than we have to expect that we will discover the one right way to interpret the Bible.

People interpret texts in all sorts of ways, often to suit the result they have already reached on other, more personal grounds. They reach conflicting answers, and they then tend to fight to defend the correctness of their own reading. For millennia, people have killed one another in the name of both legal and religious righteousness. Part of the problem of constitutional interpretation is to avoid a similar fate in American politics.

INTERPRETATION AS A FORM OF POWER

Thus what might at first appear as a dry academic exercise in interpretive theory leads to the most fundamental question in all politics: How can those who rule use power to promote community rather than destroy it? At least since Nietzsche and Durkheim, and maybe since Plato, social observers have noted that communities define their boundaries in terms of "enemies," of aliens, minorities, and the like. When communities define their existence in terms of faith, they must defend their political existence by destroying nonbelievers. Only nonbelievers, other people, can blaspheme a faith. They must die because they threaten to obliterate the community. Since reason and experience by definition often contradict faith, such threats to the community constantly occur, and the community of faith must constantly defend the faith or risk obliteration. Moreover, political leaders, if they wish to retain their moral leadership, have no choice but to escalate their commitment to the faith when it is challenged. In John Updike's book *Roger's Version* (1986), Dale, a graduate student bent on proving the existence of God through a mammoth computer analysis of samples of all data about the universe, says, "The devil is doubt." Roger, an aging professor of theology, responds:

The devil is the absence of doubt. He's what pushes people into suicide bombings, into setting up extermination camps. Doubt may give your dinner a funny taste, but it's faith that goes out and kills.

In the week I began writing this book, the late Ayatollah Khomeini declared Salman Rushdie's book *Satanic Verses* blasphemous, and his followers called for Rushdie's execution. No matter that the Koran, the object of the alleged blasphemy, appears to call at least for a trial prior to such an execution. Having lost the religious war against Islamic Iraq, the Islamic Iranians needed to reassert their moral leadership of the faith.

Here we meet political power in its rawest form: brute force and coercion. The history of western civilization suggests that this use of power inevitably escalates into the kind of warfare that destroys community. Rulers, including the late Ayatollah, seek to escape such destruction by disguising power in the cloak of authoritative legitimacy. However, when rulers base their authority to act merely on their status as rulers, the most they can achieve is a stratified political system, a system of rulers and ruled, rich and poor, noble and common, "us against them."

Fortunately, rulers possess a third and least destructive way of using political power. We may call it reason, or justification, or simply influence. Here rulers rule by trying to persuade others, by showing that an idea or an action would enhance the lives of ruler and ruled alike. This most benign form of political power explains why democracies elect rulers on the basis of their campaign statements and positions, and why appellate judges write opinions justifying their decisions. The constitutional text serves as a starting place for leaders to justify decisions and thus influence ways community members think and act. The process sustains the members' commitment to the community, even when they disagree about a particular interpretation.

This pattern, as we shall see, has much in common with biblical interpretation. We take the Bible as text seriously, but we have hardly agreed either about what it means or how to decide what it means. And how do we respond politically when biblical and constitutional interpretation intersect? We frequently learn about such intersections in news stories of lawsuits filed to resolve political conflicts over religious values. The religious basis for the abortion controversy popped up daily in the news for several weeks in the spring of 1989, when the Supreme Court heard oral argument reconsidering *Roe v. Wade*, and again when the Court announced its decision in *Webster*. We read of parents convicted of manslaughter and sentenced to jail for praying over a dying child when a trip to the hospital would have saved the child's life, and of the satanist who claims religious freedom to engage in animal torture. We even read of the potential hypocrisy of the Court itself. The Court that struck down prayer and Bible reading in the public schools, and that outlawed prayers before high school football games, begins each of its sessions with the invocation, "God save the United States and this honorable court." On June 4, 1990, the Court in *Board of Education v. Mergens* upheld the Equal Access Act of 1984 requiring public schools to allow student Bible clubs to meet on campus if such schools also allowed secular extracurricular clubs to meet. When the Court decides these seemingly inconsistent cases, we need at least some reassurance that the Court does not in such cases merely hide behind its cloak of authority. Unless its justifications honestly seek to persuade, the Court will return us to the bifurcated politics of us against them.

TWO CASES ABOUT LAW AND RELIGION

This book examines in depth two recent Supreme Court interpretations of the First Amendment's two clauses prohibiting the establishment of religion and protecting the free exercise thereof. The First Amendment seems to state our most important rights, and the first of these denies the government certain powers over religious matters. The free-exercise clause seeks to preserve each person's ability to practice her religion without governmental interference on nonreligious grounds. The establishment clause tries to prevent the problems created when the state and the church officially unite, such as by persecuting the unorthodox or taxing citizens to support a faith they don't accept. In some respects the two religion clauses support each other. When church and state join forces, they tend strongly to establish orthodoxies and to use the power of the state to punish free exercise of unorthodox religions, or to punish those who profess no religion at all. But the clauses can oppose one another. If a public school teacher or a political leader belongs to an evangelical religious faith, her religious convictions might urge her to convert her classroom students to the faith. However, the establishment clause would prevent her from freely exercising her impulse to do so through her office.

Our free-exercise case, *Goldman v. Weinberger,* concluded that the Air Force may require an officer—in this case a clinical psychologist and Orthodox rabbi—to remove his yarmulke while on duty indoors. Goldman, the Air Force said, had failed to conform to its regulation that only military policemen could wear headgear indoors. This interpretation of the free-exercise clause placed the importance of military discipline higher than Goldman's freedom to exercise an ancient requirement of his religion. As he interpreted it, his religion required him to keep his head covered before God.

The establishment case, *Edwards v. Aguillard,* struck down Louisiana's "Balanced Treatment for Creation-Science and Evolution-Science in Public Instruction Act." The Court interpreted the establishment clause of the First Amendment (as applied to the states through its incorporation into the due process clause of the Fourteenth Amendment) to prohibit Louisiana from requiring public school teachers who present evolutionary theories of biological development to teach creation-science versions, and vice versa.

I have written about only two religion cases so that we may examine their issues in depth, but we shall find that examining the Court's work in just these two cases will, as Lovejoy's epigraph for this chapter suggests, push us to reexamine many of the liberal arts and to integrate our understanding of history, philosophy of science, moral theory, and religion itself.

Studying these two cases will urge you to think of law not as a formula for calculating legal or political or moral truth but as a way of communicating and debating about our experiences. When we do this well, we may support the community even when we disagree. Each of the two cases takes the form of a debate among the justices about the nature of good law. I suggest that there are ways of assessing whether a given judge debated well or badly that don't depend on the outcome the judge reached in the case. We may have no demonstrably correct answers in law or religion, but better and worse ways to state and justify positions in law and religion do exist. Good law is possible for the same reasons good religion is possible: by one's abandoning the absolutist dogmas that kill and employing instead the virtues of honesty, courage, and openness to our capacity to care for strangers. This book does not teach any correct interpretive technique; it promotes an attitude toward the Constitution.

Hegel once said that institutions, laws, and constitutions "from which the spirit has flown" are doomed. The Constitution defines who and what we are as a nation. For many people it is the moral centerpoint of the nation, the place we go in hope of finding answers to questions about what science and morality really mean in political life. What the Supreme Court says that the Constitution means frames the deepest moral issues we face. We find that constitutional law, when taught well, gives us a sense that some good beyond economic self-interest ties us together. When taught well it satisfies a deep yearning to connect with our political community because we have experienced ways in which it is good. The Constitution serves our public lives in the same ways religion serves our private lives. They both offer hope of answers, or maybe they simply offer hope.

AUDIENCE

Studying constitutional law has for decades been a particularly popular part of a liberal education. Unfortunately, the teaching of constitutional law has tended to lose sight of its normative mission. The reason has to do partly with the increasing professionalization of our lives. Constitutional law has become either something that lawyers and judges do or something that academics study and theorize about. We academics tend either to describe what the legal process does or to teach academic theories about what law ought to be and do. Neither approach appreciates that the bulk of people who study constitutional law will become neither lawyers nor college professors. Their yearning for a heightened sense of their own capacity to judge the quality of what the Court does falls in the gap.

Let me personalize this more. Obviously I can't know much about you, but I assume you study law in the liberal arts tradition. I assume you have already spent some time in a classroom reading and debating the outcomes and reasons in legal cases. I assume you know basic legal procedures and terms and that you have at least a sketch of the 200 plus years of constitutional lawmaking by the U.S. Supreme Court. But I assume that the press of cases, in constitutional law or business law or criminal justice or whatever law you study, has left you frustrated. Frustrated because you do not have time to dig deeply enough into any one case to satisfy your own desire to judge its "goodness" well. I assume you would like to know enough about a case and the materials—the history, the precedents, the alternative moral theories, and the techniques of legal analysis—to form your own confident conclusion about the goodness of what a court has decided. I assume you are frustrated because you feel you cannot do so unless you get a law degree, and perhaps become a philosopher and historian as well. You feel that, like nearly everything else in a world dominated by "experts," law is the province of specialists. Who am I, you ask, to judge what the Supreme Court has said, or to criticize what professors tell me to believe about law?

I try to alleviate that frustration in this book. Democratic theory, which arose out of the Protestant Reformation's rejection of the Catholic Church's claim of power through expertise, presumes that you don't need to be an expert to make sound political judgments. You can develop your own sense of what you think the Constitution should mean in specific cases, without having to become a professional expert, just as you may lead a religiously meaningful life without completing formal training in theology. In other words, what follows tries to debunk the notion that you must learn the "correct" techniques of legal analysis and interpretation in order to judge the goodness of legal decisions.

Do I not contradict myself to claim that honesty, courage, and openness are the keys to good constitutional interpretation? No, I am only offering these as possibilities for you to accept or reject. I hope by the end of this book you will realize that what counts as a good or bad decision *inevitably* depends on each reader's beliefs and values about what makes people, and hence government and politics, virtuous and trustworthy or compromised and false. I hope readers will sharpen their personal political beliefs and values by accepting their responsibility for having such personal beliefs at all. The issue is never whether one can prove the superiority of one's beliefs over all others, but rather whether we take them seriously enough to talk about them coherently and to live by them. In other words, this book will meet all my objectives if, when you are done, you understand why you reject everything this book says about constitutional law.

My fondest hope for this book is that readers will see that neither religious nor legal values solve life problems in any mechanistic or automatic way. We constitute our communities and solve problems within them not by following religious or legal formulas but by trusting one another. We learn to trust each other not by contractually agreeing to abide by formulas but by talking to each other in ways that build trust, ways that reinforce our willingness to keep on talking rather than fighting when we disagree.

So constitutional interpretation, for me, ultimately revolves around how the talk of Supreme Court justices can enhance or diminish our trust in them and our willingness to converse with each other about how we are constituted. I believe that

Justice Rehnquist's opinion in *Goldman* diminishes my trust in him and in the goodness of his result. I believe that Justice Brennan's opinion in *Edwards* enhances my trust. But so does Justice Scalia's dissenting opinion in *Edwards* enhance my trust, even though Scalia vehemently disagrees with Brennan. Much of this book uses hypothetical conversations and debates to explain this approach. Your only responsibility is to formulate a coherent justification for your own position. This book's main message holds that "Because I'm powerful I can decide whatever and however I choose" or "It just feels right to me" are not acceptable arguments in any community—religious, legal, or political.

BIBLIOGRAPHIC NOTES

To clutter this text with footnotes would lend it the visual appearance of academic objectivity that belies its deeper message. A bibliography at the end of this book gives complete citations to all material indicated by a parenthetical year in the text. However, I list here and at the end of each chapter some suggestions for further reading.

John Noonan has published the best recent collection of materials combining religious documents, historical descriptions, and the constitutional law of religion in the United States: *The Believer and the Powers That Are* (1987).

Several noted professors of constitutional law who teach and write primarily for a law school audience have recently published essays on the interpretation problem that parallel mine. These include Sanford Levinson, *Constitutional Faith* (1988); Michael Perry, *Morality, Politics and Law* (1988); and Mark Tushnet, *Red, White, and Blue* (1988). In 1985 the *Southern California Law Review* devoted two long issues of its Volume 58 to a symposium on interpretation. Christopher Stone's "Introduction: Interpreting the Symposium," beginning on page 1, states several themes this chapter has introduced. For example, "[O]ne necessary element of interpretation is the potential for legitimate ambiguity. . . . [W]here we see interpretation, we should expect, in the nature of the activity, to find more than one satisfactory answer" (p. 3). Stone compares legal interpretation to literary, musical, and scientific interpretation and concludes that their common denominator is the education of the interpreter. Interpretation is subject only to the constraints of consistency and coherence, a theme this book also develops.

Hardly a week goes by without a law and religion story appearing in the newspapers. In 1989 I gathered the following clippings within two months:

- "Prophets of a Biblical America," *Wall Street Journal*, April 12, 1989, p. A14, described the Christian Reconstructionist movement, which calls for governing all of American life strictly according to biblical laws, just as Iran professes strictly following the Koran. The movement, which claims 20 million followers, would abolish the federal government and would require tithing to the church in place of taxation.

- "Mississippi Law Invades Spirit World as Man Held in Alleged Voodoo Plot," *Atlanta Journal and Constitution,* April 13, 1989, p. 12A, reported the arrest of a man on a charge of conspiracy to murder a local judge by placing a voodoo curse on him.
- "Christian Science Couple Found Guilty of Murder for Denying Girl a Doctor," *Atlanta Journal and Constitution,* April 19, 1989, p. 11A, reported the trial verdict of a six-person jury in Florida. The defendants were the first in twenty years to be so prosecuted.
- "C-Section Forced on Mom Called a Precedent," *Atlanta Constitution,* May 4, 1989, p. 1D, raised the question whether a pregnant woman may refuse a Caesarean section on religious grounds where her doctors believe the baby would not survive normal childbirth.
- "When Prayers Are Answered by Complaints," *Atlanta Constitution,* May 10, 1989, p. 8A, described objections to prayers "in Jesus' name" traditionally held at the beginning of Gwinnett County (Georgia) Commission meetings.
- "Scottish Lord Caught in Centuries-Old Dispute," *Atlanta Journal and Constitution,* May 27, 1989, p. A-21, reported that the British lord high chancellor was forced to resign from the Free Presbyterian Church of Scotland because he insisted on attending the Roman Catholic funerals of Catholic friends.
- "Supreme Court Lets Stand Ruling in Douglas Case," *Atlanta Journal and Constitution,* May 31, 1989, p. A-1, covered the results of a lawsuit by a high school band member seeking to stop the practice of Christian prayers before high school football games.
- "Scientology Dispute," *Wall Street Journal,* June 6, 1989, p. A 26, noted that the Supreme Court confirmed an IRS disallowance of tax deductions taken by those who paid money to the Church of Scientology for "spiritual auditing and training services."

CHAPTER 2

Free Exercise of Religion: The Case of the Captain's Yarmulke

The considered professional judgment of the Air Force is that the traditional outfitting of personnel in standardized uniforms encourages the subordination of personal preferences and identities in favor of the overall group mission.
—*Justice William Rehnquist*

The U.S. Constitution is the law that governs the government. Some parts of the Constitution assign powers and responsibilities to various branches of government. For example, the Congress has the power to declare war and the President possesses the power of commander-in-chief of the armed forces. Other parts of the Constitution, including the First Amendment of the Bill of Rights, which concerns us here, deny power to government. The First Amendment begins:

> Congress shall make no law respecting an establishment of religion, or prohibiting the free exercise thereof.

The amendment goes on to protect the political freedoms of speech, press, and assembly.

What do these clauses actually mean in specific cases? We will consider the free-exercise clause case first, because it is somewhat simpler and easier to teethe on. I have edited relatively little out of the two major cases in this book in order to convey the full complexity of the arguments the Justices make on both sides.

10

THE CASE

*GOLDMAN v. WEINBERGER**
475 U.S. 503 (1986)

Justice REHNQUIST delivered the opinion of the Court.

Petitioner S. Simcha Goldman contends that the Free Exercise Clause of the First Amendment to the United States Constitution permits him to wear a yarmulke while in uniform, notwithstanding an Air Force regulation mandating uniform dress for Air Force personnel. The District Court for the District of Columbia permanently enjoined the Air Force from enforcing its regulation against petitioner and from penalizing him for wearing his yarmulke. The Court of Appeals for the District of Columbia Circuit reversed on the ground that the Air Force's strong interest in discipline justified the strict enforcement of its uniform dress requirements. We granted certiorari because of the importance of the question, and now affirm.

Petitioner Goldman is an Orthodox Jew and ordained rabbi. In 1973, he was accepted into the Armed Forces Health Professions Scholarship Program and placed on inactive reserve status in the Air Force while he studied clinical psychology at Loyola University of Chicago. During his three years in the scholarship program, he received a monthly stipend and an allowance for tuition, books, and fees. After completing his Ph.D. in psychology, petitioner entered active service in the United States Air Force as a commissioned officer, in accordance with a requirement that participants in the scholarship program serve one year of active duty for each year of subsidized education. Petitioner was stationed at March Air Force Base in Riverside, California, and served as a clinical psychologist at the mental health clinic on the base.

Until 1981, petitioner was not prevented from wearing his yarmulke on the base. He avoided controversy by remaining close to his duty station in the health clinic and by wearing his service cap over the yarmulke when out of doors. But in April 1981, after he testified as a defense witness at a court-martial wearing his yarmulke but not his service cap, opposing counsel lodged a complaint with Colonel Joseph Gregory, the Hospital Commander, arguing that petitioner's practice of wearing his yarmulke was a violation of Air Force Regulation (AFR) 35-10. This regulation states in pertinent part that "[h]eadgear will not be worn . . . [w]hile indoors except by armed security police in the performance of their duties." AFR 35-10.

Colonel Gregory informed petitioner that wearing a yarmulke while on duty does indeed violate AFR 35-10, and ordered him not to violate this regulation outside the hospital. Although virtually all of petitioner's time on the base was spent in the hospital, he refused. Later, after petitioner's attorney protested to the Air Force General Counsel, Colonel Gregory revised his order to prohibit petitioner from wearing the yarmulke even in the hospital. Petitioner's request to report for duty in civilian clothing pending legal resolution of the issue was denied. The next day he received a formal letter of reprimand, and was warned that failure to obey AFR 35-10 could subject him to a court-martial. Colonel Gregory also withdrew a recommendation that petitioner's application to extend the term of his active service be approved, and substituted a negative recommendation.

Petitioner then sued respondent Secretary of Defense and others, claiming that the application of AFR 35-10 to prevent him from wearing his yarmulke infringed upon his First Amendment freedom to exercise his religious beliefs. The United States District

---

*The ellipses in my edited versions of this and the *Edwards* case indicate omission of substantive portions of the opinion's text. I have eliminated routine multiple case citations and some footnotes without ellipses. I have not renumbered the footnotes, so the gaps in the record will reveal which ones have been omitted.

Court for the District of Columbia preliminarily enjoined the enforcement of the regulation, 530 F.Supp. 12 (1981), and then after a full hearing permanently enjoined the Air Force from prohibiting petitioner from wearing a yarmulke while in uniform. Respondents appealed to the Court of Appeals for the District of Columbia Circuit, which reversed. 236 U.S. App.D.C. 248 (1984). As an initial matter, the Court of Appeals determined that the appropriate level of scrutiny of a military regulation that clashes with a constitutional right is neither strict scrutiny nor rational basis. *Id.*, at 252. Instead, it held that a military regulation must be examined to determine whether "legitimate military ends are sought to be achieved," *id.*, at 253, and whether it is "designed to accommodate the individual right to an appropriate degree." *Ibid.* Applying this test, the court concluded that "the Air Force's interest in uniformity renders the strict enforcement of its regulation permissible." *Id.*, at 257. . . .

Petitioner argues that AFR 35–10, as applied to him, prohibits religiously motivated conduct and should therefore be analyzed under the standard enunciated in *Sherbert v. Verner,* 374 U.S. 398 (1963). See also *Thomas v. Review Board,* 450 U.S. 707 (1981); *Wisconsin v. Yoder,* 406 U.S. 205 (1972). But we have repeatedly held that "the military is, by necessity, a specialized society separate from civilian society." *Parker v. Levy,* 417 U.S. 733 (1974). See also *Chappell v. Wallace,* 462 U.S. 296 (1983); *Schlesinger v. Councilman,* 420 U.S. 738 (1975); *Orloff v. Willoughby,* 345 U.S. 83 (1953). "[T]he military must insist upon a respect for duty and a discipline without counterpart in civilian life," *Schlesinger v. Councilman, supra,* 420 U.S., at 757, in order to prepare for and perform its vital role. See also *Brown v. Glines,* 444 U.S. 348 (1980).

Our review of military regulations challenged on First Amendment grounds is far more deferential than constitutional review of similar laws or regulations designed for civilian society. The military need not encourage debate or tolerate protest to the extent that such tolerance is required of the civilian state by the First Amendment; to accomplish its mission the military must foster instinctive obedience, unity, commitment, and esprit de corps. See, e.g., *Chappell v. Wallace, supra,* 462 U.S., at 300, *Greer v. Spock,* 424 U.S. 828, 843–844 (1976) (POWELL, J., concurring); *Parker v. Levy, supra,* 417 U.S., at 744. The essence of military service "is the subordination of the desires and interests of the individual to the needs of the service." *Orloff v. Willoughby, supra,* 345 U.S., at 92.

These aspects of military life do not, of course, render entirely nugatory in the military context the guarantees of the First Amendment. See, e.g., *Chappell v. Wallace, supra,* 462 U.S., at 304. But "within the military community there is simply not the same [individual] autonomy as there is in the larger civilian community." *Parker v. Levy, supra,* 417 U.S., at 751. In the context of the present case, when evaluating whether military needs justify a particular restriction on religiously motivated conduct, courts must give great deference to the professional judgment of military authorities concerning the relative importance of a particular military interest. See *Chappell v. Wallace, supra,* 462 U.S., at 305; *Orloff v. Willoughby, supra,* 345 U.S., at 93–94. Not only are courts " 'ill-equipped to determine the impact upon discipline that any particular intrusion upon military authority might have,' " *Chappell v. Wallace, supra,* 462 U.S., at 305, quoting Warren, The Bill of Rights and the Military, 37 N.Y.U.L.Rev. 181, 187 (1962), but the military authorities have been charged by the Executive and Legislative Branches with carrying out our Nation's military policy. "Judicial deference . . . is at its apogee when legislative action under the congressional authority to raise and support armies and make rules and regulations for their governance is challenged." *Rostker v. Goldberg,* 453 U.S. 57 (1981).

The considered professional judgment of the Air Force is that the traditional outfitting of personnel in standardized uniforms encourages the subordination of personal preferences and identities in favor of the overall group mission. Uniforms encourage a sense of hierarchical unity by tending to eliminate outward individual distinctions except for those of rank. The Air Force considers them as vital during peacetime as during war because its personnel must be ready to provide an effective defense on a moment's notice; the necessary habits of discipline and unity must be developed in advance of trouble. We have acknowledged that "[t]he inescapable demands of military discipline and obedience to orders cannot be taught on battlefields; the habit of immediate compliance with military procedures and orders must be virtually reflex with no time for debate or reflection." *Chappell* v. *Wallace, supra,* 462 U.S., at 300.

To this end, the Air Force promulgated AFR 35–10, a 190-page document, which states that "Air Force members will wear the Air Force uniform while performing their military duties, except when authorized to wear civilian clothes on duty." The rest of the document describes in minute detail all of the various items of apparel that must be worn as part of the Air Force uniform. It authorizes a few individualized options with respect to certain pieces of jewelry and hair style, but even these are subject to severe limitations. See AFR 35–10, Table 1–1. In general, authorized headgear may be worn only out of doors. Indoors, "[h]eadgear [may] not be worn . . . except by armed security police in the performance of their duties." A narrow exception to this rule exists for headgear worn during indoor religious ceremonies. In addition, military commanders may in their discretion permit visible religious headgear and other such apparel in designated living quarters and nonvisible items generally. See Department of Defense Directive 1300.17 (June 18, 1985).

Petitioner Goldman contends that the Free Exercise Clause of the First Amendment requires the Air Force to make an exception to its uniform dress requirements for religious apparel unless the accoutrements create a "clear danger" of undermining discipline and esprit de corps. He asserts that in general, visible but "unobtrusive" apparel will not create such a danger and must therefore be accommodated. He argues that the Air Force failed to prove that a specific exception for his practice of wearing an unobtrusive yarmulke would threaten discipline. He contends that the Air Force's assertion to the contrary is mere *ipse dixit,* with no support from actual experience or a scientific study in the record, and is contradicted by expert testimony that religious exceptions to AFR 35–10 are in fact desirable and will increase morale by making the Air Force a more humane place.

But whether or not expert witnesses may feel that religious exceptions to AFR 35–10 are desirable is quite beside the point. The desirability of dress regulations in the military is decided by the appropriate military officials, and they are under no constitutional mandate to abandon their considered professional judgment. Quite obviously, to the extent the regulations do not permit the wearing of religious apparel such as a yarmulke, a practice described by petitioner as silent devotion akin to prayer, military life may be more objectionable for petitioner and probably others. But the First Amendment does not require the military to accommodate such practices in the face of its view that they would detract from the uniformity sought by the dress regulations. The Air Force has drawn the line essentially between religious apparel which is visible and that which is not, and we hold that those portions of the regulations challenged here reasonably and evenhandedly regulate dress in the interest of the military's perceived need for uniformity. The First Amendment therefore does not prohibit them from being applied to petitioner even though their effect is to restrict the wearing of the headgear required by his religious beliefs.

The judgment of the Court of Appeals is *Affirmed.*

Justice STEVENS, with whom Justice WHITE and Justice POWELL join, concurring.

Captain Goldman presents an especially attractive case for an exception from the uniform regulations that are applicable to all other Air Force personnel. His devotion to

his faith is readily apparent. The yarmulke is a familiar and accepted sight.[1] In addition
to its religious significance for the wearer, the yarmulke may evoke the deepest respect
and admiration—the symbol of a distinguished tradition . . . and an eloquent rebuke to
the ugliness of anti-Semitism.[3] Captain Goldman's military duties are performed in a
setting in which a modest departure from the uniform regulation creates almost no
danger of impairment of the Air Force's military mission. Moreover, on the record before
us, there is reason to believe that the policy of strict enforcement against Captain
Goldman had a retaliatory motive—he had worn his yarmulke while testifying on behalf
of a defendant in a court-martial proceeding.[4] Nevertheless, as the case has been argued,
[5] I believe we must test the validity of the Air Force's rule not merely as it applies to
Captain Goldman but also as it applies to all service personnel who have sincere
religious beliefs that may conflict with one or more military commands.

Justice BRENNAN is unmoved by the Government's concern "that while a yarmulke
might not seem obtrusive to a Jew, neither does a turban to a Sikh, a saffron robe to a
Satchidananda Ashram-Integral Yogi, nor do dreadlocks to a Rastafarian." *Post.* He
correctly points out that "turbans, saffron robes, and dreadlocks are not before us in this
case," and then suggests that other cases may be fairly decided by reference to a
reasonable standard based on "functional utility, health and safety considerations, and
the goal of a polished, professional appearance." As the Court has explained, this
approach attaches no weight to the separate interest in uniformity itself. Because
professionals in the military service attach great importance to that plausible interest, it
is one that we must recognize as legitimate and rational even though personal experience
or admiration for the performance of the "rag-tag band of soldiers" that won us our

---

[1] Captain Goldman states in his brief: "Yarmulkes are generally understood to be a form of religious
observance. They are commonly seen and accepted in today's society wherever Orthodox Jews are
found. University campuses—particularly on the East Coast—have substantial numbers of young men
who wear yarmulkes. On the streets of New York City, Los Angeles, Chicago, or Miami, yarmulkes are
commonplace. They are increasingly visible in centers of commerce, including retail businesses,
brokerage houses, and stock exchanges. Attorneys wearing yarmulkes can be found in the state and
federal courthouses of New York, and attorneys wearing yarmulkes have been permitted to sit in the Bar
section of this Court and attend oral arguments." Brief for Petitioner 11.

[3] Cf. N. Belth, *A Promise to Keep* (1979) (recounting history of anti-Semitism in the United States). The
history of intolerance in our own country can be glimpsed by reviewing Justice Story's observation that
the purpose of the First Amendment was "not to countenance, much less to advance Mahometanism, or
Judaism, or infidelity, by prostrating Christianity; but to exclude all rivalry among Christian sects," 2 J.
Story, Commentaries on the Constitution of the United States § 1877, p. 594 (1851)—a view that the
Court has, of course, explicitly rejected. See *Wallace* v. *Jaffree,* 472 U.S.

[4] Before the testimony at the court martial that provoked this confrontation, Captain Goldman had
received extremely high ratings in his performance evaluations. App. 214–225. Indeed, one of the
evaluators noted, "He maintains appropriate military dress and bearing." *Id.*, at 217. Although the Air
Force stated that an officer had received one or two complaints about Captain Goldman's wearing of the
yarmulke, *id.*, at 15, 22, no complaint was acted upon until the court martial incident. . . .

[5] Captain Goldman has mounted a broad challenge to the prohibition on visible religious wear as it
applies to yarmulkes. He has not argued the far narrower ground that, even if the general prohibition is
valid, its application in his case was retaliatory and impermissible. See, e.g., Brief for Petitioner i. . . .
("The Air Force's asserted grounds for barring yarmulkes are patently unsound. . . . Indeed the
symbolic significance of our Nation's military services and the educational role of the military in
teaching the young defenders of our country the principles of liberty require acceptance of petitioner's
religious observance.")

freedom in the revolutionary war might persuade us that the Government has exaggerated the importance of that interest.

The interest in uniformity, however, has a dimension that is of still greater importance for me. It is the interest in uniform treatment for the members of all religious faiths. The very strength of Captain Goldman's claim creates the danger that a similar claim on behalf of a Sikh or a Rastafarian might readily be dismissed as "so extreme, so unusual, or so faddish an image that public confidence in his ability to perform his duties will be destroyed." *Post.* If exceptions from dress code regulations are to be granted on the basis of a multifactored test such as that proposed by Justice BRENNAN, inevitably the decision maker's evaluation of the character and the sincerity of the requestor's faith—as well as the probable reaction of the majority to the favored treatment of a member of that faith—will play a critical part in the decision. For the difference between a turban or a dreadlock on the one hand, and a yarmulke on the other, is not merely a difference in "appearance"—it is also the difference between a Sikh or a Rastafarian, on the one hand, and an Orthodox Jew on the other. The Air Force has no business drawing distinctions between such persons when it is enforcing commands of universal application.[6]

As the Court demonstrates, the rule that is challenged in this case is based on a neutral, completely objective standard—visibility. It was not motivated by hostility against, or any special respect for, any religious faith. An exception for yarmulkes would represent a fundamental departure from the true principle of uniformity that supports that rule. For that reason, I join the Court's opinion and its judgment.

Justice BRENNAN, with whom Justice MARSHALL joins, dissenting.

Simcha Goldman invokes this Court's protection of his First Amendment right to fulfill one of the traditional religious obligations of a male Orthodox Jew—to cover his head before an omnipresent God. The Court's response to Goldman's request is to abdicate its role as principal expositor of the Constitution and protector of individual liberties in favor of credulous deference to unsupported assertions of military necessity. I dissent.

I

In ruling that the paramount interests of the Air Force override Dr. Goldman's free exercise claim, the Court overlooks the sincere and serious nature of his constitutional claim. It suggests that the desirability of certain dress regulations, rather than a First Amendment right, is at issue. The Court declares that in selecting dress regulations, "military officials are under no constitutional mandate to abandon their considered professional judgment." *Ante.* If Dr. Goldman wanted to wear a hat to keep his head warm or to cover a bald spot, I would join the majority. Mere personal preferences in dress are not constitutionally protected. The First Amendment, however, restrains the

---

[6] See *United States v. Lee,* 455 U.S. 252, 263, n. 2 (1982) (STEVENS, J., concurring in the judgment) ("In my opinion, the principal reason for adopting a strong presumption against such claims is not a matter of administrative convenience. It is the overriding interest in keeping the government—whether it be the legislature or the courts—out of the business of evaluating the relative merits of differing religious claims"). Cf. *Wallace v. Jaffree* (referring to "the established principle that the Government must pursue a course of complete neutrality toward religion"); *Committee for Public Education v. Nyquist,* 413 U.S. 756, 792–793 (1973) ("A proper respect for both the Free Exercise and the Establishment Clauses compels the State to pursue a course of 'neutrality' toward religion"); *Abington School District v. Schempp,* 374 U.S. 203, 226 (1963) ("In the relationship between man and religion, the State is firmly committed to a position of neutrality").

Government's ability to prevent an Orthodox Jewish serviceman from, or punish him for, wearing a yarmulke.[1]

The Court also attempts, unsuccessfully, to minimize the burden that was placed on Dr. Goldman's rights. The fact that "the regulations don't permit the wearing of . . . a yarmulke," does not simply render military life for observant Orthodox Jews "objectionable." *Ibid.* It sets up an almost absolute bar to the fulfillment of a religious duty. Dr. Goldman spent most of his time in uniform indoors, where the dress code forbade him even from covering his head with his service cap. Consequently, he was asked to violate the tenets of his faith virtually every minute of every work day.

II

A

Dr. Goldman has asserted a substantial First Amendment claim, which is entitled to meaningful review by this Court. The Court, however, evades its responsibility by eliminating, in all but name only, judicial review of military regulations that interfere with the fundamental constitutional rights of service personnel.

Our cases have acknowledged that in order to protect our treasured liberties, the military must be able to command service members to sacrifice a great many of the individual freedoms they enjoyed in the civilian community and to endure certain limitations on the freedoms they retain. See, e.g., *Brown v. Glines,* 444 U.S. 348, 354–357; *Greer v. Spock,* 424 U.S. 828, 848 (POWELL, J., concurring); *Parker v. Levy,* 417 U.S. 733, 743–744, 751. Notwithstanding this acknowledgment, we have steadfastly maintained that " 'our citizens in uniform may not be stripped of basic rights simply because they have doffed their civilian clothes.' " *Chappell v. Wallace,* 462 U.S. 296, 304 (quoting Warren, The Bill of Rights and the Military, 37 N.Y.U.L.Rev. 181, 188 [1962]). And, while we have hesitated, due to our lack of expertise concerning military affairs and our respect for the delegated authority of a coordinate branch, to strike down restrictions on individual liberties which could reasonably be justified as necessary to the military's vital function, see, e.g., *Rostker v. Goldberg,* 453 U.S. 57, 66–67, we have never abdicated our obligation of judicial review. See, e.g., *id.,* at 67, 101 S.Ct., at 2653.

Today the Court eschews its constitutionally mandated role. It adopts for review of military decisions affecting First Amendment rights a subrational-basis standard—absolute, uncritical "deference to the professional judgment of military authorities." *Ante.* If a branch of the military declares one of its rules sufficiently important to outweigh a service person's constitutional rights, it seems that the Court will accept that conclusion, no matter how absurd or unsupported it may be.

A deferential standard of review, however, need not, and should not, mean that the Court must credit arguments that defy common sense. When a military service burdens the free exercise rights of its members in the name of necessity, it must provide, as an initial matter and at a minimum, a *credible* explanation of how the contested practice is likely to interfere with the proffered military interest.[2] Unabashed *ipse dixit* cannot outweigh a constitutional right.

In the present case, the Air Force asserts that its interests in discipline and uniformity

---

[1] The yarmulke worn by Dr. Goldman was a dark-colored skullcap measuring approximately 5 ½ inches in diameter. Brief for Petitioner 3.

[2] I continue to believe that Government restraints on First Amendment rights, including limitations placed on military personnel, may be justified only upon showing a compelling state interest which is precisely furthered by a narrowly tailored regulation. . . . My point here is simply that even under a more deferential test Dr. Goldman should prevail.

would be undermined by an exception to the dress code permitting observant male Orthodox Jews to wear yarmulkes. The Court simply restates these assertions without offering any explanation how the exception Dr. Goldman requests reasonably could interfere with the Air Force's interests. Had the Court given actual consideration to Goldman's claim, it would have been compelled to decide in his favor.

B

1

The Government maintains in its brief that discipline is jeopardized whenever exceptions to military regulations are granted. Service personnel must be trained to obey even the most arbitrary command reflexively. Non-Jewish personnel will perceive the wearing of a yarmulke by an Orthodox Jew as an unauthorized departure from the rules and will begin to question the principle of unswerving obedience. Thus shall our fighting forces slip down the treacherous slope toward unkempt appearance, anarchy, and, ultimately, defeat at the hands of our enemies.

The contention that the discipline of the armed forces will be subverted if Orthodox Jews are allowed to wear yarmulkes with their uniforms surpasses belief. It lacks support in the record of this case and the Air Force offers no basis for it as a general proposition. While the perilous slope permits the services arbitrarily to refuse exceptions requested to satisfy mere personal preferences, before the Air Force may burden free-exercise rights it must advance, at the *very least*, a rational reason for doing so.

Furthermore, the Air Force cannot logically defend the content of its rule by insisting that discipline depends upon absolute adherence to whatever rule is established. If, as General Usher admitted at trial, App. 52, the dress code codified religious exemptions from the ''no-headgear-indoors'' regulation, then the wearing of a yarmulke would be sanctioned by the code and could not be considered an unauthorized deviation from the rules.

2

The Government also argues that the services have an important interest in uniform dress, because such dress establishes the preeminence of group identity, thus fostering esprit de corps and loyalty to the service that transcends individual bonds. In its brief, the Government characterizes the yarmulke as an assertion of individuality and as a badge of religious and ethnic identity, strongly suggesting that, as such, it could drive a wedge of divisiveness between members of the services.

First, the purported interests of the Air Force in complete uniformity of dress and in elimination of individuality or visible identification with any group other than itself are belied by the service's own regulations. The dress code expressly abjures the need for total uniformity:

''(1) The American public and its elected representatives draw certain conclusions on military effectiveness based on what they see; that is, the image the Air Force presents. The image must instill public confidence and leave no doubt that the service member lives by a common standard and responds to military order and discipline.

''(2) Appearance in uniform is an important part of this image. . . . Neither the Air Force nor the public expects absolute uniformity of appearance. Each member has the right, within limits, to express individuality through his or her appearance. However, the image of a disciplined service member who can be relied on to do his or her job excludes the extreme, the unusual, and the fad.'' AFR 35–10.

It cannot be seriously contended that a serviceman in a yarmulke presents so extreme, so unusual, or so faddish an image that public confidence in his ability to perform his duties will be destroyed. Under the Air Force's own standards, then, Dr. Goldman should have and could have been granted an exception to wear his yarmulke.

The dress code also allows men to wear up to three rings and one identification bracelet of "neat and conservative," but non-uniform, design. AFR 35–10. This jewelry is apparently permitted even if, as is often the case with rings, it associates the wearer with a denominational school or a religious or secular fraternal organization. If these emblems of religious, social, and ethnic identity are not deemed to be unacceptably divisive, the Air Force cannot rationally justify its bar against yarmulkes on that basis.

Moreover, the services allow, and rightly so, other manifestations of religious diversity. It is clear to all service personnel that some members attend Jewish services, some Christian, some Islamic, and some yet other religious services. Barracks mates see Mormons wearing temple garments, Orthodox Jews wearing tzitzit, and Catholics wearing crosses and scapulars. That they come from different faiths and ethnic backgrounds is not a secret that can or should be kept from them.

I find totally implausible the suggestion that the overarching group identity of the Air Force would be threatened if Orthodox Jews were allowed to wear yarmulkes with their uniforms. To the contrary, a yarmulke worn with a United States military uniform is an eloquent reminder that the shared and proud identity of United States serviceman embraces and unites religious and ethnic pluralism.

Finally, the Air Force argues that while Dr. Goldman describes his yarmulke as an "unobtrusive" addition to his uniform, obtrusiveness is a purely relative, standardless judgment. The Government notes that while a yarmulke might not seem obtrusive to a Jew, neither does a turban to a Sikh, a saffron robe to a Satchidananda Ashram-Integral Yogi, nor do dreadlocks to a Rastafarian. If the Court were to require the Air Force to permit yarmulkes, the service must also allow all of these other forms of dress and grooming.

The Government dangles before the Court a classic parade of horribles, the specter of a brightly colored, "rag-tag band of soldiers." Brief for Respondents 20. Although turbans, saffron robes, and dreadlocks are not before us in this case and must each be evaluated against the reasons a service branch offers for prohibiting personnel from wearing them while in uniform, a reviewing court could legitimately give deference to dress and grooming rules that have a *reasoned* basis in, for example, functional utility, health and safety considerations, and the goal of a polished, professional appearance.[4] AFR 35–10 (identifying neatness, cleanliness, safety, and military image as the four elements of the dress code's "high standard of dress and personal appearance"). It is the lack of any reasoned basis for prohibiting yarmulkes that is so striking here.

Furthermore, contrary to its intimations, the Air Force has available to it a familiar standard for determining whether a particular style of yarmulke is consistent with a polished, professional military appearance—the "neat and conservative" standard by which the service judges jewelry. AFR 35–10. No rational reason exists why yarmulkes cannot be judged by the same criterion. Indeed, at argument Dr. Goldman declared himself willing to wear whatever style and color yarmulke the Air Force believes best comports with its uniform.

---

[4] For example, the Air Force could no doubt justify regulations ordering troops to wear uniforms, prohibiting garments that could become entangled in machinery, and requiring hair to be worn short so that it may not be grabbed in combat and may be kept louse-free in field conditions.

3

Department of Defense Directive 1300.17 (June 18, 1985) grants commanding officers the discretion to permit service personnel to wear religious items and apparel that are not visible with the uniform, such as crosses, temple garments, and scapulars. Justice STEVENS favors this "visibility test" because he believes that it does not involve the Air Force in drawing distinctions among faiths. *Ante.* He rejects functional utility, health, and safety considerations, and similar grounds as criteria for religious exceptions to the dress code, because he fears that these standards will allow some service persons to satisfy their religious dress and grooming obligations, while preventing others from fulfilling theirs. *Ibid.* But, the visible/not visible standard has that same effect. Furthermore, it restricts the free exercise rights of a larger number of service persons. The visibility test permits *only* individuals whose outer garments and grooming are indistinguishable from those of mainstream Christians to fulfill their religious duties. In my view, the Constitution requires the selection of criteria that permit the greatest possible number of persons to practice their faiths freely.

Implicit in Justice STEVENS' concurrence, and in the Government's arguments, is what might be characterized as a fairness concern. It would be unfair to allow Orthodox Jews to wear yarmulkes, while prohibiting members of other minority faiths with visible dress and grooming requirements from wearing their saffron robes, dreadlocks, turbans, and so forth. While I appreciate and share this concern for the feelings and the free-exercise rights of members of these other faiths, I am baffled by this formulation of the problem. What puzzles me is the implication that a neutral standard that could result in the disparate treatment of Orthodox Jews and, for example, Sikhs is *more* troublesome or unfair than the existing neutral standard that does result in the different treatment of Christians, on the one hand, and Orthodox Jews and Sikhs on the other. *Both* standards are constitutionally suspect; before either can be sustained, it must be shown to be a narrowly tailored means of promoting important military interests.

I am also perplexed by the related notion that for purposes of constitutional analysis religious faiths may be divided into two categories—those with visible dress and grooming requirements and those without. This dual category approach seems to incorporate an assumption that fairness, the First Amendment, and, perhaps, Equal Protection, require all faiths belonging to the same category to be treated alike, but permit a faith in one category to be treated differently from a faith belonging to the other category. The practical effect of this categorization is that, under the guise of neutrality and evenhandedness, majority religions are favored over distinctive minority faiths. This dual category analysis is fundamentally flawed and leads to a result that the First Amendment was intended to prevent. Under the Constitution there is only *one* relevant category—*all* faiths. Burdens placed on the free-exercise rights of members of one faith must be justified independently of burdens placed on the rights of members of another religion. It is not enough to say that Jews cannot wear yarmulkes simply because Rastafarians might not be able to wear dreadlocks.

Unless the visible/not visible standard for evaluating requests for religious exceptions to the dress code promotes a significant military interest, it is constitutionally impermissible. Justice STEVENS believes that this standard advances an interest in the "uniform treatment" of all religions. As I have shown, that uniformity is illusory, unless uniformity means uniformly accommodating majority religious practices and uniformly rejecting distinctive minority practices. But, more directly, Government agencies are not free to define their own interests in uniform treatment of different faiths. That function has been assigned to the First Amendment. The First Amendment requires that burdens on free exercise rights be justified by independent and important interests that promote the function of the agency. See, e.g., *United States v. Lee*, 455 U.S. 252, 257–258; *Thomas v. Review Bd. of Indiana Employment Security Division*, 450 U.S. 707; *Wisconsin v. Yoder*, 406 U.S. 205 (1972); *Sherbert v. Verner*, 374 U.S. 398. The only independent military interest furthered by the visibility standard is uniformity of dress. And, that interest, as I demonstrated in Part II B § 2, *supra*, does not support a prohibition against yarmulkes.

The Air Force has failed utterly to furnish a credible explanation why an exception to the dress code permitting Orthodox Jews to wear neat and conservative yarmulkes while in uniform is likely to interfere with its interest in discipline and uniformity. We cannot "distort the Constitution to approve all that the military may deem expedient." *Korematsu v. United States*, 323 U.S. 214 (1944) (Jackson, J., dissenting). Under any meaningful level of judicial review, Simcha Goldman should prevail.

III

Through our Bill of Rights, we pledged ourselves to attain a level of human freedom and dignity that had no parallel in history. Our constitutional commitment to religious freedom and acceptance of religious pluralism is one of our greatest achievements in that noble endeavor. Almost 200 years after the First Amendment was drafted, tolerance and respect for all religions still set us apart from most other countries and draws to our shores refugees from religious persecution from around the world.

Guardianship of this precious liberty is not the exclusive domain of federal courts. It is the responsibility as well of the States and of the other branches of the Federal Government. Our military services have a distinguished record of providing for many of the religious needs of their personnel. But that they have satisfied much of their constitutional obligation does not remove their actions from judicial scrutiny. Our Nation has preserved freedom of religion, not through trusting to the good faith of individual agencies of government alone, but through the constitutionally mandated vigilant oversight and checking authority of the judiciary.

It is not the province of the federal courts to second-guess the professional judgments of the military services, but we are bound by the Constitution to assure ourselves that there exists a rational foundation for assertions of military necessity when they interfere with the free exercise of religion. "The concept of military necessity is seductively broad," *Glines*, 444 U.S., at 369 (BRENNAN, J., dissenting), and military decision makers themselves are as likely to succumb to its allure as are the courts and the general public. Definitions of necessity are influenced by decision makers' experiences and values. As a consequence, in pluralistic societies such as ours, institutions dominated by a majority are inevitably, if inadvertently, insensitive to the needs and values of minorities when these needs and values differ from those of the majority. The military, with its strong ethic of conformity and unquestioning obedience, may be particularly impervious to minority needs and values. A critical function of the Religion Clauses of the First Amendment is to protect the rights of members of minority religions against quiet erosion by majoritarian social institutions that dismiss minority beliefs and practices as unimportant, because unfamiliar. It is the constitutional role of this Court to ensure that this purpose of the First Amendment be realized.

The Court and the military services[5] have presented patriotic Orthodox Jews with a

---

[5] I refer to all of the military services rather than just to the Air Force because, as the Government emphasizes in its brief, Brief for Respondents 20, n. 11, all of the uniformed services have dress and appearance regulations comparable to AFR 35–10, and the Court's decision in this case will apply to all the services. Furthermore, all Military Departments are subject to the recent Department of Defense Directive 1300.17 (June 18, 1985), which deals with the accommodation of religious practices. This directive does not provide for the type of exception sought by Dr. Goldman.

painful dilemma—the choice between fulfilling a religious obligation and serving their country. Should the draft be reinstated, compulsion will replace choice. Although the pain the services inflict on Orthodox Jewish servicemen is clearly the result of insensitivity rather than design, it is unworthy of our military because it is unnecessary. The Court and the military have refused these servicemen their constitutional rights; we must hope that Congress will correct this wrong.

Justice BLACKMUN, dissenting.

I would reverse the judgment of the Court of Appeals, but for reasons somewhat different from those respectively enunciated by Justice BRENNAN and Justice O'CONNOR. I feel that the Air Force is justified in considering not only the costs of allowing Captain Goldman to cover his head indoors, but also the cumulative costs of accommodating constitutionally indistinguishable requests for religious exemptions. Because, however, the Government has failed to make any meaningful showing that either set of costs is significant, I dissent from the Court's rejection of Goldman's claim. . . .

The problem . . . , it seems to me, is not doctrinal but empirical. The Air Force simply has not shown any reason to fear that a significant number of enlisted personnel and officers would request religious exemptions that could not be denied on neutral grounds such as safety, let alone that granting these requests would noticeably impair the overall image of the service. Cf. *Thomas* v. *Review Board of Indiana Employment Security Div.,* 450 U.S., at 719; *Sherbert* v. *Verner,* 374 U.S., at 407. The Air Force contends that the potential for such disruption was demonstrated at trial through the introduction of an Army publication discussing the beliefs and practices of a variety of religious denominations, some of which have traditions or requirements involving attire. . . . But that publication provides no indication whatsoever as to how many soldiers belong to the denominations it describes, or as to how many are likely to seek religious exemptions from the dress code.

In these circumstances, deference seems unwarranted. Reasoned military judgments, of course, are entitled to respect, but the military has failed to show that this particular judgment with respect to Captain Goldman is a reasoned one. If, in the future, the Air Force is besieged with requests for religious exemptions from the dress code, and those requests cannot be distinguished on functional grounds from Goldman's, the service may be able to argue credibly that circumstances warrant a flat rule against any visible religious apparel. That, however, would be a case different from the one at hand.

Justice O'CONNOR, with whom Justice MARSHALL joins, dissenting.

The issue posed in this case is whether, consistent with the Free Exercise Clause of the First Amendment, the Air Force may prohibit Captain Goldman, an Orthodox Jewish psychologist, from wearing a yarmulke while he is in uniform on duty inside a military hospital.

The Court rejects Captain Goldman's claim without even the slightest attempt to weigh his asserted right to the free exercise of his religion against the interest of the Air Force in uniformity of dress within the military hospital. No test for Free Exercise claims in the military context is even articulated, much less applied. It is entirely sufficient for the Court if the military perceives a need for uniformity.

Justice STEVENS acknowledges that "Captain Goldman's military duties are performed in a setting in which a modest departure from the uniform regulation creates almost no danger of impairment of the Air Force's military mission." *Ante* (concurring). Nevertheless, Justice STEVENS is persuaded that a governmental regulation based on *any* "neutral, completely objective standard," will survive a free exercise challenge.

In contrast, Justice BRENNAN recognizes that the Court "overlooks the sincere and serious nature of [the] constitutional claim." *Ante* (dissenting). He properly notes that, even with respect to military rules and regulations, the courts have a duty to weigh sincere First Amendment claims of its members against the necessity of the particular application of the rule. But Justice BRENNAN applies no particular test or standard to determine such claims.

Justice BLACKMUN focuses on the particular ways in which the military may pursue its interest in uniformity, *ante* (dissenting), but nonetheless declines "to determine the extent to which the ordinary test for inroads on religious freedom must be modified in the military context."

I believe that the Court should attempt to articulate and apply an appropriate standard for a free-exercise claim in the military context, and should examine Captain Goldman's claim in light of that standard.

Like the Court today in this case involving the military, the Court in the past has had some difficulty, even in the civilian context, in articulating a clear standard for evaluating free exercise claims that result from the application of general state laws burdening religious conduct. In *Sherbert v. Verner*, 374 U.S. 398, and *Thomas v. Review Board*, 450 U.S. 707 (1981), the Court required the States to demonstrate that their challenged policies were "the least restrictive means of achieving some compelling state interest" in order to deprive claimants of unemployment benefits when the refusal to work was based on sincere religious beliefs. *Thomas, supra,* 1432. See also *Sherbert, supra.* In *Wisconsin v. Yoder,* 406 U.S. 205 (1972), the Court noted that "only those interests of the highest order and those not otherwise served can overbalance legitimate claims to the free exercise of religion" in deciding that the Amish were exempt from a State's requirement that children attend school through the age of 16. In *United States v. Lee,* 455 U.S. 252, 257–258 (1982), the Court stated that "[t]he State may justify a limitation on religious liberty by showing that it is essential to accomplish an overriding governmental interest," and held that the Amish could not exempt themselves from the Social Security system on religious grounds. See also *Gillette v. United States,* 401 U.S. 437 (1971) (rejecting claims under the Establishment and Free Exercise Clauses to the Federal Government's refusal to give conscientious-objector status to those objecting on religious grounds only to a particular war rather than to all wars).

These tests, though similar, are not identical. One can, however, glean at least two consistent themes from this Court's precedents. First, when the government attempts to deny a Free Exercise claim, it must show that an unusually important interest is at stake, whether that interest is denominated "compelling," "of the highest order," or "overriding." Second, the government must show that granting the requested exemption will do substantial harm to that interest, whether by showing that the means adopted is the "least restrictive" or "essential," or that the interest will not "otherwise be served." These two requirements are entirely sensible in the context of the assertion of a free-exercise claim. First, because the government is attempting to override an interest specifically protected by the Bill of Rights, the government must show that the opposing interest it asserts is of especial importance before there is any chance that its claim can prevail. Second, since the Bill of Rights is expressly designed to protect the individual against the aggregated and sometimes intolerant powers of the state, the government must show that the interest asserted will in fact be substantially harmed by granting the type of exemption requested by the individual.

There is no reason why these general principles should not apply in the military, as well as the civilian, context. As this Court has stated unanimously, " 'our citizens in uniform may not be stripped of basic rights simply because they have doffed their civilian clothes.' " *Chappell v. Wallace,* 462 U.S. 296 (quoting Warren, The Bill of Rights and the Military, 37 N.Y.U.L.Rev. 181, 188 [1962]). Furthermore, the test that one can glean from this Court's decisions in the civilian context is sufficiently flexible to take into account the special importance of defending our Nation without abandoning completely the freedoms that make it worth defending.

The first question that the Court should face here, therefore, is whether the interest that the Government asserts against the religiously based claim of the individual is of unusual importance. It is perfectly appropriate at this step of the analysis to take account of the special role of the military. The mission of our armed services is to protect our Nation from those who would destroy all our freedoms. I agree that, in order to fulfill that mission, the military is entitled to take some freedoms from its members. As the Court notes, the military " 'must insist upon a respect for duty and a discipline without counterpart in civilian life.' " *Ante.* The need for military discipline and esprit de corps is unquestionably an especially important governmental interest.

But the mere presence of such an interest cannot, as the majority implicitly believes, end the analysis of whether a refusal by the Government to honor the free exercise of an individual's religion is constitutionally acceptable. A citizen pursuing even the most noble cause must remain within the bounds of the law. So, too, the Government may, even in pursuing its most compelling interests, be subject to specific restraints in doing so. The second question in the analysis of a Free Exercise claim under this Court's precedents must also be reached here: will granting an exemption of the type requested by the individual do substantial harm to the especially important governmental interest?

I have no doubt that there are many instances in which the unique fragility of military discipline and esprit de corps necessitates rigidity by the Government when similar rigidity to preserve an assertedly analogous interest would not pass constitutional muster in the civilian sphere. Compare *Greer* v. *Spock,* 424 U.S. 828 with *West Virginia Board of Education* v. *Barnette,* 319 U.S. 624, 630–634 (1943). Nonetheless, as Justice BRENNAN persuasively argues, the Government can present no sufficiently convincing proof in *this* case to support an assertion that granting an exemption of the type requested here would do substantial harm to military discipline and esprit de corps.

First, the Government's asserted need for absolute uniformity is contradicted by the Government's own exceptions to its rule. As Justice BRENNAN notes, an Air Force dress code in force at the time of Captain Goldman's service states:

> "Neither the Air Force nor the public expects absolute uniformity of appearance. Each member has the right, within limits, to express individuality through his or her appearance. However, the image of a disciplined service member who can be relied on to do his or her job excludes the extreme, the unusual and the fad." AFR 35–10.

Furthermore, the Government does not assert, and could not plausibly argue, that petitioner's decision to wear his yarmulke while indoors at the hospital presents a threat to health or safety. And finally, the District Court found as fact that in this particular case, far from creating discontent or indiscipline in the hospital where Captain Goldman worked, "[f]rom September 1977 to May 7, 1981, *no objection* was raised to Goldman's wearing of his yarmulke while in uniform." . . .

In the rare instances where the military has not consistently or plausibly justified its asserted need for rigidity of enforcement, and where the individual seeking the exemption establishes that the assertion by the military of a threat to discipline or esprit de corps is in his or her case completely unfounded, I would hold that the Government's policy of uniformity must yield to the individual's assertion of the right of free exercise of religion. On the facts of this case, therefore, I would require the Government to accommodate the sincere religious belief of Captain Goldman. Napoleon may have been correct to assert that, in the military sphere, morale is to all other factors as three is to one, but contradicted assertions of necessity by the military do not on the scales of justice bear a similarly disproportionate weight to sincere religious beliefs of the individual.

I respectfully dissent.

POSTSCRIPT

The opinions in Goldman's case appear, as best I can tell from examining the briefs and lower court opinions, to give a fairly comprehensive view of the facts. Neither side seems to have had its factual version of the case butchered. We are naturally suspicious that the Air Force may have retaliated against Goldman for his appearance as a defense witness in the court martial that precipitated the complaint. However, Goldman's lawyers chose not to make that an issue in the case. We don't know why they didn't, but because they didn't, we must assume that the Air Force did not dismiss Goldman for vindictive reasons. Goldman may have given entirely routine testimony in the court martial. Some eager advocate just out of law school may simply have insisted on making an issue of the yarmulke. In any event, Nathan Lewin, a nationally prominent First Amendment litigator, represented Goldman, and there is no reason to suspect legal negligence in the handling of his case.

There were, however, a few interesting elements in the case that the Supreme Court opinions do not reveal. For example, the evidence offered at the trial court hearing on Goldman's motion (he moved to enjoin the Air Force from enforcing its dress code against wearing yarmulkes indoors) suggested that allowances for individual religious expressions through such things as wearing a yarmulke would probably *enhance* military morale. In fact, in November 1970, Admiral Elmo Zumwalt, Chief of Naval Operations, in "Z-Gram" number 57, relaxed naval dress codes on such matters as Goldman's for just this reason.

Also the opinions had no reason to mention some minor political skirmishing that Goldman's case provoked. As a result of the Court of Appeal's reversal of Goldman's trial court victory, legislation was immediately introduced in Congress to permit the wearing of yarmulkes. The House adopted such a bill on May 24, 1984, at which point the Department of Defense forestalled action by the Senate by agreeing to do a study of conflicts between religious tenets and military requirements. The Supreme Court's ruling prompted Congress on December 4, 1987, to insert a new section in the military code, Chapter 45 of title 10 of the United States Code, which reads as follows:

"*§ 774. Religious apparel: wearing while in uniform*

"(a) GENERAL RULE.—Except as provided under subsection (b), a member of the armed forces may wear an item of religious apparel while wearing the uniform of the member's armed force.

"(b) EXCEPTIONS.—The Secretary concerned may prohibit the wearing of an item of religious apparel—

"(1) in circumstances with respect to which the Secretary determines that the wearing of the item would interfere with the performance of the member's military duties; or

"(2) if the Secretary determines, under regulations under subsection (c), that the item of apparel is not neat and conservative.

"(c) REGULATIONS.—The Secretary concerned shall prescribe regulations concerning the wearing of religious apparel by members of the armed forces under the Secretary's jurisdiction while the members are wearing the uniform. Such regulations shall be consistent with subsections (a) and (b).

"(d) RELIGIOUS APPAREL DEFINED.—In this section, the term "religious apparel" means apparel the wearing of which is part of the observance of the religious faith practiced by the member.".

(b) CLERICAL AMENDMENT.—The table of sections at the beginning of such chapter is amended by striking out the item relating to section 774 and inserting in lieu thereof the following:

"774. Religious apparel: wearing while in uniform.

"775. Applicability of chapter.".

(c) REGULATIONS.—The Secretary concerned shall prescribe the regulations required by section 774(c) of title 10, United States Code, as added by subsection (a), not later than the end of the 120-day period beginning on the date of the enactment of this Act.

THE CONSTITUTIONAL LAW OF FREE EXERCISE

Did the majority decide the rabbi captain's case well? Do the dissenters show that the majority was wrong? How can we tell? The instinctive first step toward an answer, for lawyer and layman alike, is to look at the law. Does one opinion "follow the law" better than another? This instinctive question seems the only proper question to ask, but the matter is not quite so simple. We can imagine people saying: "Look, I think the law is a corruption of God's will; I don't care whether the Court followed it," or: "The law is a tool of the capitalist pig class; it would be better if the Court could break away from the chains of our legal past and *didn't* follow the law." These responses may express entirely valid opinions, but they avoid the issues this book tackles. The question is not whether a reader likes the result but whether the decision maker decided well. An analogy would be a sporting event where your team lost but you have no doubt the referees judged well because they seemed to decide within the rules. Constitutional interpretation is the process by which the Court tries to persuade readers that it has stayed within the rules.

Chapter 1's list of methods of constitutional interpretation included following a well-developed body of Supreme Court precedents, that is, following the rules just as we expect sports referees to follow the rulebook. This and the next chapter examine the role of precedent in constitutional interpretation. The ethics of judging presumably require judges to try to follow these rules. In practice, however, following precedents is not a simple matter. Precedents conflict with each other, and the facts of each precedent differ enough from the facts of the case at hand that a judge can always find a reason not to follow it. Besides, the Court has consistently recognized its duty to overturn its own precedents if they no longer appear to state good law.

Before we turn to precedents, however, consider briefly the interpretations the literal readings of the Constitution's words might produce. When read literally, the free-exercise clause in *Goldman*—and the establishment clause in the *Edwards* case—do not apply to either case at all. The First Amendment prohibits "Congress" from making a law establishing a religion or prohibiting the free exercise of religion, and "Congress" has not acted in either of these two cases. Following the law means following precedents interpreting the law, and the religion clauses will cover the Air Force or the government of Louisiana only if the Court reads the words in a nonliteral way.

The precedents do precisely that. The First Amendment governs the military, not just Congress. For example, in 1972 a federal appellate court struck down a requirement in all three military academies that cadets, unless they filed a formal objection, must attend chapel services each week (*Anderson v. Laird*, 466 F.2d 283). The free-exercise clause has governed the states since 1940, when in *Cantwell v. Connecticut* (310 U.S. 696) the Court struck down charges against Jehovah's Witnesses who played phonograph records and solicited money on the streets of New Haven without getting prior approval. Under New Haven law, religious solicitors could get such a permit only at the discretion of a city official. The establishment clause has applied to the states since 1947, when the Supreme Court ruled in *Everson v. Board of Education* (330 U.S. 1) that the state of New Jersey did not establish a religion simply by using tax money to reimburse parents for the cost of transporting their children to school, though some of these children attended private religious schools. A year later the Court held that an Illinois school board did violate the establishment clause by allowing the voluntary teaching of Catholic, Protestant, and Jewish Bible classes to public school students on school property during regular school hours.

These precedents settled the threshold question that the lawyers in these cases took for granted: The First Amendment's religious freedoms do govern these cases. But the precedents did not resolve the substantive problems. The lawyers' serious work on these cases would begin, in one case, with a search for prior decisions that declared how broadly or narrowly the military could restrict clothing for religious reasons, and in the second case, with cases dealing with whether "creation science" counts as secular rather than sacred instruction. Of course if the lawyer found that the Supreme Court had already definitively resolved such matters, that fact would strongly discourage his spending the time and money to relitigate the issues, so it is not surprising to find that both these cases are to some degree new. But how close did some precedents come? Was there a line of precedents for each case that seemed inevitably to lead to the outcome the Court reached? It would seem there was not, since both cases provoked dissents. But perhaps one side didn't do its homework. We can tell only by scanning the cases that seem close but not "directly on point." When we do, however, we find that the precedents support both sides. Several incompatible threads, a pro-Air Force and a pro-Goldman thread, coexist in our free-exercise law. The following conversation illustrates how the precedents "go both ways."

PRECEDENTS IN *GOLDMAN:* A DIALOGUE

Imagine two students engaged in a conversation about their constitutional law course. The time is early 1990, just prior to the Supreme Court's decision in *Employment Division v. Smith* (1990), reprinted in the last chapter of this book. One really believes the Air Force was right and the other believes Goldman was right. Mary Garden, the president of her campus's Young Republicans, and Ben Bates, the head of the campus chapter of Beyond War, prepare for their final exam over a late evening pizza.

MARY: Ben, Captain Goldman doesn't have a leg to stand on. Cases from the late nineteenth century right through to 1986 consistently allow the government to interfere with individual religious expression for the public good.

BEN: I suppose you're referring to those outrageous cases that approved persecuting the Mormons.

MARY: Sure, but those cases aren't outrageous. In 1862, following a public outcry against the Mormon practice of polygamy, Congress passed a statute punishing polygamy in the U.S. territories and subjecting polygamists on conviction to a $500 fine or five years in prison. The law was finally enforced against George Reynolds, a Mormon leader who in 1875 was married to two women.

BEN: Oh for Pete's sake, Mary. Are you trying to equate marrying two wives with wearing a yarmulke?

MARY: Yes, that's just the point. Reynolds showed that under church doctrine his failure to marry polygamously could lead to his damnation. We have to assume that Reynolds and Goldman were equally sincere. Each claimed he was exercising his religious conscience. In *Reynolds v. United States* (98 U.S. 145, 1878) a unanimous Supreme Court rejected his claim. Justice Waite quoted the Virginia statute on religious freedom that Madison and Jefferson had sponsored:

> [A]fter a recital "that to suffer the civil magistrate to intrude his powers into the field of opinion, and to restrain the profession or propagation of principles on supposition of their ill tendency, is a dangerous fallacy which at once destroys all religious liberty," it is declared "that it is time enough for the rightful purposes of civil government for its officers to interfere when principles break out into overt acts against peace and good order." In these two sentences is found the true distinction between what properly belongs to the church and what to the State.

The Constitution protects religious belief, but it certainly allows the government to prohibit actions in the name of religion when those actions injure society. Do you think a bunch of marijuana smokers could avoid the law by forming the "Holy Reefer Roller Church" and smoking dope in "religious" services?

BEN: Then how come *Wisconsin v. Yoder* (406 U.S. 205, 1972) allowed the Amish to stop giving their children a formal education after the eighth grade in direct violation of state statute?

MARY: Because there was no evidence of public harm. Maintaining the Amish way of life doesn't spread immorality. Polygamy does.

BEN: And wearing a yarmulke in a hospital office spreads immorality too? Look, I agree that government can prevent harm to the general public, but it has to have some proof that it's necessary to squelch liberty to prevent the harm. In *Reynolds,* Justice Waite offered nothing like what would count as scientific proof that the religious practice of polygamy would cause any evil at all. There was no evidence that polygamy would somehow spread beyond the Mormon religion. Indeed, the conviction did not require proof that the husband had sexual relations with even one of his wives. Waite pointed out merely that "[p]olygamy has always been odious among the northern and western nations of Europe" and was punishable by death in England. The rule against polygamy applies to all, and the Court refused "to make the professed doctrines of religious belief superior to the law of the land." He just drew a moralistic conclusion that seems to me to apply just as well to the Amish. We believe education is the backbone of civilization. It's just as important as monogamy, no? The polygamy case and the Amish case flat out contradict each other.

MARY: Ben, you're not letting me make my point. I'll deal with the Amish later. Now I'm only trying to show that a body of cases from the very beginning of First Amendment law consistently can only lead to the conclusion that Goldman loses.

BEN: Okay, finish your list. At least it's good review.

MARY: In the 1880s Congress strengthened anti-Mormon legislation, first to forbid polygamists from holding office or voting, and then, in the Tucker Act of 1887, to confiscate the property of the Church of the Latter Day Saints. Worse, as a condition of voting, a man was required to take an oath that he was "not a member of any order . . . which practices bigamy" and that he would not encourage the practice of polygamy even privately. In *Davis v. Beason* (133 U.S. 333) the Court upheld the oath, and in *Romney v. United States* (136 U.S. 1) the Court upheld the confiscation.

BEN: Yeah, and denying the right to hold office, compelling an oath, and confiscation of church property were techniques used to force religious orthodoxy in the Middle Ages. That makes the Supreme Court sound like the Spanish Inquisition. Not every precedent is right, you know.

MARY: You said you'd let me finish. I'm not trying to argue right and wrong, only what the law says. The Court has never overruled *Davis*; it still sometimes cites it. For a Beyond War person you're pretty aggressive.

BEN: Sorry.

MARY: So, in 1931 in *United States v. Macintosh* (283 U.S. 605) the Supreme Court, 5 to 4, upheld denying naturalization to a chaired professor of theology at Yale for refusing to take the oath to bear arms in defense of the United States. Justice Sutherland conceded to Professor Macintosh that "We are a Christian people." However, he insisted that "unqualified allegiance to the Nation and submission and obedience to the laws of the land . . . are not inconsistent with the will of God." Macintosh wasn't even in the military, unlike Goldman, and he lost. Soon after, in 1934, the Court upheld the

University of California's requirement that all male students complete a course in military service and tactics.

BEN: But this case is different. The military stopped Goldman from engaging in a specific daily practice of his religion.

MARY: I'm not done with the precedents. In 1961 the Supreme Court upheld Pennsylvania's Sunday Closing laws against a challenge by Orthodox Jews that the laws interfered with the free exercise of their religion. If they closed their businesses on Saturdays to observe their own holy day, they would lose two days of business while their competitors lost only one. In *Braunfeld v. Brown* (366 U.S. 599) the Court insisted that the alternative might prove difficult to administer, just like an exception to the Air Force's headgear regulation. During the Vietnam War, *Gillette v. United States* (401 U.S. 437, 1971) upheld Congressional power to deny the exemption to Catholics whom the Church encouraged to object to the war on the basis of the just war doctrine. In 1981, in *Heffron v. International Society for Krishna Consciousness* (452 U.S. 640), the Court upheld the power of the state of Minnesota to limit Hare Krishna sect members soliciting alms and gifts in spite of the sect's religious obligation to move through the world begging and teaching. And in 1982 *United States v. Lee* (455 U.S. 252) rejected the religious claim of the Amish to be exempted from social security taxes because we are to bear one another's burdens (Gal. 6:2) and care for the elderly privately (1 Tim. 5:8). And, of course, in 1983 *Bob Jones University v. United States* (461 U.S. 574) denied the charitable tax exemption normally allowed religious bodies to a private college that practiced, as a matter of religious belief, racial discrimination.

BEN: I'm sure you'll ace a free-exercise question on the final, Mary, but none of those cases directly decides a free-exercise claim in the military. A precedent controls only when its facts are virtually identical, and even then the Supreme Court is free to overrule itself when it thinks its prior decision was wrong.

MARY: I've saved my best argument for last. The cases Justice Rehnquist cites at the beginning of the *Goldman* opinion do deal with the civil liberties of people in the military. These cases clearly hold that the military does not need to protect civil liberties as aggressively as does the civilian government. *Orloff* (1953) held that one lawfully drafted into the Army loses the right of *habeas corpus* to question his assignment. In 1976 the famous baby doctor Benjamin Spock, then a presidential candidate on an anti-Vietnam War platform, lost his request to give a partisan speech and distribute campaign literature on a military base. The government, represented by then Solicitor General Robert Bork, prevailed on the claim that there is no general constitutional right to give political speeches or distribute literature on a military reservation. *Brown v. Glines* (1980) denied a serviceman the right to circulate on an Air Force base a petition complaining about grooming standards and intended for members of Congress and the Defense Department. Regulations required the plaintiff to obtain prior approval from his commander, a kind of censorship we do not allow in civilian life. In 1981 in the *Rostker* case the Court found no unconstitutional discrimination in the draft law that drafted only men, and in *Chappell v. Wallace* (1983) the Court denied Navy enlisted men the right to recover damages from superior officers who practiced racial discrimination against them. This consistent string of cases clearly upholds the power of the military to modify civil rights, and the majority in *Goldman* clearly followed the law.

BEN: Your long boring string of cases. . . .

MARY: Wait, I'm still not done. Although the issues have not reached the Supreme Court, many state and lower federal decisions in the last twenty years have limited free religious exercise by authorizing hospitals to give blood transfusions against the religious will of the patient, by enjoining snake handling and drinking poison to honor Mark 16:15–18, by upholding federal approval of building dams and ski resorts on sacred Indian lands, by refusing to allow Black Muslims to hold religious services in prisons, and by upholding the firing of a public school teacher who had become a Sikh and who refused to remove her white clothing and turban in violation of a school policy against wearing "religious dress" while on duty.

BEN: And all these cases lead to only one conclusion, right?

MARY: Right. These cases flatly refute Goldman's claim. These cases prove that, while the Constitution protects beliefs and conscience in religious matters, it does not limit governmental interference with actions. When a rule regulating action and behavior applies equally to all and has generally desirable benefits for society at large, the claim of religious freedom must give way. Indeed these cases do so even against a background of evidence suggesting prejudice against specific religions, like the Mormons, and when the rule in practice has a disproportionately negative effect on one religious sect, as the refusal to honor selective conscientious objection did on Catholics during Vietnam. The headgear rule which Goldman refused to obey did not interfere with belief, nor did it single out any religious practice. Like the rule prohibiting polygamy, it applied equally to all and served the valid purpose of maintaining service discipline.

BEN: All right, I've let you have your say. You want me to believe that the weight of all these cases can lead to only one conclusion—your conclusion. I have two responses. First, the weight of who wins and loses in the precedents doesn't tell us what the law means. I'll match the weight of my list of winners and losers with the weight of your list any day. And second, precisely because I can, we have to look beyond case outcomes to find out what the law means. We have to look at the reasons and the justifications the courts give for their results. When we do, we'll find that Goldman was absolutely right. Sure, all your cases are "the law," but I don't think Rehnquist followed them. In the first place, your nineteenth-century cases don't help your position at all. There's nothing in our law that makes wearing a yarmulke either a crime or a threat to public safety. It won't destroy the fabric of family life as polygamy might, so *Reynolds* doesn't apply. And *Davis* is one of the worst opinions the Supreme Court ever issued. Imagine today how long it would take the courts to strike down a law requiring voters to take an oath that they did not advocate legalizing marijuana, or that they did not favor abortion.

MARY: But *Davis* is still on the books.

BEN: That doesn't make it right. We can debate that later. Now you have to hear my boring list. Starting in 1925 the Court began to defend liberty interests comparable to Goldman's. In *Pierce v. Society of Sisters* (268 U.S. 510) the Supreme Court held that the liberty guaranteed by the Fourteenth Amendment required the State of Oregon to allow children to choose to get educated in religious schools rather than public schools. This theme carries through all the cases you've cited. The Constitution requires the government to tip in favor of protecting our liberties unless and until it can show—not just assert, like the Air Force did, but show through plausible evidence and argument—that the religious practice will harm society at large. The *Cantwell* case in 1940 struck down the New Haven censorship law because the bureaucrat could deny anyone the right to promote his religious beliefs without any showing that the advocacy would do any harm.

And then come the famous cases. *West Virginia State Board of Education v. Barnette* (319 U.S. 624, 1943) stands as one of the most resounding civil liberties victories in our constitutional history. Here the Supreme Court prohibited the states from compelling schoolchildren to salute the flag against their religious convictions. Law professors and journalists alike had savaged the earlier decision, *Minersville School District v. Gobitis* (310 U.S. 586, 1940), on the ground that, in forcing Jehovah's Witness children and parents to choose between violating the Commandment against worshipping a false god, the flag, or going without an education (and, in the case of the parents, risking prosecution for truancy), the Court had condoned exactly what we would fight against in Nazi Germany. By 1943 that war had materialized, yet Justice Jackson went further than the Court had in *Pierce*. For Jackson the issue was not simply whether the rule bore a reasonable relation to a useful purpose, patriotism. Instead Jackson wrote:

> If there is any fixed star in our constitutional constellation, it is that no official, high or petty, can prescribe what shall be orthodox in politics, nationalism, religion, or other matters of opinion or force citizens to confess by word or act their faith therein. If there are any circumstances which permit an exception, they do not now occur to us. . . . We think the action . . . invades the sphere of intellect and spirit which it is the purpose of the First Amendment of our Constitution to reserve from *all* official control.

"*All* official control." That's strong language. Jackson was no dummy. He doesn't distinguish between belief and action. He talks of matters of the spirit, and when he wrote "all official control," we know the military must have crossed his mind.

MARY: But the military rights cases Rehnquist cites clearly reject that liberal a reading.

BEN: I admit that in practice most cases don't go this far. But the cases still require the government to show how interference with a religious liberty serves a compelling state interest. Take the unemployment compensation case. Suppose an employee belongs to a sabbatarian religion and is fired from a job for refusing to work on Saturdays. Does it violate the free exercise of that person's religion for the state to deny her unemployment compensation while she seeks a job that does not require Saturday work? *Sherbert v. Verner* (374 U.S. 398, 1963) held yes. The state insisted that this case could lead to a flood of phony unemployment claims, but the Court didn't buy that. The Court held that the state could win only if it established that a "compelling state interest" would be served by denying the benefits. The Court noted that the state had introduced no evidence to support its claim that the ruling would open up a run on unemployment funds by phony and fraudulent claims. A mere abstract possibility of disruption did not suffice to outweigh the religious freedom claim. This is just like Goldman's case. The trial produced *no* evidence that wearing the yarmulkes would do any harm. The California Supreme Court upheld the use of an illegal substance, peyote, by Navajo Indians in religious services by the same reasoning. It concluded that in practice the use of the drug was confined to the religious service and that there was no evidence of harm to the participants, their families, or outsiders. The California court noted that peyote was not merely a part of the worship service, like bread and wine in the Christian Eucharist, but was itself an object of worship. Those who consumed it outside the religious ritual committed a sacrilege (*People v. Woody*, 61 Cal 2d 716, 1964).

MARY: That's no precedent here.

BEN: It doesn't have to be. I'm only trying to show you that our legal system, indeed our entire political system, assumes that we're free, we have liberty, and that government can take away our liberty only after it shows that doing so is necessary to achieve some greater good. But you want precedents—let's talk about the Amish. In 1972 the Court, in probably its strongest free exercise decision, ruled that the state of Wisconsin could not compel Amish parents to send their children to school—any approved school at all— beyond the eighth grade. Wisconsin law required all children to attend school through the age of 16. The opinion followed the lead taken in *Sherbert*. The trial had produced no evidence that the less educated Amish children were more likely to become criminals or to end up as burdens on the social welfare rolls of Wisconsin. Indeed the evidence showed the opposite. So in Goldman's case it's the government that doesn't have a leg to stand on. The military has not shown a compelling interest against allowing Jewish officers to wear yarmulkes in settings fully comparable to civilian settings. It has at best introduced abstract speculations. Goldman should have won. The precedents consistently tip the scales in favor of free exercise until the government introduces compelling evidence of the harm it causes. Besides, this line of cases draws no distinction between beliefs and practices. The First Amendment does guarantee the free *exercise* of religion, not merely freedom of conscience. If the Constitution excuses children from a patriotic exercise in wartime and excuses children from the obligation to get a complete education on the basis of their religion, and if the Constitution requires spending taxpayer money on those unemployed only by virtue of their religious convictions, it's crazy not to excuse Goldman from the headgear rule. The Air Force had accepted him and his yarmulke for several years. Judging from the evidence in the case, his yarmulke was harmless. Rehnquist is a madman!

MARY: Calm down, Ben.

BEN: I'm only trying to keep us awake. I really think both your long list and mine are boring as hell.

MARY: But they're the law! I hate to tell you, but you're ignoring two things. First, remember those cases Rehnquist cited at the beginning of his opinion? They all say that the "compelling state interest test" does *not* apply to the military. In those cases the military didn't really prove that circulating petitions about grooming or giving a speech would have any serious harmful effects. The military just asserted it.

BEN: No, you miss my point. It's not that the military really proved anything in some final objective sense. What matters is that the Court insisted on looking into the matter for itself. In *Chappell* the Court insisted on actually investigating the question of whether allowing damage suits would injure the military chain of command. The Court found that it would. And in *Brown* the Court insisted that the Air Force actually show that the speech could interfere with military effectiveness and that the anti-speech regulation was narrowly designed to protect effectiveness and no more. In *Goldman* Justice Rehnquist, the great advocate of self-restraint, makes brand new law. For the first time the Supreme Court takes the pressure off the military to justify its actions. The law now says we'll take the military's word for it without proof.

MARY: And that's the second thing you forgot. You yourself just pointed out how the Court has revised constitutional law across our history. Well, why not here?

BEN: But Mary, you started out saying that the weight of all these precedents proved Rehnquist was right. If you now argue that the Court can change its precedents, you shoot down your own argument. I'm only trying to show that you can argue the cases both ways, that the cases don't really prove that one side is necessarily right.

MARY: Yes they do. They add up to a clear moral statement that military defense takes priority over individual liberty. You can't run a military any other way.

BEN: And I can counter that by appealing to history. The whole history of democracy is to prevent the military from having this kind of unchecked power. So we're at a standoff.

MARY: No we're not. I'll concede that the cases by themselves don't dictate the result in some automatic or mechanistic sense. But principles emerge from lines of cases. The principle is the idea the cases together stand for, the idea that holds them together and makes them coherent. And from the polygamy case forward, the courts have said that the government can protect itself from harm at the expense of liberties. In World War II the Court upheld military orders requiring American citizens of Japanese ancestry living in Western states to go to "relocation centers" without any proof that they were disloyal or that their presence made enemy infiltration or sabotage more likely.

BEN: That was one of the worst decisions of all time! You're not defending that result, are you?

MARY: No, I'm just reporting what the law is and that Justice Rehnquist's opinion coherently follows the law. The Supreme Court isn't some moral legislator. We can disagree and work to change or improve the law, but Rehnquist did nothing illegal. His opinion is perfectly good law, and that's all we can say in judgment of the Court.

BEN: Aha! Now you say that there's no provable right answer. I agree. The weight of cases doesn't produce one automatically right result. But we do make—we can't avoid making—moral judgments about the cases. The judges can't help making moral judgments every time they decide. That's what doing justice is all about. I say the principle that holds the cases together, including the cases Rehnquist cites, requires the government, even in the military, to reassure us that it's necessary to invade liberties. The dissenters in *Goldman* make just this moral claim.

MARY: But Ben, we believe in a government of law, not of men. Rehnquist's morality is that he follows the law and does not let his moral values get in the way. He is faithful to our history. In terms of the law's morality, he made the correct decision.

BEN: And I say he didn't. He ignores that people seeking religious liberty founded this nation. He ignores the moral foundation of all those precedents you cite. After all, judges decided all those precedent cases too. Unless you think they come from some constitutional stork, sooner or later we have to face the fact that people make precedents the way they make babies. To decide if a case is right, we have to decide if we agree with the morality the law expresses.

CONCLUSION

Ben and Mary may think they have come to a standoff, but they do agree that the legal meaning of lines of cases depends on the principles that tie them together. The difficulty is that each side constructs an equally good list. For review, you might try identifying pairs of cases from these lists that seem to contradict each other. Would the *Reynolds* court that decided the fate of the Mormons have agreed with Justice

Jackson in *Barnette* exempting Jehovah's Witnesses from compulsory flag salute? Does the Sunday closing case agree with *Sherbert*, which required paying unemployment compensation to sabbatarians?

The main point of this dialogue, however, underscores that listing and arguing about the cases this way is futile and therefore boring. The long boring lists miss some essential expectation we have of justice. Both debaters agree, when pressed, that we must look behind the written precedents to larger questions of morality and history to decide whether we agree with a decision. After the next chapter's case we shall look at whether history and moral theory can tell us any better than precedents which choice to make.

BIBLIOGRAPHIC NOTES

The opinions in *Goldman* together with Ben and Mary's legal debate canvass virtually all the significant free-exercise precedents in our constitutional history. Since the *Goldman* decision, the Court has decided two significant free-exercise cases. In *Hobbie v. Unemployment Appeals Commission* (107 S.Ct. 1046, 1987) the Court decided, over Justice Rehnquist's dissent, that a worker who joined the Seventh-day Adventist Church after working for an employer for several years, and who was then fired for her refusal to work on her Sabbath, deserved unemployment compensation. The majority insisted that the state could deny such benefits only after proving a compelling state interest in doing so. Here the state made no such showing and lost. The second case, the focus of the last chapter, held that the State of Oregon could deny unemployment benefits to persons fired for ingesting peyote in a Native American religious ceremony.

The *Goldman* decision itself did not receive major coverage in the law reviews. Most of the coverage occurred either in canvasses of the Court's work for that term or in short essays usually called "notes" and written by law students. Nearly all these comments criticized the majority. See, for example, the review of the 1985 Term in 100 *Harvard Law Review* 163 (1986): "[O]nly an almost blind obeisance to military officialdom can explain the result in *Goldman*." See also critical comments in "Civil Liberty and Military Necessity," 113 *Military Law Review* 31 (1986); "The 'Core'–'Periphery' Dichotomy in First Amendment Free Exercise Clause Doctrine," 72 *Cornell Law Review* 827 (1987); "First Amendment Rights of Military Personnel: Denying Rights to Those Who Defend Them," 62 *New York University Law Review* 855 (1987).

For more general treatments of free-exercise law see John Arthur, *The Unfinished Constitution* (1989), Chapter 6; Leo Pfeffer, *God, Caesar, and the Constitution* (1975); Michael E. Smith, "The Special Place of Religion in the Constitution" (1983); Leonard Levy, *The Establishment Clause* (1986).

CHAPTER 3

Establishment Law:
Genesis v. *Charles Darwin*

The Court has been particularly vigilant in monitoring compliance with the Establishment Clause in elementary and secondary schools. Families entrust public schools with the education of their children, but condition their trust on the understanding that the classroom will not purposely be used to advance religious views that may conflict with the private beliefs of the student and his or her family. Students in such institutions are impressionable, and their attendance is involuntary.

—*Justice William Brennan*

In 1791 the First Amendment presumably sought to prevent the national government from adopting an official religion, as England did under Henry VIII and Elizabeth I. We saw in the last chapter that the Supreme Court has applied the establishment clause to the states through the Fourteenth Amendment's clause prohibiting the state from depriving a person of life, liberty, or property without due process of law. This is a curious interpretation because a number of colonies, particularly in New England, gave official support to specific Christian sects at the founding, and the establishment clause in 1789 reassured them that the Congress could not interfere with those practices. How, then, did the Fourteenth Amendment, which wrote the Union victory in the Civil War into the Constitution, change that? How does establishing a religion deprive a person of liberty without due process? And why would teaching religion alongside science in the schools violate the establishment principle at all? "Balanced treatment" hardly equals the official adoption of a particular sect.

    Edwards v. Aguillard held that Louisiana illegally established a religion when its legislature required public schools to give "balanced treatment" to evolution and creation science whenever either is taught. The opinions in this case raise the scientific, historical, moral, and religious questions that underlie the First Amendment more directly than the opinions in *Goldman* did. This chapter makes the same point about religious establishment that the last chapter made about free-exercise law. Neither the Constitution nor what the Supreme Court had said about it provided an unambiguously correct solution to the creation-science case. The following chapters address the historical and moral issues directly. In the previous chapter, you read the majority and dissenting opinions first and then, through the debate, wove the precedents back into the opinions. This chapter reviews the establishment cases chronologically before presenting the Court's opinions. In this way you will be able to read the creation-science opinions already knowing the precedents on which judges on different sides of the issue could draw to justify their conclusion. We begin with the argument for upholding Louisiana's "balanced treatment" statute.

"WE ARE A RELIGIOUS PEOPLE"

If the First Amendment only prohibits the establishment of a particular religious sect, we might read the Constitution implicitly to endorse the nation's Christian origins. If so, Louisiana's balanced treatment law, which requires merely offering scientific evidence of a sudden creation alongside evidence of long-term evolution, comes nowhere near official state endorsement of a particular religious sect. We now review the many cases which support the position that the state can constitutionally accommodate and reinforce religious, and specifically Christian, values without officially establishing a religion.

1811. In New York State one Ruggles, who had in public stated that "Jesus Christ was a bastard, and his mother must be a whore," was charged with the common-law crime of blasphemy against Christianity. New York's highest court upheld his conviction, fine ($500) and imprisonment for three months, stating that protecting Christianity was not an establishment because Christianity itself was essential to the survival of civil government. "[W]hatever strikes at the root of Christianity, tends manifestly to the dissolution of civil government" *The People against Ruggles* (8 Johns. 225). This case, of course, predates the incorporation of the establishment clause into the Fourteenth Amendment's limits on the states. It illustrates how originally the First Amendment establishment clause prohibited Congress from interfering with the states if and when the states chose to establish religions of their own. (For decades after the founding, Massachusetts by law compelled church attendance at least once every three months and distributed tax revenues to incorporated churches in proportion to church membership. Connecticut, whose state constitution guaranteed religious freedom, for many decades required witnesses to take their oath on a Protestant Bible. In several New England states Jews were not permitted to vote or hold office well into the nineteenth century.)

1892. It would be easier to disregard *Ruggles* as irrelevant and anachronistic had not the Supreme Court declared much the same message in *Holy Trinity Church v. United States* (143 U.S. 457). In this case Congress, to protect jobs for Americans, had made it unlawful for "any person . . . in any manner whatsoever, to prepay the transportation . . . of any alien . . . into the United States . . . under contract . . . to perform labor or service of any kind in the United States. . . ." Holy Trinity had arranged for the transportation of an Englishman to become its pastor. The Supreme Court, ignoring the statute's repeated use of the inclusive word "any," held that Congress obviously did not intend the law to cover Christian ministers. Christianity is part of our common law, said the Court, and "this is a Christian nation."

1952. While the Court in 1948 prohibited voluntary Bible classes on school property during school hours, the Court seemed to go out of its way to approve a state policy allowing children to leave school to attend religious studies elsewhere. Justice Douglas's language seemed to reaffirm the spirit of *Ruggles* and *Holy Trinity* when he wrote:

> We are a religious people whose institutions presuppose a Supreme Being. We guarantee the freedom to worship as one chooses. We sponsor an attitude on the part of government that shows no partiality to any one group and that lets each flourish according to the zeal of its adherents and the appeal of its dogma. When the state encourages religious instruction or cooperates with religious authorities by adjusting the schedule of public events to sectarian needs, it follows the best of our traditions. For it then respects the religious nature of our people and accommodates the public service to their spiritual needs.

The spirit of accommodation in this case, *Zorach v. Clauson* (343 U.S. 306), seems entirely consistent with requiring teachers to contrast more and less religious views on the science of creation.

1961. We have already seen how the Court found no conflict between Sunday closing laws and religious free exercise. In *McGowen v. Maryland* (366 U.S. 420) the Court found that Sunday closing did not conflict with the establishment clause. The fact that there is an obvious Christian influence on the choice of Sunday as the mandatory day of rest does not mean that the law establishes a religion. It also serves the valid secular purpose of shielding the maximum number of citizens from the temptations of commercial life and allowing more families to get together than would the choice of any other day.

1970. Churches and other religious organizations, like private, church-run schools, have traditionally received a variety of tax breaks. State and local governments exempt them from property taxes and they receive not-for-profit status under the Internal Revenue Code. In *Walz v. Tax Commission of the City of New York* (397

U.S. 664), the Supreme Court approved this practice. It insisted that most churches engage directly in charity work, thus relieving government and taxpayers of some of that burden. Moreover, churches that do no charity work but merely preach and teach religion have a secular stabilizing influence on the community. *Walz* presumably justifies the inclusion in Title VII of the 1964 Civil Rights Act of a prohibition against discrimination in employment decisions on the basis of religion, but at the same time allows an exemption for religious employers, who may discriminate by hiring members of their own sects.

1983. The Court decided two cases in 1983 that rejected establishment arguments. In the first, *Mueller v. Allen* (463 U.S. 388), it upheld a Minnesota law allowing parents to deduct expenditures for tuition, books, supplies, and transportation, up to a $700 ceiling, for their children's education. The Court deemed irrelevant that tuition-paying parents of children in private, and hence predominantly religious, schools would benefit from this law far more than would parents of public school children who pay no such tuition. Justice Rehnquist stressed that this law made no formal distinction on the basis of religion. In the second case, *Marsh v. Chambers* (463 U.S. 783), the Court approved the practice of the Nebraska legislature of paying a chaplain to conduct prayers at the beginning of legislative sessions. The majority opinion pointed out that the same Congress that endorsed the original Bill of Rights also authorized payment of a chaplain for itself.

1984. Lynch v. Donnelly (465 U.S. 668), the famous Pawtucket, Rhode Island, creche case, held that just as we allow "In God We Trust" on our currency and allow Congress to designate Christmas a national holiday and allow public museums to purchase and display religious works of art, so the city can pay for the display of a manger scene on private property as part of the merchant's annual Christmas display. "The display is sponsored by the city to celebrate the Holiday and to depict the origins of that Holiday. These are legitimate secular purposes," wrote Chief Justice Burger.

1985. A federal appellate court upheld providing chaplains out of taxpayer monies for military bases in *Katcoff v. Marsh* (755 F.2d 223).

Does Louisiana's creation-science law meet the criteria these cases endorse? Louisiana does not permit teaching it as religious doctrine per se; the law does not symbolically endorse Christianity directly, as do the creche or chaplain prayer or "In God We Trust" on U.S. currency. *Zorach*, no mere holdover from a rejected past, strongly supports government action that will accommodate differing religious interests. Hence, even if, as in the case of Sunday closing laws, the creation-science statute serves the religious interests of some, that impact is part of the very accommodation *Zorach* affirms. That case, of course, involved religious training on private property, but the Nebraska chaplain's prayers and the creche, both legal and both explicitly religious, occur in public.

THOMAS JEFFERSON'S "WALL OF SEPARATION"

No metaphor occurs more frequently in establishment clause law than does Thomas Jefferson's famous phrase. In his New Year's Day, 1802, letter to the Baptist Association of Danbury, Connecticut, President Jefferson wrote that the establishment and free-exercise clauses built "a wall of separation between Church and State." The Baptists had been the victims of official state persecution, especially in colonial Virginia, and have until very recently strongly advocated strict separation of church and state, so Jefferson's comment may have had a political motive. Nevertheless the metaphor has played a dramatic role in twentieth-century establishment law. Here are the cases that would condemn Louisiana's effort to teach, even indirectly, a biblically based version of science.

1947. Everson, the first modern establishment case, approved giving transportation money to parents of schoolchildren, but the Court seemed more concerned with expanding the reach of the establishment clause. For the majority Justice Black wrote:

> The "establishment of religion" clause of the First Amendment means at least this: Neither a state nor the Federal Government can set up a church. Neither can pass laws which aid one religion, aid all religions, or prefer one religion over another. Neither can force nor influence a person to go to or to remain away from church against his will or force him to profess a belief or disbelief in any religion. No person can be punished for entertaining or professing religious beliefs or disbeliefs, for church attendance or non-attendance. No tax in any amount, large or small, can be levied to support any religious activities or institutions, whatever they may be called, or whatever form they may adopt to teach or practice religion. Neither a state nor the Federal Government can, openly or secretly, participate in the affairs of any religious organizations or groups and vice versa. In the words of Jefferson, the clause against establishment of religion by law was intended to erect "a wall of separation between church and state." . . .

1948. McCollum v. Board of Education (333 U.S. 203), which forbade Bible classes on school grounds during school time, repeated the theme. Again Justice Black:

> Here not only are the State's tax-supported public school buildings used for the dissemination of religious doctrines. The State also affords sectarian groups an invaluable aid in that it helps to provide pupils for their religious classes through the use of the State's compulsory public school machinery. This is not separation of Church and State.

1962. In *Engel v. Vitale* (370 U.S. 421), the first of the famous school prayer cases which held unconstitutional the nondenominational prayer composed by the New

York Regents, Justice Black invoked more directly the historical experience that generated the establishment clause:

> The purposes underlying the Establishment Clause rested on the belief that a union of government and religion tends to destroy government and to degrade religion. The history of the governmentally established religion, both in England and in this country, showed that whenever government had allied itself with one particular form of religion, the inevitable result had been that it had incurred the hatred, disrespect, and even contempt of those who held contrary beliefs. That same history showed that many people had lost their respect for any religion that had relied upon the support of government to spread its faith. Another purpose of the Establishment Clause rested upon an awareness of the historical fact that governmentally established religions and religious persecutions go hand in hand.

Engel seemed so clearly an establishment benchmark that Justice Brennan's dissent in the creche case complained that the Court had undermined the foundation of modern establishment law in a throwback to *Holy Trinity*:

> By insisting that such a distinctly sectarian message [the creche] is merely an unobjectionable part of our "religious heritage," . . . the Court takes a long step backwards to the days when Justice Brewer could arrogantly declare for the Court that "this is a Christian nation." . . . Those days, I had thought, were forever put behind us by the Court's decision in *Engel v. Vitale* . . . , in which we rejected a similar argument advanced by the State of New York that its Regent's Prayer was simply an acceptable part of our "spiritual heritage."

1963. Abington School District v. Schempp (374 U.S. 203) struck down a Pennsylvania state law requiring reading without comment at least ten verses of the Bible at the beginning of each school day. Students could be excused from the exercise with written permission from their parent or guardian.

1968. Epperson v. Arkansas (393 U.S. 97) comes as close as any on these lists to controlling *Edwards*. In 1928, shortly after the famous *Scopes* monkey trial (where the Tennessee Supreme Court upheld a statute forbidding the teaching of Darwinian evolution), Arkansas passed a statute making it unlawful for a teacher in a state-supported school "to teach the theory or doctrine that mankind ascended or descended from a lower order of animals" or "to adopt or use in any such institution a textbook that teaches" this theory. Justice Fortas's majority opinion held the restriction invalid on two grounds. First, making it a crime for a teacher to teach a scientific theory violates the First Amendment free expression rights of the teacher. Second, the purpose of the Arkansas law was not neutral as to religion; it did not simply forbid teaching any theory of evolution at all. Instead, the law attempted "to blot out a particular theory because of its supposed conflict with the Biblical account, literally read." The law therefore violated the establishment clause. Note, however, how the case provides fuel for both sides in the Louisiana case. Louisiana did not prohibit the teaching of evolution. Its requirement of balance is neutral. It seems to meet Justice Black's test. On the other hand, the law does limit the teacher's freedom to teach. Yet all curricular requirements do so. The Constitution has never granted teachers the freedom to teach anything they wish. Indeed, in 1979 a federal appellate court struck down on First Amendment grounds an elective course in Transcendental Meditation that compelled its students to attend a Hindu ceremony sung in Sanskrit, during which students would select their personal mantra.

1971. Lemon v. Kurtzman (403 U.S. 602) began a line of cases, continuing for over a decade, that sorted out the extent to which states could use public funds to support religious schools. *Lemon* "codified" the prior law on the subject into a "three-pronged test": "First, the statute must have a secular legislative purpose; second, its principal or primary effect must be one that neither advances nor inhibits religion . . . ; finally, the statute must not foster 'an excessive government entanglement with religion.' " According to the Court, a statute violates the First Amendment if it violates any one of these three tests. Thus *Lemon* permitted public funding of school lunches in sectarian schools because good nutrition has a secular purpose that neither promotes nor inhibits religion nor requires governmental interference in the daily management of the school. However, the Court struck down state provision of instructional materials for religious schools, because for government to make sure that the materials were not used to teach religion would cause excessive entanglement of the state and religion. Subsequent cases permitted providing counseling and therapy for students at religious schools off school grounds but held unconstitutional funding for teacher salary supplements; tuition reimbursement for parents of private-school children; maps, magazines, and tape recorders for children; and payment to public school teachers to teach nonreligious subjects in religious schools. Nearly all of these decisions rested on the second and third prongs of the test. In nearly every case the Court conceded the secular purpose of improving the quality of education per se but held that the effect would either advance religion or require too much government supervision of religious schools to ensure that advancing religion did not happen.

1980. Stone v. Graham (449 U.S. 39) struck down a Kentucky statute requiring the posting of the Ten Commandments in every public classroom. Private funding paid for the physical copies. The Court found no secular purpose, despite the fact that the legislature had required printing at the bottom of every copy that the Commandments are a secular foundation of "the fundamental legal code of Western Civilization and the Common Law of the United States."

1985. Wallace v. Jaffree (105 S. CT. 2479) struck down an Alabama law that allowed in public schools a period of silence "for meditation or voluntary prayer." The Court noted that Alabama already had on its books a presumptively valid law requiring a minute of silence for voluntary meditation. It concluded that adding the reference to prayer could have only a religious purpose; indeed the sponsor of the bill in the Alabama legislature said at trial that the only purpose of the bill was to return voluntary prayer to the school. In 1985 the Court also struck down a Connecticut law forbidding employers from requiring employees to work on their Sabbath, regardless of which day of the week the employee observed. The Court could find only a sacred purpose here, namely to give a job benefit to people classified by religion that the nonreligious cannot receive. *Estate of Thornton v. Caldor, Inc.* (472 U.S. 703).

THE CASE

The opinions in this case make most of the arguments on both sides clear to the layperson. However, one procedural aspect of this case may affect evaluations of these opinions: as in *Goldman*, the trial court decided this case not by holding a full trial but by holding hearings on a motion, a kind of mini-trial without a jury. The plaintiff filed, and the trial court granted, a motion for summary judgment, which made a full trial unnecessary. The plaintiff won the summary judgment by prevailing on a matter of law and a matter of fact. The plaintiff, using the first prong of the *Lemon* test, insisted that the statute failed because teaching the belief in the abrupt appearance of complex life forms could have no secular purpose. A trial judge may grant summary judgment only after giving the factual allegations a reading most favorable to the loser. Here, therefore, the trial judge found that after reading the facts Louisiana's way, one would nevertheless have to conclude that the only purpose of the law was to advance religion. We have trials to find the facts, but the judge knew key facts prior to the trial because the plaintiff introduced during pretrial proceedings the record of the legislative debate, and the defendant introduced affidavits of the scientific nature of creationism. The trial judge decided that nothing the parties might prove at a trial could change the conclusion that the only purpose of creation science was to advance religion. Justice Brennan and the Supreme Court majority agreed, but Justices Scalia and Rehnquist vehemently disagreed. Their dissent is long, but we cannot judge the goodness of this result without reviewing the dissent carefully. If, as the dissenters believe, a trial might bring forward evidence that the statute *did* have a secular purpose, then it would pass the *Lemon* test, and therefore it was wrong to grant summary judgment. The dissenters also believe that the purpose prong of *Lemon* is itself bad law and the Court should abandon it, and therefore the trial court should not have granted summary judgment either. The law had never been enforced and hence nobody had yet gathered any factual evidence about whether teaching creationism in practice would serve a secular purpose. Nor could it be known in advance whether such teaching would substantially advance or inhibit religion.

EDWARDS v. AGUILLARD

482 U.S. 578 (1987)

Justice BRENNAN delivered the opinion of the Court.

The question for decision is whether Louisiana's "Balanced Treatment for Creation-Science and Evolution-Science in Public School Instruction" Act (Creationism Act), La.Rev.Stat.Ann. §§ 17:286.1–17:286.7, is facially invalid as violative of the Establishment Clause of the First Amendment.

I

The Creationism Act forbids the teaching of the theory of evolution in public schools unless accompanied by instruction in "creation science." § 17:286–4A. No school is required to teach evolution or creation science. If either is taught, however, the other must also be taught. *Ibid.* The theories of evolution and creation science are statutorily defined as "the scientific evidences for [creation or evolution] and inferences from those scientific evidences." §§ 17.286.3(2) and (3).

Appellees, who include parents of children attending Louisiana public schools, Louisiana teachers, and religious leaders, challenged the constitutionality of the Act in District Court, seeking an injunction and declaratory relief. Appellants, Louisiana officials charged with implementing the Act, defended on the ground that the purpose of the Act is to protect a legitimate secular interest, namely, academic freedom. Appellees attacked the Act as facially invalid because it violated the Establishment Clause and made a motion for summary judgment. The District Court granted the motion. *Aguillard v. Treen*, 634 F.Supp. 426 (ED La.1985). The court held that there can be no valid secular reason for prohibiting the teaching of evolution, a theory historically opposed by some religious denominations. The court further concluded that "the teaching of 'creation-science' and 'creationism,' as contemplated by the statute, involves teaching 'tailored to the principles' of a particular religious sect or group of sects." *Id.*, at 427 (citing *Epperson v. Arkansas*, 393 U.S. 97, 106, 89 S.Ct. 266, 271–72, 21 L.Ed.2d 228 [1968]). The District Court therefore held that the Creationism Act violated the Establishment Clause either because it prohibited the teaching of evolution or because it required the teaching of creation science with the purpose of advancing a particular religious doctrine.

The Court of Appeals affirmed. 765 F.2d 1251 (CA5 1985). The court observed that the statute's avowed purpose of protecting academic freedom was inconsistent with requiring, upon risk of sanction, the teaching of creation science whenever evolution is taught. *Id.*, at 1257. The court found that the Louisiana legislature's actual intent was "to discredit evolution by counterbalancing its teaching at every turn with the teaching of creationism, a religious belief." *Ibid.* Because the Creationism Act was thus a law furthering a particular religious belief, the Court of Appeals held that the Act violated the Establishment Clause. A suggestion for rehearing en banc was denied over a dissent. 778 F.2d 225 (CA5 1985). We now affirm.

II

The Establishment Clause forbids the enactment of any law "respecting an establishment of religion."[3] The Court has applied a three-pronged test to determine whether

---

[3] The First Amendment states: "Congress shall make no law respecting an establishment of religion. . . ." Under the Fourteenth Amendment, this "fundamental concept of liberty" applies to the States. *Cantwell v. Connecticut*, 310 U.S. 296 (1940).

legislation comports with the Establishment Clause. First, the legislature must have adopted the law with a secular purpose. Second, the statute's principal or primary effect must be one that neither advances nor inhibits religion. Third, the statute must not result in an excessive entanglement of government with religion. *Lemon v. Kurtzman*, 403 U.S. 602, 612–613 (1971).[4] State action violates the Establishment Clause if it fails to satisfy any of these prongs.

In this case, the Court must determine whether the Establishment Clause was violated in the special context of the public elementary and secondary school system. States and local school boards are generally afforded considerable discretion in operating public schools. See *Bethel School District No. 403 v. Fraser*, 478 U.S. 675 (1986); *Tinker v. Des Moines Independent Community School Dist.*, 393 U.S. 503 (1969). "At the same time . . . we have necessarily recognized that the discretion of the States and local school boards in matters of education must be exercised in a manner that comports with the transcendent imperatives of the First Amendment." *Board of Education v. Pico*, 457 U.S. 853, 864 (1982).

The Court has been particularly vigilant in monitoring compliance with the Establishment Clause in elementary and secondary schools. Families entrust public schools with the education of their children, but condition their trust on the understanding that the classroom will not purposely be used to advance religious views that may conflict with the private beliefs of the student and his or her family. Students in such institutions are impressionable and their attendance is involuntary. See, e.g., *Grand Rapids School Dist.* v. *Ball*, 473 U.S. 373, 383 (1985); *Wallace* v. *Jaffree*, 472 U.S. 38 (1985); *Meek* v. *Pittenger*, 421 U.S. 349, 369 (1975); *Abington School Dist.* v. *Schempp*, 374 U.S. 203, 252253 (1963) (BRENNAN, J., concurring). The State exerts great authority and coercive power through mandatory attendance requirements, and because of the students' emulation of teachers as role models and the children's susceptibility to peer pressure.[5] See *Bethel School Dist. No. 403* v. *Fraser, supra*; *Wallace* v. *Jaffree, supra*, (O'CONNOR, J., concurring in judgment). Furthermore, "[t]he public school is at once the symbol of our democracy and the most pervasive means for promoting our common destiny. In no activity of the State is it more vital to keep out divisive forces than in its schools. . . ." *Illinois ex rel. McCollum* v. *Board of Education*, 333 U.S. 203, 231 (1948) (opinion of Frankfurter, J.).

Consequently, the Court has been required often to invalidate statutes which advance religion in public elementary and secondary schools. See, e.g., *Grand Rapids School Dist.* v. *Ball, supra* (school district's use of religious school teachers in public schools); *Wallace* v. *Jaffree, supra* (Alabama statute authorizing moment of silence for school prayer); *Stone* v. *Graham*, 449 U.S. 39 (1980) (posting copy of Ten Commandments on

---

[4] The *Lemon* test has been applied in all cases since its adoption in 1971, except in *Marsh* v. *Chambers*, 463 U.S. 783 (1983), where the Court held that the Nebraska legislature's practice of opening a session with a prayer by a chaplain paid by the State did not violate the establishment clause. The Court based its conclusion in that case on the historical acceptance of the practice. Such a historical approach is not useful in determining the proper roles of church and state in public schools, since free public education was virtually nonexistent at the time the Constitution was adopted. See *Wallace v. Jaffree*, 472 U.S. 38 (1985) (O'CONNOR, J., concurring in judgment) (citing *Abington School Dist. v. Schempp*, 374 U.S. 203, 238, and n. 7 [1963] [BRENNAN, J., concurring]).

[5] The potential for undue influence is far less significant with regard to college students, who voluntarily enroll in courses. "This distinction warrants a difference in constitutional results." *Abington School Dist. v. Schempp, supra*, at 253, 83 S.Ct., at 1587 (BRENNAN, J., concurring). Thus, for instance, the Court has not questioned the authority of state colleges and universities to offer courses on religion or theology. See *Widmar v. Vincent*, 454 U.S. 263 (1981) (POWELL, J.); *id.*, at 281 (STEVENS, J., concurring in judgment).

public classroom wall); *Epperson v. Arkansas*, 393 U.S. 97 (1968) (statute forbidding teaching of evolution); *Abington School District v. Schempp, supra* (daily reading of Bible); *Engel v. Vitale*, 370 U.S. 421, 430 (1962) (recitation of "denominationally neutral" prayer).

Therefore, in employing the three-pronged *Lemon* test, we must do so mindful of the particular concerns that arise in the context of public elementary and secondary schools. We now turn to the evaluation of the Act under the *Lemon* test.

III

Lemon's first prong focuses on the purpose that animated adoption of the Act. "The purpose prong of the *Lemon* test asks whether government's actual purpose is to endorse or disapprove of religion." *Lynch v. Donnelly*, 465 U.S. 668 (1984) (O'CONNOR, J., concurring). A governmental intention to promote religion is clear when the State enacts a law to serve a religious purpose. This intention may be evidenced by promotion of religion in general, see *Wallace v. Jaffree, supra* (Establishment Clause protects individual freedom of conscience "to select any religious faith or none at all"), or by advancement of a particular religious belief, e.g., *Stone v. Graham, supra* (invalidating requirement to post Ten Commandments, which are "undeniably a sacred text in the Jewish and Christian faiths"); *Epperson v. Arkansas, supra* (holding that banning the teaching of evolution in public schools violates the First Amendment since "teaching and learning" must not "be tailored to the principles or prohibitions of any religious sect or dogma"). If the law was enacted for the purpose of endorsing religion, "no consideration of the second or third criteria [of *Lemon*] is necessary." *Wallace v. Jaffree, supra*, at 56. In this case, the petitioners have identified no clear secular purpose for the Louisiana Act.

True, the Act's stated purpose is to protect academic freedom. La.Rev.Stat.Ann. § 17:286.2 (West 1982). This phrase might, in common parlance, be understood as referring to enhancing the freedom of teachers to teach what they will. The Court of Appeals, however, correctly concluded that the Act was not designed to further that goal.[6] We find no merit in the State's argument that the "legislature may not [have] use[d] the terms 'academic freedom' in the correct legal sense. They might have [had] in mind, instead, a basic concept of fairness; teaching all of the evidence." Tr. of Oral Arg. 60. Even if "academic freedom" is read to mean "teaching all of the evidence" with respect to the origin of human beings, the Act does not further this purpose. The goal of providing a more comprehensive science curriculum is not furthered either by outlawing the teaching of evolution or by requiring the teaching of creation science.

---

[6] The Court of Appeals stated that: "[a]cademic freedom embodies the principle that individual instructors are at liberty to teach that which they deem to be appropriate in the exercise of their professional judgment." 765 F.2d, at 1257. But, in the State of Louisiana, courses in public schools are prescribed by the State Board of Education and teachers are not free, absent permission, to teach courses different from what is required. Tr. of Oral Arg. 44–46. "Academic freedom," at least as it is commonly understood, is not a relevant concept in this context. Moreover, as the Court of Appeals explained, the Act "requires, presumably upon risk of *sanction* or *dismissal* for failure to comply, the teaching of creation-science whenever evolution is taught. Although states may prescribe public school curriculum concerning science instruction under ordinary circumstances, the compulsion inherent in the Balanced Treatment Act is, on its face, inconsistent with the idea of academic freedom as it is universally understood." 765 F.2d, at 1257 (emphasis in original). The Act actually serves to diminish academic freedom by removing the flexibility to teach evolution without also teaching creation science, even if teachers determine that such curriculum results in less effective and comprehensive science instruction.

A

While the Court is normally deferential to a State's articulation of a secular purpose, it is required that the statement of such purpose be sincere and not a sham. . . . As Justice O'CONNOR stated in *Wallace*: "It is not a trivial matter, however, to require that the legislature manifest a secular purpose and omit all sectarian endorsements from its laws. That requirement is precisely tailored to the Establishment Clause's purpose of assuring that Government not intentionally endorse religion or a religious practice." 472 U.S., at 75 (concurring in judgment).

It is clear from the legislative history that the purpose of the legislative sponsor, Senator Bill Keith, was to narrow the science curriculum. During the legislative hearings, Senator Keith stated: "My preference would be that neither [creationism nor evolution] be taught." 2 App. E621. Such a ban on teaching does not promote—indeed, it undermines—the provision of a comprehensive scientific education.

It is equally clear that requiring schools to teach creation science with evolution does not advance academic freedom. The Act does not grant teachers a flexibility that they did not already possess to supplant the present science curriculum with the presentation of theories, besides evolution, about the origin of life. Indeed, the Court of Appeals found that no law prohibited Louisiana public schoolteachers from teaching any scientific theory. 765 F.2d, at 1257. As the president of the Louisiana Science Teachers Association testified, "[a]ny scientific concept that's based on established fact can be included in our curriculum already, and no legislation allowing this is necessary." 2 App. E616. The Act provides Louisiana schoolteachers with no new authority. Thus the stated purpose is not furthered by it.

The Alabama statute held unconstitutional in *Wallace v. Jaffree, supra*, is analogous. In *Wallace*, the State characterized its new law as one designed to provide a one-minute period for mediation. We rejected that stated purpose as insufficient, because a previously adopted Alabama law already provided for such a one-minute period. Thus, in this case, as in *Wallace*, "[a]ppellants have not identified any secular purpose that was not fully served by [existing state law] before the enactment of [the statute in question]." 472 U.S., at 59.

Furthermore, the goal of basic "fairness" is hardly furthered by the Act's discriminatory preference for the teaching of creation science and against the teaching of evolution.[7] While requiring that curriculum guides be developed for creation science, the Act says nothing of comparable guides for evolution. Similarly, research services are supplied for creation science but not for evolution. § 17:286.7B. Only "creation scientists" can serve on the panel that supplies the resource services. *Ibid.* The Act forbids school boards to discriminate against anyone who "chooses to be a creation-scientist" or to teach "creationism," but fails to protect those who choose to teach evolution or any other non-creation science theory, or who refuse to teach creation science. § 17:286.4C.

If the Louisiana legislature's purpose was solely to maximize the comprehensiveness and effectiveness of science instruction, it would have encouraged the teaching of all scientific theories about the origins of humankind.[8] But under the Act's requirements,

---

[7] The Creationism Act's provisions appear among other provisions prescribing the courses of study in Louisiana's public schools. These other provisions, similar to those in other states, prescribe courses of study in such topics as driver training, civics, the Constitution, and free enterprise. None of these other provisions, apart from those associated with the Creationism Act, nominally mandates "equal time" for opposing opinions within a specific area of learning. See, e.g., La.Rev.Stat.Ann. §§ 17:261–17:281.

[8] The dissent concludes that the Act's purpose was to protect the academic freedom of students, and not that of teachers. *Post*, at 2601. Such a view is not at odds with our conclusion that if the Act's purpose was to provide comprehensive scientific education (a concern shared by students and teachers, as well as parents), that purpose was not advanced by the statute's provisions. *Supra*, at 2579.

teachers who were once free to teach any and all facets of this subject are now unable to do so. Moreover, the Act fails even to ensure that creation science will be taught, but instead requires the teaching of this theory only when the theory of evolution is taught. Thus we agree with the Court of Appeals' conclusion that the Act does not serve to protect academic freedom, but has the distinctly different purpose of discrediting "evolution by counterbalancing its teaching at every turn with the teaching of creation science. . . ." 765 F.2d, at 1257.

B

Stone v. Graham, invalidated the State's requirement that the Ten Commandments be posted in public classrooms. "The Ten Commandments are undeniably a sacred text in the Jewish and Christian faiths, and no legislative recitation of a supposed secular purpose can blind us to that fact." 449 U.S., at 41. As a result, the contention that the law was designed to provide instruction on a "fundamental legal code" was "not sufficient to avoid conflict with the First Amendment." *Ibid.* Similarly *Abington School District v. Schempp* held unconstitutional a statute "requiring the selection and reading at the opening of the school day of verses from the Holy Bible and the recitation of the Lord's Prayer by the students in unison," despite the proffer of such secular purposes as the "promotion of moral values, the contradiction to the materialistic trends of our times, the perpetuation of our institutions and the teaching of literature." 374 U.S., at 223.

As in *Stone* and *Abington*, we need not be blind in this case to the legislature's preeminent religious purpose in enacting this statute. There is a historic and contemporaneous link between the teachings of certain religious denominations and the teaching of evolution. It was this link that concerned the Court in *Epperson v. Arkansas*, 393 U.S. 97 (1968), which also involved a facial challenge to a statute regulating the teaching of evolution. In that case, the Court reviewed an Arkansas statute that made it unlawful for an instructor to teach evolution or to use a textbook that referred to this scientific theory. Although the Arkansas anti-evolution law did not explicitly state its predominant religious purpose, the Court could not ignore that "[t]he statute was a product of the upsurge of 'fundamentalist' religious fervor" that has long viewed this particular scientific theory as contradicting the literal interpretation of the Bible. *Id.*, 393 U.S., at 98.[10] After reviewing the history of anti-evolution statutes, the Court determined that "there can be no doubt that the motivation for the [Arkansas] law was the same [as other anti-evolution statues]: to suppress the teaching of a theory which, it was thought, 'denied' the divine creation of man." *Id.*, at 109. The Court found that there

---

Moreover, it is astonishing that the dissent, to prove its assertion, relies on a section of the legislation, which was eventually deleted by the legislature. Compare § 3702 in App. E292 (text of section prior to amendment) with La.Rev.Stat.Ann. § 17:286.2. The dissent contends that this deleted section—which was explicitly rejected by the Louisiana legislature—reveals the legislature's "obviously intended meaning of the statutory terms 'academic freedom.' " *Post*, at 2601. Quite to the contrary, Boudreaux, the main expert relief on by the sponsor of the Act, cautioned the legislature that the words "academic freedom" meant "freedom to teach science." App. E429. His testimony was given at the time the legislature was deciding whether to delete this section of the Act.

[10] The Court evaluated the statute in light of a series of anti-evolution statutes adopted by state legislatures dating back to the Tennessee statute that was the focus of the celebrated *Scopes* trial in 1927. *Epperson v. Arkansas*, 393 U.S., at 98, 101, n. 8, and 109. The Court found the Arkansas statute comparable to this Tennessee "monkey law," since both gave preference to "religious establishments which have as one of their tenets or dogmas the instantaneous creation of man." *Id.*, at 103, n. 11 (quoting *Scopes v. State*, 154 Tenn. 105, 126, 289 S.W. 363, 369 [1927] [CHAMBLISS, J., concurring]).

can be no legitimate state interest in protecting particular religions from scientific views "distasteful to them," *id.*, at 107, and concluded "that the First Amendment does not permit the State to require that teaching and learning must be tailored to the principles or prohibitions of any religious sect or dogma," *id.*, at 106.

These same historic and contemporaneous antagonisms between the teachings of certain religious denominations and the teaching of evolution are present in this case. The preeminent purpose of the Louisiana legislature was clearly to advance the religious viewpoint that a supernatural being created humankind.[11] The term "creation science" was defined as embracing this particular religious doctrine by those responsible for the passage of the Creationism Act. Senator Keith's leading expert on creation science, Edward Boudreaux, testified at the legislative hearings that the theory of creation science included belief in the existence of a supernatural creator. See 1 App. E421–422 (noting that "creation scientists" point to high probability that life was "created by an intelligent mind").[12] Senator Keith also cited testimony from other experts to support the creation-science view that "a creator [was] responsible for the universe and everything in it."[13] 2 App. E497. The legislative history therefore reveals that the term "creation science," as contemplated by the legislature that adopted this Act, embodies the religious belief that a supernatural creator was responsible for the creation of humankind.

Furthermore, it is not happenstance that the legislature required the teaching of a theory that coincided with this religious view. The legislative history documents that the Act's primary purpose was to change the science curriculum of public schools in order to provide persuasive advantage to a particular religious doctrine that rejects the factual basis of evolution in its entirety. The sponsor of the Creationism Act, Senator Keith, explained during the legislative hearings that his disdain for the theory of evolution resulted from the support that evolution supplied to views contrary to his own religious beliefs. According to Senator Keith, the theory of evolution was consonant with the "cardinal principle[s] of religious humanism, secular humanism, theological liberalism, aetheistism [*sic*]." 1 App. E312–313; see also 2 App. E499–500. The state senator repeatedly stated that scientific evidence supporting his religious views should be included in the public school curriculum to redress the fact that the theory of evolution incidentally coincided with what he characterized as religious beliefs antithetical to his own.[14] The legislation therefore sought to alter the science curriculum to reflect endorsement of a religious view that is antagonistic to the theory of evolution.

---

[11] While the belief in the instantaneous creation of humankind by a supernatural creator may require the rejection of every aspect of the theory of evolution, an individual instead may choose to accept some or all of this scientific theory as compatible with his or her spiritual outlook. See Tr. of Oral Arg. 23–29.

[12] Boudreaux repeatedly defined creation science in terms of a theory that supports the existence of a supernatural creator. See, *e.g.*, 2 App. E501–502 (equating creation science with a theory pointing "to conditions of a creator"); 1 App. E153–154 ("Creation . . . requires the direct involvement of a supernatural intelligence"). The lead witness at the hearings introducing the original bill, Luther Sunderland, described creation science as postulating "that everything was created by some intelligence or power external to the universe." *Id.*, at E9–10.

[13] Senator Keith believed that creation science embodied this view: "One concept is that a creator however you define a creator was responsible for everything that is in this world. The other concept is that it just evolved." *Id.*, at E280. Besides Senator Keith, several of the most vocal legislators also revealed their religious motives for supporting the bill in the official legislative history. See, *e.g.*, *id.*, at E441, E443 (Sen. Saunders noting that bill was amended so that teachers could refer to the Bible and other religious texts to support the creation-science theory); 2 App. E561–E562, E610 (Rep. Jenkins contending that the existence of God was a scientific fact).

[14] See, *e.g.*, 1 App. E74–E75 (noting that evolution is contrary to his family's religious beliefs); *id.*, at E313 (contending that evolution advances religions contrary to his own); *id.*, at E357 (stating that

In this case, the purpose of the Creationism Act was to restructure the science curriculum to conform with a particular religious viewpoint. Out of many possible science subjects taught in the public schools, the legislature chose to affect the teaching of the one scientific theory that historically has been opposed by certain religious sects. As in *Epperson*, the legislature passed the Act to give preference to those religious groups which have as one of their tenets the creation of humankind by a divine creator. The "overriding fact" that confronted the Court in *Epperson* was "that Arkansas' law selects from the body of knowledge a particular segment which it proscribes for the sole reason that it is deemed to conflict with . . . a particular interpretation of the Book of Genesis by a particular religious group." 393 U.S., at 103. Similarly, the Creationism Act is designed *either* to promote the theory of creation science which embodies a particular religious tenet by requiring that creation science be taught whenever evolution is taught *or* to prohibit the teaching of a scientific theory disfavored by certain religious sects by forbidding the teaching of evolution when creation science is not also taught. The Establishment Clause, however, "forbids *alike* the preference of a religious doctrine or the prohibition of theory which is deemed antagonistic to a particular dogma." *Id.*, at 106107 (emphasis added). Because the primary purpose of the Creationism Act is to advance a particular religious belief, the Act endorses religion in violation of the First Amendment.

We do not imply that a legislature could never require that scientific critiques of prevailing scientific theories be taught. Indeed, the Court acknowledge in *Stone* that its decision forbidding the posting of the Ten Commandments did not mean that no use could ever be made of the Ten Commandments, or that the Ten Commandments played an exclusively religious role in the history of Western Civilization. 449 U.S., at 42. In a similar way, teaching a variety of scientific theories about the origins of humankind to schoolchildren might be validly done with the clear secular intent of enhancing the effectiveness of science instruction. But because the primary purpose of the Creationism Act is to endorse a particular religious doctrine, the Act furthers religion in violation of the Establishment Clause.[15]

In this case, appellees' motion for summary judgment rested on the plain language of the Creationism Act, the legislative history and historical context of the Act, the specific sequence of events leading to the passage of the Act, the State Board's report on a survey of school superintendents, and the correspondence between the Act's legislative sponsor and its key witnesses. Appellants contend that affidavits made by two scientists, two theologians, and an education administrator raise a genuine issue of material fact and that summary judgment was therefore barred. The affidavits define creation science as "origin through abrupt appearance in complex form" and allege that such a viewpoint constitutes a true scientific theory. See App. to Brief for Appellants A–7 to A–40.

We agree with the lower courts that these affidavits do not raise a genuine issue of material fact. The existence of "uncontroverted affidavits" does not bar summary judgment. Moreover, the postenactment testimony of outside experts is of little use in determining the Louisiana legislature's purpose in enacting this statute. The Louisiana

---

evolution is "almost a religion" to science teachers); *id.*, at E418 (arguing that evolution is cornerstone of some religions contrary to his own); 2 App. E763–E764 (author of model bill, from which Act is derived, sent copy of the model bill to Senator Keith and advised that "I view this whole battle as one between God and anti-God forces. . . . if evolution is permitted to continue . . . it will continue to be made to appear that a Supreme Being is unnecessary . . .").

[15] Neither the District Court nor the Court of Appeals found a clear secular purpose, while both agreed that the Creationism Act's primary purpose was to advance religion. "When both courts below are unable to discern an arguably valid secular purpose, this Court normally should hesitate to find one." *Wallace* v. *Jaffree*, 472 U.S., at 66 (POWELL, J., concurring).

legislature did hear and rely on scientific experts in passing the bill,[17] but none of the persons making the affidavits produced by the appellants participated in or contributed to the enactment of the law or its implementation.[18] The District Court, in its discretion, properly concluded that a Monday-morning "battle of the experts" over possible technical meanings of terms in the statute would not illuminate the contemporaneous purpose of the Louisiana legislature when it made the law.[19] We therefore conclude that the District Court did not err in finding that appellants failed to raise a genuine issue of material fact, and in granting summary judgment.

The Louisiana Creationism Act advances a religious doctrine by requiring either the banishment of the theory of evolution from public school classrooms or the presentation of a religious viewpoint that rejects evolution in its entirety. The Act violates the Establishment Clause of the First Amendment because it seeks to employ the symbolic and financial support of government to achieve a religious purpose. The judgment of the Court of Appeals therefore is
Affirmed.

Justice POWELL, with whom Justice O'CONNOR joins, concurring.
I write separately to note certain aspects of the legislative history, and to emphasize that nothing in the Court's opinion diminishes the traditionally broad discretion accorded state and local school officials in the selection of the public school curriculum.

I
. . . .
B

In June 1980, Senator Bill Keith introduced Senate Bill 956 in the Louisiana legislature. The stated purpose of the bill was to "assure academic freedom by requiring the teaching of the theory of creation ex nihilo in all public schools where the theory of evolution is taught." 1 App. E-1.[2] The bill defined the "theory of creation ex nihilo" as "the belief that the origin of the elements, the galaxy, the solar system, of life, of all the species of plants and animals, the origin of man, and the original of all things and their processes and relationships were created ex nihilo and fixed by God." *Id.*, at E-1a— E-1b. This theory was referred to by Senator Keith as "scientific creationism." *Id.*, at E-2.

---

[17] The experts, who were relied upon by the sponsor of the bill and the legislation's other supporters, testified that creation science embodies the religious view that there is a supernatural creator of the universe.

[18] Appellants contend that the affidavits are relevant because the term "creation science" is a technical term similar to that found in statutes that regulate certain scientific or technological developments. Even assuming *arguendo* that "creation science" is a term of art as represented by Appellants, the definition provided by the relevant agency provides a better insight than the affidavits submitted by appellants in this case. In a 1981 survey conducted by the Louisiana Department of Education, the school superintendents in charge of implementing the provisions of the Creationism Act were asked to interpret the meaning of "creation science" as used in the statute. About 75 percent of Louisiana's superintendents stated that they understood "creation science" to be a religious doctrine. 2 App. E798–E799. Of this group, the largest proportion of superintendents interpreted creation science, as defined by the Act, to mean the literal interpretation of the Book of Genesis. The remaining superintendents believed that the Act required teaching the view that "the universe was made by a creator." *Id.*, at E799.

[19] The Court has previously found the postenactment elucidation of the meaning of a statute to be of little relevance in determining the intent of the legislature contemporaneous to the passage of the statute. See *Wallace* v. *Jaffree*, 472 U.S., at 57, n. 45 (O'CONNOR, J., concurring in judgment).

While a Senate committee was studying scientific creationism, Senator Keith introduced a second draft of the bill, requiring balanced treatment of "evolution-science" and "creation-science." *Id.*, at E–108. Although the Keith bill prohibited "instruction in any religious doctrine or materials," *id.*, at E–302, it defined "creation-science" to include

> "the scientific evidences and related inferences that indicate (a) sudden creation of the universe, energy, and life from nothing; (b) the insufficiency of mutation and natural selection in bringing about development of all living kinds from a single organism; (c) changes only within fixed limits or originally created kinds of plants and animals; (d) separate ancestry for man and apes; (e) explanation of the earth's geology by catastrophism, including the occurrence of a worldwide flood; and (f) a relatively recent inception of the earth and living kinds." *Id.*, at E–298—E–299.

Significantly, the model act on which the Keith bill relied was also the basis for a similar statute in Arkansas. See *McLean v. Arkansas Board of Education*, 529 F.Supp. 1255 (ED Ark.1982). The District Court in *McLean* carefully examined this model act, particularly the section defining creation-science, and concluded that "[b]oth [its] concepts and wording . . . convey an inescapable religiosity." *Id.*, at 1265. The court found that "[t]he ideas of [this section] are not merely similar to the literal interpretation of Genesis; they are identical and parallel to no other story of creation." *Ibid.*

The complaint in *McLean* was filed on May 27, 1981. On May 28, the Louisiana Senate committee amended the Keith bill to delete the illustrative list of scientific evidences. According to the legislator who proposed the amendment, it was "not intended to try to gut [the bill] in any way, or defeat the purpose [for] which Senator Keith introduced [it]," 1 App. E–432, and was not viewed as working "any violence to the bill." *Id.*, at E–438. Instead, the concern was "whether this should be an all inclusive list." *Ibid.*

The legislature then held hearings on the amended bill, that became the Balanced Treatment Act under review. The principal creation-scientist to testify in support of the Act was Dr. Edward Boudreaux. He did not elaborate on the nature of creation-science except to indicate that the "scientific evidences" of the theory are "the objective information of science [that] point[s] to conditions of a creator." 2 *id.*, at E–501—E–502. He further testified that the recognized creation-scientists in the United States, who "numbe[r] something like a thousand [and] who hold doctorate and masters degrees in all areas of science," are affiliated with either or both the Institute for Creation Research and the Creation Research Society. *Id.*, at E–503—E–504. Information on both of these organizations is part of the legislative history, and a review of their goals and activities sheds light on the nature of creation-science as it was presented to, and understood by, the Louisiana legislature.

The Institute for Creation Research is an affiliate of the Christian Heritage College in San Diego, California. The Institute was established to address the "urgent need for our nation to return to belief in a personal, omnipotent Creator, who has a purpose for His

---

Creation "*ex nihilo*" means creation "from nothing" and has been found to be an "inherently religious concept." *McLean v. Arkansas Board of Education*, 529 F.Supp. 1255, 1266 (ED Ark.1982). The District Court in *McLean* found:

"The argument that creation from nothing in [section] 4(a)(1) [of the substantially similar Arkansas Balanced Treatment Act] does not involve a supernatural deity has no evidentiary or rational support. To the contrary, 'creation out of nothing' is a concept unique to Western religions. In traditional Western religious thought, the conception of a creator of the world is a conception of God. Indeed, creation of the world 'out of nothing' is the ultimate religious statement because God is the only actor." *Id.*, at 1265.

creation and to whom all people must eventually give account." 1 *id.*, at E–197. A goal of the Institute is "a revival of belief in special creation as the true explanation of the origin of the world." Therefore, the Institute currently is working on the "development of new methods for teaching scientific creationism in public schools." *Id.*, at E–197— E–199. The Creation Research Society (CRS) is located in Ann Arbor, Michigan. A member must subscribe to the following statement of belief: "The Bible is the written word of God, and because it is inspired throughout, all of its assertions are historically and scientifically true." 2 *id.*, at E–583. To study creation-science at the CRS, a member must accept "that the account of origins in Genesis is a factual presentation of simple historical truth." *Ibid.*[3]

C

When, as here, "both courts below are unable to discern an arguably valid secular purpose, this Court normally should hesitate to find one." *Wallace v. Jaffree, supra*, 472 U.S., at 66 (POWELL, J., concurring). My examination of the language and the legislative history of the Balanced Treatment Act confirms that the intent of the Louisiana legislature was to promote a particular religious belief. The legislative history of the Arkansas statute prohibiting the teaching of evolution examined in *Epperson v. Arkansas*, 393 U.S. 97 (1968), was strikingly similar to the legislative history of the Balanced Treatment Act. In *Epperson.* the Court found:

> "It is clear that fundamentalist sectarian conviction was and is the law's reason for existence. Its antecedent, Tennessee's 'monkey law,' candidly stated its purpose: to make it unlawful 'to teach any theory that denies the story of the Divine Creation of man as taught in the Bible, and to teach instead that man has descended from a lower order of animals.' Perhaps the sensational publicity attendant upon the *Scopes* trial induced Arkansas to adopt less explicit language. It eliminated Tennessee's reference to 'the story of the Divine creation of man' as taught in the Bible, but there is no doubt that the motivation for the law was the same: to suppress the teaching of a theory which, it was thought, 'denied' the divine creation of man." *Id.*, at 107–109.

Here, it is clear that religious belief is the Balanced Treatment Act's "reason for existence." The tenets of creation-science parallel the Genesis story of creation,[4] and

---

[3] The District Court in *McLean* noted three other elements of the CRS statement of belief to which members must subscribe:

"[i] All basic types of living things, including man, were made by direct creative acts of God during Creation Week as described in Genesis. Whatever biological changes have occurred since Creation have accomplished only changes within the original created kinds. [ii] The great Flood described in Genesis, commonly referred to as the Noachian Deluge, was an historical event, worldwide in its extent and effect. [iii] Finally, we are an organization of Christian men of science, who accept Jesus Christ as our Lord and Savior. The account of the special creation of Adam and Eve as one man and one woman, and their subsequent Fall into sin, is the basis for our belief in the necessity of a Savior for all mankind. Therefore, salvation can come only thru (sic) accepting Jesus Christ as our Savior." 529 F.Supp., at 1260, n. 7.

[4] After hearing testimony from numerous experts, the District Court in *McLean* concluded that "[t]he parallels between [the definition section of the model act] and Genesis are quite specific." *Id.*, at 1265, n. 19. It found the concepts of "sudden creation from nothing," a worldwide flood of divine origin, and "kinds" to be derived from Genesis; "relatively recent inception" to mean "an age of the earth from 6,000 to 10,000 years" and to be based "on the geneology of the Old Testament using the rather astronomical ages assigned to the patriarchs"; and the "separate ancestry of man and ape" to focus on "the portion of the theory of evolution which Fundamentalists find most offensive." *Ibid.* (citing *Epperson* v. *Arkansas*, 393 U.S. 97 [1968]).

this is a religious belief. "[N]o legislative recitation of a supposed secular purpose can blind us to that fact." *Stone* v. *Graham*, 449 U.S. 39, 41 (1980). Although the Act as finally enacted does not contain explicit reference to its religious purpose, there is no indication in the legislative history that the deletion of "creation *ex nihilo*" and the four primary tenets of the theory were intended to alter the purpose to teaching creation-science. Instead, the statements of purpose of the sources of creation-science in the United States make clear that their purpose is to promote a religious belief. I find no persuasive evidence in the legislative history that the legislature's purpose was any different. The fact that the Louisiana legislature purported to add information to the school curriculum rather than detract from it as in *Epperson* does not affect my analysis. Both legislatures acted with the unconstitutional purpose of structuring the public school curriculum to make it compatible with a particular religious belief: the "divine creation of man."

That the statute is limited to the scientific evidences supporting the theory does not render its purpose secular. In reaching its conclusion that the Act is unconstitutional, the Court of Appeals "[did] not deny that the underpinnings of creationism may be supported by scientific evidence." 765 F.2d 1251, 1256 (1985). And there is no need to do so. Whatever the academic merit of particular subjects or theories, the Establishment Clause limits the discretion of state officials to pick and choose among them for the purpose of promoting a particular religious belief. The language of the statute and its legislative history convince me that the Louisiana legislature exercised its discretion for this purpose in this case.

II

As a matter of history, schoolchildren can and should properly be informed of all aspects of this Nation's religious heritage. I would see no constitutional problem if schoolchildren were taught the nature of the Founding Father's religious beliefs and how these beliefs affected the attitudes of the times and the structure of our government.[6] Courses in comparative religion of course are customary and constitutionally appropriate. In fact, since religion permeates our history, a familiarity with the nature of religious beliefs is necessary to understand many historical as well as contemporary events.[8] In addition, it is worth noting that the Establishment Clause does not prohibit *per se* the educational use of religious documents in public school education. Although this Court has recognized that the Bible is "an instrument of religion," *Abington School District* v. *Schempp, supra*, 374 U.S., at 224, it also has made clear that the Bible "may constitutionally be used in an appropriate study of history, civilization, ethics, comparative religion, or the like." *Stone* v. *Graham*, 449 U.S., at 42. The book is, in fact, "the

---

[6] There is an enormous variety of religions in the United States. The Encyclopedia of American Religions (2d ed. 1987) describes 1,347 religious organizations. The United States Census Bureau groups the major American religions into: Buddhist Churches of America; Eastern Churches; Jews; Old Catholic, Polish National Catholic, and Armenian Churches; the Roman Catholic Church; Protestants; and Miscellaneous. Statistical Abstract of the United States 50 (106th ed. 1986).

Our country has become strikingly multi-religious as well as multi-racial and multi-ethnic. This fact, perhaps more than anything one could write, demonstrates the wisdom of including the Establishment Clause in the First Amendment. States' proposals for what became the Establishment Clause evidence the goal of accommodating competing religious beliefs. See, e.g., New York's Resolution of Ratification reprinted in 2 Documentary History of the Constitution 190, 191 (1894) ("[N]o Religious Sect or Society ought to be favoured or established by Law in preference of others").

[8] For example, the political controversies in Northern Ireland, the Middle East, and India cannot be understood properly without reference to the underlying religious beliefs and the conflicts they tend to generate.

world's all-time best seller"[9] with undoubted literary and historic value apart from its religious content. The Establishment Clause is properly understood to prohibit the use of the Bible and other religious documents in public school education only when the purpose of the use is to advance a particular religious belief.

III

In sum, I find that the language and the legislative history of the Balanced Treatment Act unquestionably demonstrate that its purpose is to advance a particular religious belief. Although the discretion of state and local authorities over public school curricula is broad, "the First Amendment does not permit the State to require that teaching and learning must be tailored to the principles or prohibitions of any religious sect or dogma." *Epperson v. Arkansas*, 393 U.S., at 106, 89 S.Ct., at 271. Accordingly, I concur in the opinion of the Court and its judgment that the Balanced Treatment Act violates the Establishment Clause of the Constitution.

Justice SCALIA, with whom THE CHIEF JUSTICE joins, dissenting.

Even if I agreed with the questionable premise that legislation can be invalidated under the Establishment Clause on the basis of its motivation alone, without regard to its effects, I would still find no justification for today's decision. The Louisiana legislators who passed the "Balanced Treatment for Creation-Science and Evolution-Science Act," each of whom had sworn to support the Constitution,[1] were well aware of the potential Establishment Clause problems and considered that aspect of the legislation with great care. After seven hearings and several months of study, resulting in substantial revision of the original proposal, they approved the Act overwhelmingly and specifically articulated the secular purpose they meant it to serve. Although the record contains abundant evidence of the sincerity of that purpose (the only issue pertinent to this case), the Court today holds, essentially on the basis of "its visceral knowledge regarding what *must* have motivated the legislators," 778 F.2d 225, 227 (CA5 1985) (GEE, J., dissenting) (emphasis added), that the members of the Louisiana Legislature knowingly violated their oaths and then lied about it. I dissent. Had requirements of the Balanced Treatment Act that are not apparent on its face been clarified by an interpretation of the Louisiana Supreme Court, or by the manner of its implementation, the Act might well be found unconstitutional; but the question of its constitutionality cannot rightly be disposed of on the gallop, by impugning the motives of its supporters.

I

This case arrives here in the following posture: The Louisiana Supreme Court has never been given an opportunity to interpret the Balanced Treatment Act, State officials have never attempted to implement it, and it has never been the subject of a full evidentiary hearing. We can only guess at its meaning. We know that it forbids instruction in either "creation-science" or "evolution-science" without instruction in the other, § 17:286.4A, but the parties are sharply divided over what creation science consists of. Appellants insist that it is a collection of educationally valuable scientific data that has been censored from classrooms by an embarrassed scientific establishment. Appellees insist it is not science at all but thinly veiled religious doctrine. Both interpretations of the intended meaning of that phrase find considerable support in the legislative history.

---

[9] See *New York Times*, May 10, 1981, § 2, p. 24, col. 3; N. McWhirter, 1986 *Guiness Book of World Records* 144 (the Bible is the world's most widely distributed book).

[1] Article VI, clause 3 of the Constitution provides that "the Members of the several State Legislatures . . . shall be bound by Oath or Affirmation, to support this Constitution."

At least at this stage in the litigation, it is plain to me that we must accept appellants' view of what the statute means. To begin with, the statute itself *defines* "creation-science" as "the *scientific evidences* for creation and inferences from those *scientific evidences.*" § 17:286.3(2) (emphasis added). If, however, that definition is not thought sufficiently helpful, the means by which the Louisiana Supreme Court will give the term more precise content is quite clear—and again, at this stage in the litigation, favors the appellants' view. "Creation science" is unquestionably a "term of art," see Brief for 72 Nobel Laureates, et al. as *Amici Curiae* 20, and thus, under Louisiana law, is "to be interpreted according to [its] received meaning and acceptation with the learned in the art, trade or profession to which [it] refer[s]." La.Civ. Code Ann., Art. 15 (West 1952).[2] The only evidence in the record of the "received meaning and acceptation" of "creation science" is found in five affidavits filed by appellants. In those affidavits, two scientists, a philosopher, a theologian, and an educator, all of whom claim extensive knowledge of creation science, swear that it is essentially a collection of scientific data supporting the theory that the physical universe and life within it appeared suddenly and have not changed substantially since appearing. See App. to Juris. Statement A19 (Kenyon); *id.*, at A36 (Morrow); *id.*, at A41 (Miethe). These experts insist that creation science is a strictly scientific concept that can be presented without religious reference. See *id.*, at A19–A20, A35 (Kenyon); *id.*, at A36–A38 (Morrow); *id.*, at A40, A41, A43 (Miethe); *id.*, at A47, A48 (Most); *id.*, at A49 (Clinkert). At this point, then, we must assume that the Balanced Treatment Act does *not* require the presentation of religious doctrine.

Nothing in today's opinion is plainly to the contrary, but what the statute means and what is requires are of rather little concern to the Court. Like the Court of Appeals, 765 F.2d 1251, 1253, 1254 (CA5 1985), the Court finds it necessary to consider only the motives of the legislators who supported the Balanced Treatment Act, *ante*. After examining the statute, its legislative history, and its historical and social context, the Court holds that the Louisiana Legislature acted without "a secular legislative purpose" and that the Act therefore fails the "purpose" prong of the three-part test set forth in *Lemon v. Kurtzman*, 403 U.S. 602, 612. As I explain below, I doubt whether that "purpose" requirement of *Lemon* is a proper interpretation of the Constitution; but even if it were, I could not agree with the Court's assessment that the requirement was not satisfied here.

This Court has said little about the first component of the *Lemon* test. Almost invariably, we have effortlessly discovered a secular purpose for measures challenged under the Establishment Clause, typically devoting no more than a sentence or two to the matter. . . . In fact, only once before deciding *Lemon*, and twice since, have we invalidated a law for lack of a secular purpose. See *Wallace v. Jaffree*, 472 U.S. 38, 105 S.Ct. 2479, 86 L.Ed.2d 29 (1985); *Stone v. Graham*, 449 U.S. 39, 101 S.Ct. 192, 66 L.Ed.2d 199 (1980) *(per curiam)*; *Epperson v. Arkansas*, 393 U.S. 97, 89 S.Ct. 266, 21 L.Ed.2d 228 (1968).

Nevertheless, a few principles have emerged from our cases, principles which should, but to an unfortunately large extent do not, guide the Court's application of *Lemon* today. It is clear, first of all, that regardless of what "legislative purpose" may mean in other contexts, for the purpose of the *Lemon* test it means the "actual" motives of those responsible for the challenged action. Thus, if those legislators who supported the Balanced Treatment Act *in fact* acted with a "sincere" secular purpose, the Act survives

---

[2] Thus the popular dictionary definitions cited by Justice POWELL, *ante* (concurring opinion), and appellees, see Brief for Appellees 25, 26; Tr. of Oral Arg. 32, 34, are utterly irrelevant, as are the views of the school superintendents cited by the majority, *ante*, n. 17. Three quarters of those surveyed had "[n]o" or "[l]imited" knowledge of "creation-science theory," and not a single superintendent claimed "[e]xtensive" knowledge of the subject. 2 App. E798.

the first component of the *Lemon* test, regardless of whether that purpose is likely to be achieved by the provisions they enacted.

Our cases have also confirmed that when the *Lemon* Court referred to "a secular . . . purpose," 403 U.S., at 612, it meant "*a* secular purpose." The author of *Lemon*, writing for the Court, has said that invalidation under the purpose prong is appropriate when "there [is] *no question* that the statute or activity was motivated *wholly* by religious considerations." *Lynch v. Donnelly*, 465 U.S. 668, 680 (1984) (BURGER, C.J.) (emphasis added); *Wallace v. Jaffree, supra*, 472 U.S., at 56 ("the First Amendment requires that a statute must be invalidated if it is *entirely* motivated by a purpose to advance religion") (emphasis added; footnote omitted). In all three cases in which we struck down laws under the Establishment Clause for lack of a secular purpose, we found that the legislature's sole motive was to promote religion. See *Wallace v. Jaffree, supra*, at 56, 57, 60; *Stone v. Graham, supra*, 449 U.S., at 41, 43, n. 5; *Epperson v. Arkansas, supra*, 393 U.S., at 103; see also *Lynch v. Donnelly, supra*, 465 U.S., at 680, (describing *Stone* and *Epperson* as cases in which we invalidated laws "motivated wholly by religious considerations"). Thus, the majority's invalidation of the Balanced Treatment Act is defensible only if the record indicates that the Louisiana Legislature had *no* secular purpose. . . .

Our cases in no way imply that the Establishment Clause forbids legislators merely to act upon their religious convictions. We surely would not strike down a law providing money to feed the hungry or shelter the homeless if it could be demonstrated that, but for the religious beliefs of the legislators, the funds would not have been approved. Also, political activism by the religiously motivated is part of our heritage. Notwithstanding the majority's implication to the contrary, we do not presume that the sole purpose of a law is to advance religion merely because it was supported strongly by organized religions or by adherents of particular faiths. See *Walz v. Tax Comm'n of New York City, supra*, 397 U.S., at 670. To do so would deprive religious men and women of their right to participate in the political process. Today's religious activism may give us the Balanced Treatment Act, but yesterday's resulted in the abolition of slavery, and tomorrow's may bring relief for famine victims.

Similarly, we will not presume that a law's purpose is to advance religion merely because it " 'happens to coincide or harmonize with the tenets of some or all religions,' " *Harris v. McRae, supra*, at 319, or because it benefits religion, even substantially. We have, for example, turned back Establishment Clause challenges to restrictions on abortion funding, *Harris v. McRae, supra*, and to Sunday closing laws, *McGowan v. Maryland, supra*, despite the fact that both "agre[e] with the dictates of [some] Judaeo-Christian religions. . . . In many instances, the Congress or state legislatures conclude that the general welfare of society, wholly apart from any religious considerations, demands such regulation." *Ibid.* On many past occasions we have had no difficulty finding a secular purpose for governmental action far more likely to advance religion than the Balanced Treatment Act. See, *e.g., Mueller v. Allen*, 463 U.S., at 394–395 (tax deduction for expenses of religious education; *Meek v. Pittenger*, 421 U.S., at 363, 95 S.Ct., at 1762 (aid to religious schools); *Committee for Public Education & Religious Liberty v. Nyquist*, 413 U.S., at 773, 93 S.Ct., at 2965 (same); *Lemon v. Kurtzman*, 403 U.S., at 613, 91 S.Ct., at 2111 (same); *Walz v. Tax Comm'n of New York City, supra*, 397 U.S., at 672, 90 S.Ct., at 1413 (tax exemption for church property); *Board of Education v. Allen, supra*, 392 U.S., at 243, 88 S.Ct. Thus, the fact that creation science coincides with the beliefs of certain religions, a fact upon which the majority relies heavily, does not itself justify invalidation of the Act.

Finally, our cases indicate that even certain kinds of governmental actions undertaken with the specific intention of improving the position of religion do not "advance religion'' as that term is used in *Lemon*. 403 U.S., at 613. Rather, we have said that in at least two circumstances government *must* act to advance religion, and that in a third it *may* do so.

First, since we have consistently described the Establishment Clause as forbidding not only state action motivated by the desire to *advance* religion, but also that intended to "disapprove," "inhibit," or evince "hostility" toward religion, see, *e.g.*, *ante* ("disapprove") (quoting *Lynch v. Donnelly, supra*, 465 U.S., at 690); *Lynch v. Donnelly, supra*, at 673 ("hostility"); *Committee for Public Education & Religious Liberty v. Nyquist, supra*, 413 U.S., at 788 ("'inhibi[t]'"); and since we have said that governmental "neutrality" toward religion is the preeminent goal of the First Amendment, see *e.g.*, *Grand Rapids School District v. Ball*, 473 U.S., at 382; *Roemer v. Maryland Public Works Bd.*, 426 U.S. 736, 747; *Committee for Public Education & Religious Liberty v. Nyquist, supra*, 413 U.S., at 792–793; a State which discovers that its employees are inhibiting religion must take steps to prevent them from doing so, even though its purpose would clearly be to advance religion. *Cf. Walz v. Tax Comm'n of New York City, supra*, 397 U.S., at 673. Thus, if the Louisiana Legislature sincerely believed that the State's science teachers were being hostile to religion, our cases indicate that it could act to eliminate that hostility without running afoul of *Lemon's* purpose test.

Second, we have held that intentional governmental advancement of religion is sometimes required by the Free Exercise Clause. For example, in *Thomas v. Review Bd., Indiana Employment Security Div.*, 450 U.S. 707 (1981); *Wisconsin v. Yoder*, 406 U.S. 205 (1972); and *Sherbert v. Verner*, 374 U.S. 398 (1963), we held that in some circumstances States must accommodate the beliefs of religious citizens by exempting them from generally applicable regulations. We have not yet come close to reconciling *Lemon* and our Free Exercise cases, and typically we do not really try. It is clear, however, that members of the Louisiana Legislature were not impermissibly motivated for purpose of the *Lemon* test if they believed that approval of the Balanced Treatment Act was *required* by the Free Exercise Clause.

We have also held that in some circumstances government may act to accommodate religion, even if that action is not required by the First Amendment. . . . Thus, few would contend that Title VII of the Civil Rights Act of 1964, which both forbids religious discrimination by private-sector employers, 78 Stat. 255, 42 U.S.C. § 2000e-2(a)(1), and requires them reasonably to accommodate the religious practices of their employees, § 2000e(j), violates the Establishment Clause, even though its "purpose" is, of course, to advance religion, and even though it is almost certainly not required by the Free Exercise Clause. While we have warned that at some point, accommodation may devolve into "an unlawful fostering of religion," *Hobbie v. Unemployment Appeals Comm'n of Fla., supra*, 480 U.S., at _____ , we have not suggested precisely (or even roughly) where that point might be. It is possible, then, that even if the sole motive of those voting for the Balanced Treatment Act was to advance religion, and its passage was not actually required, or even believed to be required, by either the Free Exercise or Establishment Clauses, the Act would nonetheless survive scrutiny under *Lemon's* purpose test.

One final observation about the application of that test: Although the Court's opinion gives no hint of it, in the past we have repeatedly affirmed "our reluctance to attribute unconstitutional motives to the States." *Mueller v. Allen, supra*, 463 U.S., at 394; see also *Lynch v. Donnelly*, 465 U.S., at 699 (BRENNAN, J., dissenting). . . . Whenever we are called upon to judge the constitutionality of an act of a state legislature, "we must have 'due regard to the fact that this Court is not exercising a primary judgment but is sitting in judgment upon those who also have taken the oath to observe the Constitution and who have the responsibility for carrying on government.' '' *Rostker v. Goldberg, supra*, 453 U.S., at 64. This is particularly true, we have said, where the legislature has specifically considered the question of a law's constitutionality. *Ibid.*

With the foregoing in mind, I now turn to the purposes underlying adoption of the Balanced Treatment Act.

II

A

We have relatively little information upon which to judge the motives of those who supported the Act. About the only direct evidence is the statute itself and transcripts of the seven committee hearings at which it was considered. Unfortunately, several of those hearings were sparsely attended, and the legislators who were present revealed little about their motives. We have no committee reports, no floor debates, no remarks inserted into the legislative history, no statement from the Governor, and no post-enactment statements or testimony from the bill's sponsor or any other legislators. Compare *Wallace v. Jaffree*, 472 U.S. 38, 43, 56–57 (1985). Nevertheless, there is ample evidence that the majority is wrong in holding that the Balanced Treatment Act is without secular purpose.

At the outset, it is important to note that the Balanced Treatment Act did not fly through the Louisiana Legislature on wings of fundamentalist religious fervor—which would be unlikely, in any event, since only a small minority of the State's citizens belong to fundamentalist religious denominations. See B. Quinn, H. Anderson, M. Bradley, P. Goetting, & P. Shriver, Churches and Church Membership in the United States 16 (1982). The Act had its genesis (so to speak) in legislation introduced by Senator Bill Keith in June 1980. After two hearings before the Senate Committee on Education, Senator Keith asked that his bill be referred to a study commission composed of members of both houses of the Louisiana Legislature. He expressed hope that the joint committee would give the bill careful consideration and determine whether his arguments were "legitimate." 1 App. E29–E30. The committee met twice during the interim, heard testimony (both for and against the bill) from several witnesses, and received staff reports. Senator Keith introduced his bill again when the legislature reconvened. The Senate Committee on Education held two more hearings and approved the bill after substantially amending it (in part over Senator Keith's objection). After approval by the full Senate, the bill was referred to the House Committee on Education. That committee conducted a lengthy hearing, adopted further amendments, and sent the bill on to the full House, where it received favorable consideration. The Senate concurred in the House amendments and on July 20, 1981, the Governor signed the bill into law.

Senator Keith's statements before the various committees that considered the bill hardly reflect the confidence of a man preaching to the converted. He asked his colleagues to "keep an open mind" and not to be "biased" by misleading characterizations of creation science. *Id.*, at E33. He also urged them to "look at this subject on its merits and not on some preconceived idea." *Id.*, at E34; see also 2 *id.*, at E491. Senator Keith's reception was not especially warm. Over his strenuous objection, the Senate Committee on Education voted 5–1 to amend his bill to deprive it of any force; as amended, the bill merely gave teachers *permission* to balance the teaching of creation science or evolution with the other. 1 *id.*, at E442–E461. The House Committee restored the "mandatory" language to the bill by a vote of only 6–5, 2 *id.*, at E626–E627, and both the full House (by vote of 52–35), *id.*, at E700–E706, and full Senate (23–15), *id.*, at E735–E738, had to repel further efforts to gut the bill.

The legislators understood that Senator Keith's bill involved a "unique" subject, 1 *id.*, at E106 (Rep. M. Thompson), and they were repeatedly made aware of its potential constitutional problems, see, *e.g., id.*, at E26–E28 (McGehee); *id.*, at E38–E39 (Sen. Keith); *id.*, at E241–E242 (Rossman); *id.*, at E257 (Probst); *id.*, at E261 (Beck); *id.*, at E282 (Sen. Keith). Although the Establishment Clause, including its secular purpose requirement, was of substantial concern to the legislators, they eventually voted overwhelmingly in favor of the Balanced Treatment Act: The House approved it 71–19 (with 15 members absent), 2 *id.*, at E716–E722; the Senate 26–12 (with all members present), *id.*, at E741–E744. The legislators specifically designated the protection of "academic freedom" as the purpose of the Act. La.Rev.Stat. § 17:286.2. We cannot accurately assess whether this purpose is a "sham," *ante*, at 2579, until we first examine the evidence presented to the legislature far more carefully than the Court has done.

Before summarizing the testimony of Senator Keith and his supporters, I wish to make clear that I by no means intend to endorse its accuracy. But my views (and the views of this Court) about creation science and evolution are (or should be) beside the point. Our task is not to judge the debate about teaching the origins of life, but to ascertain what the members of the Louisiana Legislature believed. The vast majority of them voted to approve a bill which explicitly stated a secular purpose; what is crucial is not their *wisdom* in believing that purpose would be achieved by the bill, but their *sincerity* in believing it would be.

Most of the testimony in support of Senator Keith's bill came from the Senator himself and from scientists and educators he presented, many of whom enjoyed academic credentials that may have been regarded as quite impressive by members of the Louisiana Legislature. To a substantial extent, their testimony was devoted to lengthy, and, to the layman, seemingly expert scientific expositions on the origin of life. See, *e.g.*, 1 App. E11–E18 (Sunderland); *id.*, at E50–E60 (Boudreaux); *id.*, at E86–E89 (Ward); *id.*, at E130–E153 (Boudreaux paper); *id.*, at E321–E326 (Boudreaux); *id.*, at E423–E428 (Sen. Keith). These scientific lectures touched upon, *inter alia*, biology, paleontology, genetics, astronomy, astrophysics, probability analysis, and biochemistry. The witnesses repeatedly assured committee members that "hundreds and hundreds" of highly respected, internationally renowned scientists believed in creation science and would support their testimony. See, *e.g., id.*, at E5 (Sunderland); *id.*, at E76 (Sen. Keith); *id.*, at E100–E101 (Reiboldt); *id.*, at E327–E328 (Boudreaux); 2 *id.*, at E503–E504 (Boudreaux).

Senator Keith and his witnesses testified essentially as set forth in the following numbered paragraphs:

(1) There are two and only two scientific explanations for the beginning of life[3]— evolution and creation science. 1 *id.*, at E6 (Sunderland); *id.*, at E34 (Sen. Keith); *id.*, at E280 (Sen. Keith); *id.*, at E417–E418 (Sen. Keith). Both are bona fide "sciences." *Id.*, at E6–E7 (Sunderland); *id.*, at E12 (Sunderland); *id.*, at E416 (Sen. Keith); *id.*, at E427 (Sen. Keith); 2 *id.*, at E491–E492 (Sen. Keith); *id.*, at E497–E498 (Sen. Keith). Both posit a theory of the origin of life and subject that theory to empirical testing. Evolution posits that life arose out of inanimate chemical compounds and has gradually evolved over millions of years. Creation science posits that all life forms now on earth appeared suddenly and relatively recently and have changed little. Since there are only two possible explanations of the origin of life, any evidence that tends to disprove the theory of evolution necessarily tends to prove the theory of creation science, and vice versa. For example, the abrupt appearance in the fossil record of complex life, and the extreme

---

[3] Although creation scientists and evolutionists also disagree about the origin of the physical universe, both proponents and opponents of Senator Keith's bill focused on the question of the beginning of life.

rarity of transitional life forms in that record, are evidence for creation science. 1 *id.*, at E7 (Sunderland); *id.*, at E12–E18 (Sunderland); *id.*, at E45–E60 (Boudreaux); *id.*, at E67 (Harlow); *id.*, at E130–E153 (Boudreaux paper); *id.*, at E423–E428 (Sen. Keith).

(2) The body of scientific evidence supporting creation science is as strong as that supporting evolution. In fact, it may be *stronger*. *Id.*, at E214 (Young statement); *id.*, at 310 (Sen. Keith); *id.*, at E416 (Sen. Keith); 2 *id.*, at E492 (Sen. Keith). The evidence for evolution is far less compelling than we have been led to believe. Evolution is not a scientific "fact," since it cannot actually be observed in a laboratory. Rather, evolution is merely a scientific theory or "guess." 1 *id.*, at E20–E21 (Morris); *id.*, at E85 (Ward); *id.*, at E100 (Reiboldt); *id.*, at E328–E329 (Boudreaux); 2 *id.*, at E506 (Boudreaux). It is a very bad guess at that. The scientific problems with evolution are so serious that it could accurately be termed a "myth." 1 *id.*, at E85 (Ward); *id.*, at E92–E93 (Kalivoda); *id.*, at E95–E97 (Sen. Keith); *id.*, at E154 (Boudreaux paper); *id.*, at E329 (Boudreaux); *id.*, E453 (Sen. Keith); 2 *id.*, at E505–E506 (Boudreaux); *id.*, at E516 (Young).

(3) Creation science is educationally valuable. Students exposed to it better understand the current state of scientific evidence about the origin of life. 1 *id.*, at E19 (Sunderland); *id.*, at E39 (Sen. Keith); *id.*, at E79 (Kalivoda); *id.*, at E308 (Sen. Keith); 2 *id.*, at E513–E514 (Morris). Those students even have a better understanding of evolution. 1 *id.*, at E19 (Sunderland). Creation science can and should be presented to children without any religious content. *Id.*, at E12 (Sunderland); *id.*, at E22 (Sanderford); *id.*, at E35–E36 (Sen. Keith); *id.*, at E101 (Reiboldt); *id.*, E279–E280 (Sen. Keith); *id.*, at E282 (Sen. Keith).

(4) Although creation science is educationally valuable and strictly scientific, it is now being censored from or misrepresented in the public schools. *Id.*, at E19 (Sunderland); *id.*, at E21 (Morris); *id.*, at E34 (Sen. Keith); *id.*, at E37 (Sen. Keith); *id.*, at E42 (Sen. Keith); *id.*, at E92 (Kalivoda); *id.*, at E97–E98 (Reiboldt); *id.*, at E214 (Young statement); *id.*, at E218 (Young statement); *id.*, at E280 (Sen. Keith); *id.*, at E309 (Sen. Keith); 2 *id.*, at E513 (Morris). Evolution, in turn, is misrepresented as an absolute truth. 1 *id.*, at E63 (Harlow); *id.*, at E74 (Sen. Keith); *id.*, at E81 (Kalivoda); *id.*, at E214 (Young statement); 2 *id.*, at E507 (Harlow); *id.*, at E513 (Morris); *id.*, at E516 (Young). Teachers have been brainwashed by an entrenched scientific establishment composed almost exclusively of scientists to whom evolution is like a "religion." These scientists discriminate against creation scientists so as to prevent evolution's weaknesses from being exposed. 1 *id.*, at E61 (Boudreaux); *id.*, at E63–E64 (Harlow); *id.*, at E78–E79 (Kalivoda); *id.*, at E80 (Kalivoda); *id.*, at E95–E97 (Sen. Keith); *id.*, at E129 (Boudreaux paper); *id.*, at E218 (Young statement); *id.*, at E357 (Sen. Keith); *id.*, at E430 (Boudreaux).

(5) The censorship of creation science has at least two harmful effects. First, it deprives students of knowledge of one of the two scientific explanations for the origin of life and leads them to believe that evolution is proven fact; thus, their education suffers and they are wrongly taught that science has proven their religious beliefs false. Second, it violates the Establishment Clause. The United States Supreme Court has held that secular humanism is a religion. *Id.*, at E36 (Sen. Keith) (referring to *Torcaso v. Watkins*, 367 U.S. 488, 495, n. 11, 81 S.Ct. 1680, 1683, n. 11, 6 L.Ed.2d 982 [1961]); 1 App. E418 (Sen. Keith); 2 *id.*, at E499 (Sen. Keith). Belief in evolution is a central tenet of that religion. 1 *id.*, at E282 (Sen. Keith); *id.*, at E312–E313 (Sen. Keith); *id.*, at E317 (Sen. Keith); *id.*, at E418 (Sen. Keith); 2 *id.*, at E499 (Sen Keith). Thus, by censoring creation science and instructing students that evolution is fact, public school teachers are *now* advancing religion in violation of the Establishment Clause. 1 *id.*, at E2–E4 (Sen. Keith); *id.*, at E36–E37, E39 (Sen. Keith); *id.*, at E154–E155 (Boudreaux paper); *id.*, at E281–E282 (Sen. Keith); *id.*, at E313 (Sen. Keith); *id.*, at E315–E316 (Sen. Keith); *id.*, at E317 (Sen. Keith); 2 *id.*, at E499–E500 (Sen. Keith).

Senator Keith repeatedly and vehemently denied that his purpose was to advance a particular religious doctrine. At the outset of the first hearing on the legislation, he testified, "We are not going to say today that you should have some kind of religious instructions in our schools. . . . We are not talking about religion today. . . . I am not proposing that we take the Bible in each science class and read the first chapter of Genesis." 1 *id.*, at E35. At a later hearing, Senator Keith stressed that "to . . . teach religion and disguise it as creationism . . . is not my intent. My intent is to see to it that our textbooks are not censored." *Id.*, at E280. He made many similar statements throughout the hearings. See, e.g., *id.*, at E41; *id.*, at E282; *id.*, at E310; *id.*, at E417; see also *id.*, at E44 (Boudreaux); *id.*, at E80 (Kalivoda).

We have no way of knowing, of course, how many legislators believed the testimony of Senator Keith and his witnesses. But in the absence of evidence to the contrary,[4] we have to assume that many of them did. Given that assumption, the Court today plainly errs in holding that the Louisiana Legislature passed the Balanced Treatment Act for exclusively religious purposes.

B

Even with nothing more than this legislative history to go on, I think it would be extraordinary to invalidate the Balanced Treatment Act for lack of a valid secular purpose. Striking down a law approved by the democratically elected representatives of the people is no minor matter. "The cardinal principle of statutory construction is to save and not to destroy. We have repeatedly held that as between two possible interpretations of a statute, by one of which it would be unconstitutional and by the other valid, our plain duty is to adopt that which will save the act." *NLRB v. Jones & Laughlin Steel Corp.*, 301 U.S.1 (1937). So, too, it seems to me, with discerning statutory purpose. Even if the legislative history were silent or ambiguous about the existence of a secular purpose—and here it is not—the statute should survive *Lemon*'s purpose test. But even more validation than mere legislative history is present here. The

---

[4] Although appellees and *amici* dismiss the testimony of Senator Keith and his witnesses as pure fantasy, they did not bother to submit evidence of that to the District Court, making it difficult for us to agree with them. The State, by contrast, submitted the affidavits of two scientists, a philosopher, a theologian, and an educator, whose academic credentials are rather impressive. See App. to Juris. Statement A17–A18 (Kenyon); *id.*, at A36 (Morrow); *id.*, at A39–A40 (Miethe); *id.*, at A46–A47 (Most); *id.*, at A49 (Clinkert). Like Senator Keith and his witnesses, the affiants swear that evolution and creation science are the only two scientific explanations for the origin of life, see *id.*, at A19–A20 (Kenyon); *id.*, at A38 (Morrow); *id.*, at A41 (Miethe); that creation science is strictly scientific, see *id.*, at A18 (Kenyon); *id.*, at A36 (Morrow); *id.*, at A40–A41 (Miethe); *id.*, at A49 (Clinkert); that creation science is simply a collection of scientific data that supports the hypothesis that life appeared on earth suddenly and has changed little, see *id.*, at A19 (Kenyon); *id.*, at A36 (Morrow); *id.*, at A41 (Miethe); that hundreds of respected scientists believe in creation science, see *id.*, at A20 (Kenyon); that evidence for creation science is as strong as evidence for evolution, see *id.*, at A21 (Kenyon); *id.*, at A34–A35 (Kenyon); *id.*, at A37–A38 (Morrow); that creation science is educationally valuable, see *id.*, at A19 (Kenyon); *id.*, at A36 (Morrow); *id.*, at A38–A39 (Morrow); *id.*, at A49 (Clinkert); that creation science can be presented without religious content, see *id.*, at A19 (Kenyon); *id.*, at A35 (Kenyon); *id.*, at A36 (Morrow); *id.*, at A40 (Miethe); *id.*, at A43–A44 (Miethe); *id.*, at A47 (Most); *id.*, at A49 (Clinkert); and that creation science is now censored from classrooms while evolution is misrepresented as proven fact, see *id.*, at A20 (Kenyon); *id.*, at A35 (Kenyon); *id.*, at A39 (Morrow); *id.*, at A50 (Clinkert). It is difficult to conclude on the basis of these affidavits—the only substantive evidence in the record—that the laymen serving in the Louisiana Legislature must have disbelieved Senator Keith or his witnesses.

Louisiana Legislature explicitly set forth its secular purpose ("protecting academic freedom") in the very text of the Act. La.Rev.Stat. § 17:286.2 (West 1982). We have in the past repeatedly relied upon or deferred to such expressions. . . . The Court seeks to evade the force of this expression of purpose by stubbornly misinterpreting it, and then finding that the provisions of the Act do not advance that misinterpreted purpose, thereby showing it to be a sham. The Court first surmises that "academic freedom" means "enhancing the freedom of teachers to teach what they will," *ante*, at 2578— even though "academic freedom" in that sense has little scope in the structured elementary and secondary curriculums with which the Act is concerned. Alternatively, the Court suggests that it might mean "maximiz[ing] the comprehensiveness and effectiveness of science instruction," *ante*, at 2579—though that is an exceeding strange interpretation of the words, and one that is refuted on the very face of the statute. See § 17:286.5. Had the Court devoted to this central question of the meaning of the legislatively expressed purpose a small fraction of the research into legislative history that produced its quotations of religiously motivated statements by individual legislators, it would have discerned quite readily what "academic freedom" meant: *students'* freedom from *indoctrination*. The legislature wanted to ensure that students would be free to decide for themselves how life began, based upon a fair and balanced presentation of the scientific evidence—that is, to protect "the right of each [student] voluntarily to determine what to believe (and what not to believe) free of any coercive pressures from the State." *Grand Rapids School District v. Ball*, 473 U.S., at 385. The legislature did not care *whether* the topic of origins was taught; it simply wished to ensure that *when* the topic was taught, students would receive " 'all of the evidence' " (quoting Tr. of Oral Arg. 60).

As originally introduced, the "purpose" section of the Balanced Treatment Act read: "This Chapter is enacted for the purposes of protecting academic freedom . . . *of students* . . . and assisting *students* in their search for truth." 1 App. E292 (emphasis added). Among the proposed findings of fact contained in the original version of the bill was the following: "Public school instruction in only evolution-science . . . *violates the principle of academic freedom because it denies students a choice between scientific models and instead indoctrinates them in evolution science alone.*" *Id.*, at E295 (emphasis added).[5] Senator Keith unquestionably understood "academic freedom." See *id.*, at E36 (purpose of bill is "to protect academic freedom by providing student choice"); *id.*, at E283 (purpose of bill is to protect "academic freedom" by giving students a "choice" rather than subjecting them to "indoctrination on origins").

If one adopts the obviously intended meaning of the statutory terms "academic freedom," there is no basis whatever for concluding that the purpose they express is a "sham." To the contrary, the Act pursues that purpose plainly and consistently. It requires that, whenever the subject of origins is covered, evolution be "taught as a theory, rather than as proven scientific fact" and that scientific evidence inconsistent with the theory of evolution (*viz.*, "creation science") be taught as well.

---

[5] The majority finds it "astonishing" that I would cite a portion of Senator Keith's original bill that was later deleted as evidence of the Legislature's understanding of the phrase "academic freedom." *Ante*, at 2580, n. 8. What is astonishing is the majority's implication that the deletion of that section deprives it of value as a clear indication of what the phrase meant—there and in the other, retained, sections of the bill. The Senate Committee on Education deleted most of the lengthy "purpose" section of the bill (with Senator Keith's consent) because it resembled legislative "findings of fact," which, committee members felt, should generally not be incorporated in legislation. The deletion had absolutely nothing to do with the manner in which the section described "academic freedom." See 1 App. E314–E320; *id.*, at E440–E442.

La.Rev.Stat.Ann. § 17:286.4A (West 1982). Living up to its title of "*Balanced Treatment* for Creation-Science and Evolution-Science Act," § 17:286.1, it treats the teaching of creation the same way. It does *not* mandate instruction in creation science, § 17:286.5; *forbids* teachers to present creation science "as proven scientific fact," § 17:286.4A; and *bans* the teaching of creation science unless the theory is (to use the Court's terminology) "discredit[ed] ' . . . at every turn' " with the teaching of evolution (quoting 765 F.2d, at 1257). It surpasses understanding how the Court can see in this a purpose "to restructure the science curriculum to conform with a particular religious viewpoint," "to provide a persuasive advantage to a particular religious doctrine," "to promote the theory of creation science which embodies a particular religious tenet," *ante,* and "to endorse a particular religious doctrine."

The Act's reference to "creation" is not convincing evidence of religious purpose. The Act defines creation science as "*scientific evidenc[e],*" § 17:286.3(2) (emphasis added), and Senator Keith and his witnesses repeatedly stressed that the subject can and should be presented without religious content. We have no basis on the record to conclude that creation science need be anything other than a collection of scientific data supporting the theory that life abruptly appeared on earth. See n. 4, *supra.* Creation science, its proponents insist, no more must explain *whence* life came than evolution must explain whence came the inanimate materials from which it says life evolved. But even if that were not so, to posit a past creator is not to posit the eternal and personal God who is the object of religious veneration. Indeed, it is not even to posit the "*unmoved* mover" hypothesized by Aristotle and other notably nonfundamentalist philosophers. Senator Keith suggested this when he referred to "a creator *however you define a creator.*" 1 App. E280 (emphasis added).

The Court cites three provisions of the Act which, it argues, demonstrate a "discriminatory preference for the teaching of creation science" and no interest in "academic freedom." First, the Act prohibits discrimination only against creation scientists and those who teach creation science. § 17:286.4C. Second, the Act requires local school boards to develop and provide to science teachers "a curriculum guide on presentation of creation-science." § 17:286.7A. Finally, the Act requires the governor to designate seven creation scientists who shall, upon request, assist local school boards in developing the curriculum guides. § 17.286.7B. But none of these provisions casts doubt upon the sincerity of the legislators' articulated purpose of "academic freedom"—unless, of course, one gives that term the obviously erroneous meanings preferred by the Court. The Louisiana legislators had been told repeatedly that creation scientists were scorned by most educators and scientists, who themselves had an almost religious faith in evolution. It is hardly surprising, then, that in seeking to achieve a balanced, "nonindoctrinating" curriculum, the legislators protected from discrimination only those teachers whom they thought were *suffering* from discrimination. (Also, the legislators were undoubtedly aware of *Epperson v. Arkansas,* 393 U.S. 97 [1968], and thus could quite reasonably have concluded that discrimination against evolutionists was already prohibited.) The two provisions respecting the development of curriculum guides are also consistent with "academic freedom" as the Louisiana Legislature understood the term. Witnesses had informed the legislators that, because of the hostility of most scientists and educators to creation science, the topic had been censored from or badly misrepresented in elementary and secondary school texts. In light of the unavailability of works on creation science suitable for classroom use (a fact appellees concede, see Brief for Appellees 27, 40) and the existence of ample materials on evolution, it was entirely reasonable for the Legislature to conclude that science teachers attempting to implement the Act would need a curriculum guide on creation science, but not on evolution, and that those charged with developing the guide would need an easily accessible group of creation scientists. Thus, the provisions of the Act of so much concern to the Court *support* the conclusion that the Legislature acted to advance "academic freedom."

The legislative history gives ample evidence of the sincerity of the Balanced Treatment Act's articulated purpose. Witness after witness urged the legislators to support the Act so that students would not be "indoctrinated" but would instead be free to decide for themselves, based upon a fair presentation of the scientific evidence, about the origin of life. See, *e.g.*, 1 App. E18 (Sunderland) ("all that we are advocating" is presenting "scientific data" to students and "letting [them] make up their own mind[s]"); *id.*, at E19–E20 (Sunderland) (Students are now being "indoctrinated" in evolution through the use of "censored school books. . . . All that we are asking for is [the] open unbiased education in the classroom . . . your students deserve"); *id.*, at E21 (Morris) ("A student cannot [make an intelligent decision about the origin of life] unless he is well informed about both [evolution and creation science]"); *id.*, at E22 (Sanderford) ("We are asking very simply [that] . . . creationism [be presented] alongside . . . evolution and let people make their own mind[s] up"); *id.*, at E23 (Young) (the bill would require teachers to live up to their "obligation to present all theories" and thereby enable "students to make judgments themselves"); *id.*, at E44 (Boudreaux) ("Our intention is truth and as a scientist, I am interested in truth"); *id.*, at E60–E61 (Boudreaux) ("[W]e [teachers] are guilty of a lot of brainwashing. . . . We have a duty to . . . [present the] truth" to students "at all levels from gradeschool on through the college level"); *id.*, at E79 (Kalivoda) ("This [hearing] is being held I think to determine whether children will benefit from freedom of information or if they will be handicapped educationally by having little or no information about creation"); *id.*, at E80 (Kalivoda) ("I am not interested in teaching religion in schools. . . . I am interested in the truth and [students] having the opportunity to hear more than one side"); *id.*, at E98 (Reiboldt) ("The students have a right to know there is an alternate creationist point of view. They have a right to know the scientific evidences which suppor[t] that alternative"); *id.*, at E218 (Young statement) (passage of the bill will ensure that "communication of scientific ideas and discoveries may be unhindered"); 2 *id.*, at E514 (Morris) ("[A]re we going to allow [students] to look at evolution, to look at creationism, and to let one or the other stand or fall on its own merits, or will we by failing to pass this bill . . . deny students an opportunity to hear another viewpoint?"); *id.*, at E516–E517 (Young) ("We want to give the children here in this state an equal opportunity to see both sides of the theories"). Senator Keith expressed similar views. See *e.g.*, 1 *id.*, at E36; *id.*, at E41; *id.*, at E280; *id.*, at E283.

Legislators other than Senator Keith made only a few statements providing insight into their motives, but those statements cast no doubt upon the sincerity of the Act's articulated purpose. The legislators were concerned primarily about the manner in which the subject of origins was presented in Louisiana schools—specifically, about whether scientifically valuable information was being censored and students misled about evolution. Representatives Cain, Jenkins, and F. Thompson seemed impressed by the scientific evidence presented in support of creation science. See 2 *id.*, at E530 (Rep. F. Thompson); *id.*, at E533 (Rep. Cain); *id.*, at E613 (Rep. Jenkins). At the first study commission hearing, Senator Picard and Representative M. Thompson questioned Senator Keith about Louisiana teachers' treatment of evolution and creation science. See 1 *id.*, at E71–E74. At the close of the hearing, Representative M. Thompson told the audience:

"We as members of the committee will also receive from the staff information of what is currently being taught in the Louisiana public schools. We really want to see [it]. I . . . have no idea in what manner [biology] is presented and in what manner the creationist theories [are] excluded in the public school[s]. We want to look at what the status of the situation is." *Id.*, at E104.

Legislators made other comments suggesting a concern about censorship and misrepresentation of scientific information. See, *e.g.*, *id.*, at E386 (Sen. McLeod); 2 *id.*, at E527 (Rep. Jenkins); *id.*, at E528 (Rep. M. Thompson); *id.*, at E534 (Rep. Fair).

It is undoubtedly true that what prompted the Legislature to direct its attention to the misrepresentation of evolution in the schools (rather than the inaccurate presentation of other topics) was its awareness of the tension between evolution and the religious beliefs of many children. But even appellees concede that a valid secular purpose is not rendered impermissible simply because its pursuit is prompted by concern for religious sensitivities. Tr. of Oral Arg. 43, 56. If a history teacher falsely told her students that the bones of Jesus Christ had been discovered, or a physics teacher that the Shroud of Turin had been conclusively established to be inexplicable on the basis of natural causes, I cannot believe (despite the majority's implication to the contrary, see *ante*, at 2582) that legislators or school board members would be constitutionally prohibited from taking corrective action, simply because that action was prompted by concern for the religious beliefs of the misinstructed students.

In sum, even if one concedes, for the sake of argument, that a majority of the Louisiana Legislature voted for the Balanced Treatment Act partly in order to foster (rather than merely eliminate discrimination against) Christian fundamentalist beliefs, our cases establish that that alone would not suffice to invalidate the Act, so long as there was a genuine secular purpose as well. We have, moreover, no adequate basis for disbelieving the secular purpose set forth in the Act itself, or for concluding that it is a sham enacted to conceal the legislators' violation of their oaths of office. I am astonished by the Court's unprecedented readiness to reach such a conclusion, which I can only attribute to an intellectual predisposition created by the facts and the legend of *Scopes v. State*, 154 Tenn. 105, 289 S.W. 363 (1927)—an instinctive reaction that any governmentally imposed requirements bearing upon the teaching of evolution must be a manifestation of Christian fundamentalist repression. In this case, however, it seems to me the Court's position is the repressive one. The people of Louisiana, including those who are Christian fundamentalists, are quite entitled, as a secular matter, to have whatever scientific evidence there may be against evolution presented in their schools, just as Mr. Scopes was entitled to present whatever scientific evidence there was for it. Perhaps what the Louisiana Legislature has done is unconstitutional because there *is* no such evidence, and the scheme they have established will amount to no more than a presentation of the Book of Genesis. But we cannot say that on the evidence before us in this summary judgment context, which includes ample uncontradicted testimony that "creation science" is a body of scientific knowledge rather than revealed belief. *Infinitely* less can we say (or should we say) that the scientific evidence for evolution is so conclusive that no one could be gullible enough to believe that there is any real scientific evidence to the contrary, so that the legislation's stated purpose must be a lie. Yet that illiberal judgment, that *Scopes*-in-reverse, is ultimately the basis on which the Court's facile rejection of the Louisiana Legislature's purpose must rest.

Since the existence of secular purpose is so entirely clear, and thus dispositive, I will not go on to discuss the fact that, even if the Louisiana Legislature's purpose were exclusively to advance religion, some of the well established exceptions to the impermissibility of that purpose might be applicable—the validating intent to eliminate a perceived discrimination against a particular religion, to facilitate its free exercise, or to accommodate it. I am not in any case enamored of those amorphous exceptions, since I think them no more than unpredictable correctives to what is (as the next Part of this opinion will discuss) a fundamentally unsound rule. It is surprising, however, that the

Court does not address these exceptions, since the context of the legislature's action gives some reason to believe they may be applicable.[6]

Because I believe that the Balanced Treatment Act had a secular purpose, which is all the first component of the *Lemon* test requires, I would reverse the judgment of the Court of Appeals and remand for further consideration.

III

I have to this point assumed the validity of the *Lemon* "purpose" test. In fact, however, I think the pessimistic evaluation that THE CHIEF JUSTICE made of the totality of *Lemon* is particularly applicable to the "purpose" prong; it is "a constitutional theory [that] has no basis in the history of the amendment it seeks to interpret, is difficult to apply and yields unprincipled results." *Wallace v. Jaffree*, 472 U.S., at 112 (REHNQUIST, J., dissenting).

Our cases interpreting and applying the purpose test have made such a maze of the Establishment Clause that even the most conscientious governmental officials can only guess what motives will be held unconstitutional. We have said essentially the following: Government may not act with the purpose of advancing religion, except when forced to do so by the Free Exercise Clause (which is now and then); or when eliminating existing governmental hostility to religion (which exists sometimes); or even when merely accommodating governmentally uninhibited religious practices, except that at some point (it is unclear where) intentional accommodation results in the fostering of religion, which is of course unconstitutional.

But the difficulty of knowing what vitiating purpose one is looking for is as nothing compared with the difficulty of knowing how or where to find it. For while it is possible to discern the objective "purpose" of a statute (*i.e.*, the public good at which its provisions appear to be directed), or even the formal motivation for a statute where that is explicitly set forth (as it was, to no avail, here), discerning the subjective motivation of those enacting the statute is, to be honest, almost always an impossible task. The number of possible motivations, to begin with, is not binary, or indeed even finite. In the present case, for example, a particular legislator need not have voted for the Act either because he wanted to foster religion or because he wanted to improve education. He may have thought the bill would provide jobs for his district, or may have wanted to make amends with a faction of his party he had alienated on another vote, or he may

---

[6] As the majority recognizes, *ante*, at 2581–2582, Senator Keith sincerely believed that "secular humanism is a bona fide religion," 1 App. E36; see also *id.*, at E418; 2 *id.*, at E499, and that "evolution is the cornerstone of that religion," 1 *id.*, at E418; see also *id.*, at E282; *id.*, at E312–E313; *id.*, at E317; 2 *id.*, at E499. The Senator even told his colleagues that this Court had "held" that secular humanism was a religion. See 1 *id.*, at E36; *id.*, at E418; 2 *id.*, at E499. (In *Torcaso v. Watkins*, 367 U.S. 488, 495, n. 11, 81 S.Ct. 1680, 1684, n. 11, 6 L.Ed.2d 982 (1961), we did indeed refer to "Secular Humanism" as a "religio[n].") Senator Keith and his supporters raised the "religion" of secular humanism *not*, as the majority suggests, to explain the source of their "disdain for the theory of evolution," *ante*, at 2581–2582, but to convince the Legislature that the State of Louisiana was *violating the Establishment Clause* because its teachers were misrepresenting evolution as fact and depriving students of the information necessary to question that theory. 1 App. E2–E4 (Sen. Keith); *id.*, at E36–E37, E39 (Sen. Keith); *id.*, at E154–E155 (Boudreaux paper); *id.*, at E281–E282 (Sen. Keith); *id.*, at E317 (Sen. Keith); 2 *id.*, at E499–E500 (Sen. Keith). The Senator repeatedly urged his colleagues to pass his bill to *remedy* this Establishment Clause violation by ensuring state neutrality in religious matters, see, *e.g.*, 1 *id.*, at E36; *id.*, at E39; *id.*, at E313, surely a permissible purpose under *Lemon*. Senator Keith's argument may be questionable, but nothing in the statute or its legislative history gives us reason to doubt his sincerity or that of his supporters.

have been a close friend of the bill's sponsor, or he may have been repaying a favor he owed the Majority Leader, or he may have hoped the Governor would appreciate his vote and make a fundraising appearance for him, or he may have been pressured to vote for a bill he disliked by a wealthy contributor or by a flood of constituent mail, or he may have been seeking favorable publicity, or he may have been reluctant to hurt the feelings of a loyal staff member who worked on the bill, or he may have been settling an old score with a legislator who opposed the bill, or he may have been mad at his wife who opposed the bill, or he may have been intoxicated and utterly *un*motivated when the vote was called, or he may have accidentally voted "yes" instead of "no," or, of course, he may have had (and very likely did have) a combination of some of the above and many other motivations. To look for *the sole purpose* of even a single legislator is probably to look for something that does not exist.

Putting that problem aside, however, where ought we to look for the individual legislator's purpose? We cannot of course assume that every member present (if, as is unlikely, we know who or even how many they were) agreed with the motivation expressed in a particular legislator's pre-enactment floor or committee statement. Quite obviously, "[w]hat motivates one legislator to make a speech about a statute is not necessarily what motivates scores of others to enact it." *United States v. O'Brien*, 391 U.S. 367, 384 (1968). Can we assume, then, that they all agree with the motivation expressed in the staff-prepared committee reports they might have read—even though we are unwilling to assume that they agreed with the motivation expressed in the very statute that they voted for? Should we consider post-enactment floor statements? Or post-enactment testimony from legislators, obtained expressly for the lawsuit? Should we consider media reports on the realities of the legislative bargaining? All of these sources, of course, are eminently manipulable. Legislative histories can be contrived and sanitized, favorable media coverage orchestrated, and post-enactment recollections conveniently distorted. Perhaps most valuable of all would be more objective indications—for example, evidence regarding the individual legislators' religious affiliations. And if that, why not evidence regarding the fervor or tepidity of their beliefs?

Having achieved, through these simple means, an assessment of what individual legislators intended, we must still confront the question (yet to be addressed in any of our cases) how *many* of them must have the invalidating intent. If a state senate approves a bill by vote of 26 to 25, and only one of the 26 intended solely to advance religion, is the law unconstitutional? What if 3 of the 26 had that intent? What if 3 of the 26 had the impermissible intent, but 3 of the 25 voting against the bill were motivated by religious hostility or were simply attempting to "balance" the votes of their impermissibly motivated colleagues? Or is it possible that the intent of the bill's sponsor is alone enough to invalidate it—on a theory, perhaps, that even though everyone else's intent was pure, what they produced was the fruit of a forbidden tree?

Because there are no good answers to these questions, this Court has recognized from Chief Justice Marshall, see *Fletcher v. Peck*, 6 Cranch 87 (1810), to Chief Justice Warren, *United States v. O'Brien, supra*, 391 U.S. at 383–384, that determining the subjective intent of legislators is a perilous enterprise. It is perilous, I might note, not just for the judges who will very likely reach the wrong result, but also for the legislators who find that they must assess the validity of proposed legislation—and risk the condemnation of having voted for an unconstitutional measure—not on the basis of what the legislation contains, nor even on the basis of what they themselves intend, but on the basis of what *others* have in mind.

Given the many hazards involved in assessing the subjective intent of governmental decision makers, the first prong of *Lemon* is defensible, I think, only if the text of the Establishment Clause demands it. That is surely not the case. The Clause states that "Congress shall make no law respecting an establishment of religion." One could argue, I suppose, that any time Congress acts with the *intent* of advancing religion, it has enacted a "law respecting an establishment of religion"; but far from being an unavoidable reading, it is quite an unnatural one. . . . It is, in short, far from an inevitable reading of the Establishment Clause that it forbids all governmental action intended to advance religion; and if not inevitable, any reading with such untoward consequences must be wrong.

In the past we have attempted to justify our embarrassing Establishment Clause jurisprudence[7] on the ground that it "sacrifices clarity and predictability for flexibility." *Committee for Public Education & Religious Liberty v. Regan*, 444 U.S., at 662. One commentator has aptly characterized this as "a euphemism . . . for . . . the absence of any principled rationale." Choper, *supra*, n. 7, at 681. I think it time that we sacrifice some "flexibility" for "clarity and predictability." Abandoning *Lemon*'s purpose test—a test which exacerbates the tension between the Free Exercise and Establishment Clauses, has no basis in the language or history of the amendment, and, as today's decision shows, has wonderfully flexible consequences—would be a good place to start.

POSTSCRIPT

Although Justice Powell's concurring opinion mentions it only in passing, the Court's perception of the merits of creation science must have been deeply influenced by the opinion of the trial court in *McLean v. Arkansas Board of Education*. As Powell points out, Louisiana's law, with the exception of the legislature's strategic deletion of the Genesis-based definition of creation science, followed the same pattern as the Arkansas law that Judge Overton struck down in *McLean*. That opinion reveals more about the origins of the bill. The model bill was actually drafted by Mr. Paul Ellwanger, a respiratory therapist from Anderson, South Carolina. Attorneys in the Arkansas litigation took Mr. Ellwanger's deposition. Judge Overton's opinion describes what Ellwanger revealed in his depositions:

> Mr. Ellwanger does not believe creation science is a science. In a letter to Pastor Robert E. Hays he states, "While neither evolution nor creation can qualify as a

---

[7] Professor Choper summarized our school aid cases thusly:

"[A] provision for therapeutic and diagnostic health services to parochial school pupils by public employees is invalid if provided *in* the parochial school, but not if offered at a neutral site, even if in a mobile unit adjacent to the parochial school. Reimbursement to parochial schools for the expense of administering teacher-prepared tests required by state law is invalid, but the state may reimburse parochial schools for the expense of administering state-prepared tests. The state may lend school textbooks to parochial school pupils because, the Court has explained, the books can be checked in advance for religious content and are 'self-policing'; but the state may not lend other seemingly self-policing instructional items such as tape recorders and maps. The state may pay the cost of bus transportation to parochial schools, which the Court has ruled are 'permeated' with religion; but the state is forbidden to pay for field trip transportation visits 'to governmental, industrial, cultural, and scientific centers designed to enrich the secular studies of students.' " Choper, The Religion Clauses of the First Amendment: Reconciling the Conflict, 41 U.Pitt.L.Rev. 673, 680–681 (1980) (footnotes omitted).

Since that was written, more decisions on the subject have been rendered, but they leave the theme of chaos securely unimpaired. See, *e.g.*, *Aguilar v. Felton*, 473 U.S. 402 (1985); *Grand Rapids School District v. Ball*, 473 U.S. 373 (1985).

scientific theory, and since it is virtually impossible at this point to educate the whole world that evolution is not a true scientific theory, we have freely used these terms—the evolution theory and the theory of scientific creationism—in the bill's text." . . .

Ellwanger's correspondence on the subject shows an awareness that [Arkansas] Act 590 is a religious crusade, coupled with the desire to conceal the fact. In a letter to State Senator Bill Keith of Louisiana, he says, "I view this whole battle as one between God and anti-God forces, though I know there are a large number of evolutionists who believe in God." And further, ". . . it behooves Satan to do all he can to thwart our efforts and confuse the issue at every turn." Yet Ellwanger suggests to Senator Keith, "If you have a clear choice between having grassroots leaders of this statewide bill promotion effort to be ministerial or non-ministerial, be sure to opt for the non-ministerial. It does the bill no good to have ministers out there in the public forum and the adversary will surely pick at this point."

Judge Overton's opinion also describes in detail the testimony of Marianne Wilson, the science curriculum supervisor for the largest school district in Arkansas. In anticipation of the enforcement of the act, she along with a committee of science teachers researched ways of teaching creation science scientifically. She and the committee concluded that creation science could not be taught scientifically, that it was purely religious. Ms. Wilson testified that she found "all available creationists' materials unacceptable because they were permeated with religious references and reliance upon religious beliefs." Moreover, the State of Arkansas in its defense offered no text or writing of any kind in evidence to refute Ms. Wilson's conclusion.

ANOTHER DIALOGUE

BEN: This one's easy. Creation science is a simple oxymoron. All the majority says is that religion and science don't mix. Since the Constitution prohibits the government from advancing religion, and creation science is by definition religious, the state can't require it.

MARY: But we're a religious nation, Ben. We pledge allegiance to a nation under God, we have "In God We Trust" on our coins, and from 1811 onward courts have said government can frame policy on religious grounds. The polygamy case is still good free-exercise law, and yet our views about marriage come from our religion. Justice Scalia is absolutely right that requiring balanced treatment is nowhere near what the establishment clause prohibits, which is that the state officially adopt one religious sect as an official state religion.

BEN: Then how come the Supreme Court has been such a stickler about denying almost all forms of financial aid to religiously based private schools? The law is very clear. The state cannot pass laws whose purpose is to advance religion, and creation science is a religious belief. All the cases you cite fall into one of two categories, either they have a generalized and psychologically innocuous reference to God, with no specific religious sectarian connotation, or they allow the representation of religious symbols in the context of our history and traditions. Not one of these cases allows government to promote a specific religious sect, like a fundamentalist Christian reading of Genesis.

MARY: But the Court says the law fails the purpose test. I'd cheerfully strike the law down if after the schools implemented it we found evidence in a trial that the law's effect promoted religion. But an important purpose is secular.

BEN: You mean the academic freedom argument?

MARY: Yes.The precedents are crystal clear about one thing. The mere fact that a public policy, like Sunday closing laws, coincides with religion doesn't violate the establishment clause. In fact, it would violate both the free exercise and free speech rights of Christians to prohibit teaching the *secular*, that is the scientific, evidence against evolution.

BEN: The academic freedom argument in this case is a total crock. Nothing in Louisiana law prohibited any teacher from teaching—from scientifically teaching—the evidence for creationism and showing how religious arguments are constructed. It's plainly incoherent to say the purpose was to advance a freedom that was already there.

MARY: No, that's just where Scalia is right. Academic freedom does not refer only to teachers' freedom, it also refers to the freedom of students to get more than one point of view. You can hardly deny that, given the harsh application of the *Lemon* test, the schools might be nervous about doing so. This law reassures the schools that they can provide more information and develop respect for different perspectives without breaking the law.

BEN: Look, do you believe in a young earth? Do you believe dinosaur fossils are found in lower layers of sedimentary rock because during the Flood dinosaurs sank first (because they were heavier and couldn't swim), but human and mammal fossils are found in higher sedimentary layers because people are lighter and could swim and sank a few hours later? It's no more possible to teach creationism scientifically than it is to teach that the sun goes around the earth.

MARY: Of course I don't believe in a young earth, but you're distorting the argument. You're talking effects and entanglement, not purpose, and without a trial there's no proof of either. The philosophy of modern science teaches that theories are always tentative and open to revision by counter or conflicting evidence. It violates the principle of modern science and freedom of speech to deny students access to conflicting data. This purpose is far more secular than having "In God We Trust" on coins. The fact that it has some secondary relationship to religion is no more important here than it is in the Sunday closing cases. Why do we give tax breaks to churches who practice snake handling and don't spend a dime on charity?

BEN: Mary, it warms my heart to hear you embrace science's skepticism. That's just the point I pushed against your dogmatism about the law in our yarmulke debate. But here you're creating a ridiculous fiction. The purpose of Louisiana's law *had* to be to promote fundamentalist Christianity. Otherwise the legislature would have called for balanced treatment of all alternatives to evolution, not just the Genesis interpretation.

MARY: You're creating the fiction. The law allows just that. Do you really believe there's a third alternative to evolution and creationism? If there is, I haven't the foggiest idea what it could be. The legislature, as Scalia points out, *deleted* from the bill all the direct and even indirect references to Genesis. Why not say that the legislature intended to pass a bill whose purpose would meet the *Lemon* test in just the way Sunday closing laws do and allowing chaplains in the military does?

BEN: Because that way the Court allows people to manipulate the legislative record, as Mr. Ellwanger advised, to put a secular cosmetic face on a religious policy.

MARY: But that argument cuts both ways. The majority's reading in *Edwards* allows a clever opponent of a bill to give a religious speech in the legislature in favor of it and scuttle an otherwise valid statute.

BEN: No. *Edwards* is just like the case that prohibited posting the Ten Commandments. There's a difference between speculating scientifically about religious possibilities and making all your science conform to religion. The legislature isn't saying let's speculate about whether big bang origins of the universe imply a God; this is specific biology dictated by the creationist story of one religion, the story of Genesis, and that's illegal.

MARY: But Scalia was still right. The issue as far as purpose goes is whether the legislature sincerely thought it was creating secular policy, policy at least as secular as Sunday closing laws. The record simply doesn't give us any reason to doubt their sincerity.

BEN: If you believe that, you believe in the Easter Bunny. The issue is not what they actually thought. Scalia gives us the right answer to an irrelevant question, namely that we can't tell what they thought. So what? The legal question is, what purpose does it serve—what problem does it solve—to pass a bill with those particular clauses in it and designed by Christian fundamentalists. The answer is that this bill is incoherent unless its only purpose is to promote religion.

MARY: In some ways I do believe in the Easter Bunny, and Santa Claus, but let's save that for the philosophy class. Look, Ben, we're back to the same argument we had about the yarmulke. I think our law has to provide some basis for us to trust the most important governmental institutions like the military and the elected legislature. Nobody can prove anything for certain in this world, but law isn't science. It's more like religion. Your position ends up pulling the rug out from under the very processes that we must have faith in. We need political faith just as we do religious faith, and your kind of law destroys political faith.

CONCLUSION

Chapter 2's debate concluded that we must look to history and moral theory to get behind the conflicting precedents. Here it appears we must look at the nature of science and religion itself to evaluate establishment policy. The next three chapters do so. Please bear in mind, however, that much of the controversy about the creation-science ruling was over whether to have a full constitutional debate at all. The defendants, it appears, never had their day in court. Does the Constitution give them at least this right?

BIBLIOGRAPHIC NOTES

For an overview of establishment law from one who endorses strict separation of church and state, see Leonard Levy, *The Establishment Clause* (1986). Levy's selective bibliography provides sources for both separationist positions like his own and the more traditional nonpreferentialist position. John Arthur's *The Unfinished Constitution* (1989), which I noted at the end of Chapter 2, traces the competing views of establishment law back to the differences between federalists and anti-federalists (republicans) at the time of the founding. He believes all constitutional law operates within that fundamental tension without resolving it.

A thorough review of establishment cases since World War II is one of the most frustrating jurisprudential exercises imaginable. The cases, especially those ostensibly relying on *Lemon*, often seem to split microscopic hairs. *Wolman v. Walter* (1977) approved governmental assistance for testing, diagnostic, and therapeutic services in sectarian schools but denied aid for instructional equipment and services for field trips. Louis Fisher has provided a detailed tour of this dank, dark, and confused jurisprudential jungle in his *American Constitutional Law* (1990), pp. 707721.

The law review coverage of *Edwards* was not particularly kind to the majority opinion. The *Harvard Law Review*'s annual summary of the Supreme Court's leading cases criticized relying on the purpose test of *Lemon* because doing so invites creation scientists to try harder to mask their intentions in a revised statute. "A full trial would certainly have produced a record, as it did in *McLean v. Arkansas Board of Education*, from which the Court could conclude once and for all that creation-science is not a scientific theory, but rather a religious doctrine" (101 *Harvard Law Review* 197, 1987). For a spirited defense of the scientific acceptability of creationism, though not of the sort envisioned by Paul Ellwanger and company, see Gary Leedes, "Monkeying Around with the Establishment Clause and Bashing Creation Science," 22 *Richmond Law Review* 149 (1988) and the subsequent exchange with Lucien J. Dhooge in the same issue.

For the Supreme Court's latest word on the inherent conflict between the free exercise clause and the establishment clause, see *Board of Education* v. *Mergens*, 110 L.Ed. 2d 191, decided June 4, 1990. The Court held that the establishment clause does not prohibit Congress from requiring public secondary schools to make school facilities available to student religious groups whenever those schools allow any other "noncurriculum related student groups" to meet on school premises.

CHAPTER 4

The History of Church and State: Two Lectures

[E]xperience witnesseth that ecclesiastical establishments, instead of maintaining the purity and efficacy of Religion, have had a contrary operation. During almost fifteen centuries has the legal establishment of Christianity been on trial. What have been its fruits? More or less in all places, pride and indolence of the Clergy, ignorance and servility of the laity, in both, superstition, bigotry, and persecution.

—James Madison

Chapter 1 described the political aspects of constitutional interpretation. It listed various ways judges might go about interpreting the supreme law of the land. These interpretive theories turn out to be problematic, first because judges do not practice them consistently, and second because, even if they did practice one interpretive theory consistently, they could still use it to justify decisions on all sides of a case. Ben and Mary both tried to argue from precedent, but the precedents did not prove that one side should win. Good interpretation does not depend on finding the correct legal technique and using it properly. Good interpretation describes a way of defending a position so that those who disagree with the decision nevertheless trust the decider. Trusting the decider in turn strengthens the community to which both citizen and decider belong.

Chapters 2 and 3 illustrated this perspective on constitutional interpretation in two ways. First they described how the most conventional methods of legal reasoning, reading the words of a legal text literally and following precedents, do not provide answers to constitutional questions. Both cases contain opinions that disagree about what precedents mean and whether the Court should follow them at all. Justice Scalia disagrees with the Court's application of the purpose prong of *Lemon* to the Louisiana statute. At the same time, he would, if he had the votes, abandon the purpose prong altogether. Second, these two chapters illustrated legal conversations. The cases *are* debates, debates among political actors struggling to specify the values that make our polity good. Ben and Mary struggled in the same way. We seek ways of knowing whether these debates and conversations are good, and ways of knowing our own political values so that we too can converse well about them.

This chapter reviews another interpretive theory. Does our history reveal some deep structure of political life, some conditions of human affairs so clear in our culture that they tell us what the Constitution means? Both sides in the last chapters' legal debates appealed to history for support because cultures, nations, and the formal legal systems they create can do no more than express their histories. The historical origins of the First Amendment confront us with the fact that the contest for power between church and state has dominated Western civilization since Jesus' lifetime. Some of the books in the bibliographic note at the end of this chapter exceed a thousand pages on the subject. Yet, as I have already written, democracy empowers us to evaluate what the Supreme Court does without mastering thousands of pages of dense and, for the most part, remote history.

This chapter presents another kind of debate: two hypothetical lectures by historians to a general audience. These lecturers reach different conclusions about the two cases you have read and, more generally, about the historically valid ways of reading the Constitution. Each speaker hopes to persuade a lay audience that one reading of our history presents a coherent basis for judging what the Court has decided. I label these the individualist reading and the communitarian reading. These two lectures serve in part to introduce you to the main contours of Western history. Their main function, however, like that of the debates in the last chapters, is to illustrate how serious seekers of truth may reach opposing but equally credible conclusions from the same sources of information.

LECTURE I: THE HISTORICAL BASIS OF LIBERAL INDIVIDUALISM

Keynote Address to the 1990 Annual Meeting of the National Bar Association

Dr. Janet Taylor, Professor of History, U.S. University

Good evening. You attorneys and judges are no doubt more aware than I how frequently our courts confront an endless series of cases pitting the government against individual belief. Some of these may seem pretty trivial, like the *Goldman* case, where the Court allowed the Air Force to enforce a neutral headgear rule against an Orthodox Jew who insisted on wearing a yarmulke. Some cases, like the Arkansas and Louisiana creation-science decisions, raise the most fundamental (no pun intended) questions about modern scientific and moral knowledge. But from my perspective, both cases are equally important. In the next hour or so I shall sketch how Western history created our modern political philosophy of liberalism. I shall show that the origins of liberalism and of our Constitution boil down to only one conclusion: that the Supreme Court must insist that government aggressively protect the individual except when we can be virtually certain that the individual's actions hurt other individuals or the polity.

From the individualist perspective, the Court majority surely erred in the yarmulke case and may well have erred in the creation-science case as well. Liberalism requires protecting the rights of unconventional individuals, and creation scientists are unconventional just as Captain Goldman was. History and our Constitution both command government to avoid ideological commitments. The genuine protection of liberty is the only solution to the historical problem of persecution and bloodshed in the name of orthodoxy.

Tonight I shall sketch the familiar outlines of Western history to show, mostly by the weight of repetition, how pervasive persecution has been and why we must guard against it so vigilantly. I shall tilt this review toward the history of anti-Semitism; we shall discover anti-Semitic edicts that, like the Court's ruling in *Goldman*, rest on the principle, "I'm right, I'm in charge, and you do what I say without question." It is precisely this principle that our history tells us we must reject if we are to survive, and we can protect it only by aggressively defending individual dignity. As Justice Brennan told Nat Hentoff (*The New Yorker,* March 12, 1990, p. 70), "Look, pal. We've always known—the Framers knew—that liberty is a fragile thing. A very fragile thing."

Christianity and the End of the Roman Empire

Part of the modern mythology of Christianity tells of Romans persecuting Christians in decaying Rome by publicly feeding them to lions. The Emperor Nero first actively persecuted Christians in 64 A.D. No emperor officially endorsed tolerance for Christians for the next 200 years, but Christians, despite persecutions, rose to positions in Roman government. As contests for power in Rome grew bloodier, however, the Emperor Diocletian in about 300 A.D. sought to destroy all Christian churches and libraries and to remove Christians from office, particularly from the military. When Constantine conquered Rome in 312, saying God had given him the victory, his conversion initiated the process, completed in 381, of adopting Christianity as the official religion of the empire.

That move at once enmeshed the Empire in religious politics. Bishops held political office and church decisions became binding in Roman courts. The government granted special legal privileges to the clergy and financially supported educational efforts to spread the faith and to build churches. And not surprisingly, Constantine immediately sought to enforce religious orthodoxy. In October of 315 he ordered:

> It is Our will that Jews and their elders and patriarchs shall be informed that if, after the issuance of this law, any of them should dare to attempt to assail with stones or with any other kind of madness . . . any person who has fled their feral sect and has resorted to the worship of God, such assailant shall be immediately delivered to the flames and burned, with all his accomplices.

From then until its final collapse, the Empire issued hundreds more of such edicts, against Donatists, Manicheans, and other schismatics and Jews. Some samples:

381 A.D.: We forbid all heretics to hold unlawful assemblies within the towns. If factions should attempt to do anything, We order that their madness shall be banished and that they shall be driven away from the very walls of the cities, in order that Catholic churches throughout the whole world may be restored to all orthodox bishops who hold the Nicene faith.

391 A.D.: If any persons should betray the holy faith and should profane holy baptism, they shall be segregated from the community of all men, shall be disqualified from giving testimony, and, as We have previously ordained, . . . they shall inherit from no person, and by no person shall they be designated heirs.

408 A.D.: The new and unaccustomed audacity of the Donatists, heretics, and Jews has disclosed that they wish to throw into confusion the sacraments of the Catholic faith. Such audacity is a pestilence and a contagion if it should spring forth and spread abroad more widely. We command, therefore, that the penalty of a just chastisement shall be inflicted upon those persons who attempt anything that is contrary and opposed to the Catholic sect.

Orders such as these initiated precedents for discrimination and persecution that have lasted practically to our own day. An order prohibiting Jews from holding any office in which they might impose a penalty on a Christian originated in 439 A.D. and spread slowly to many European jurisdictions. Poland did not eliminate this clause from its statutes until 1931.

The Dark Ages

For 500 years after the collapse of Rome, populations were too dispersed and institutions too weak to pose any new church-and-state problems. Nations as we know them today were, for practical purposes, nonexistent in Europe, and towns were by and large little more than market centers. The Church of Rome, dwarfed by the power of the Eastern church in Constantinople, survived, but not so much as a centrally administered Roman bureaucracy as through the slow spread of monastic life. Virtually all religious life fell under the practical control of feudal lords and kings. The unifying work of Charlemagne, crowned Emperor of the Romans in 800, accelerated the Christianizing of Europe, but the feudal politics of the time resembled tribal politics more than it did the administrative glory of Rome.

Yet the underlying mood of ignorance and superstition during the Dark Ages only reinforced the prevalence of persecution. Maurice Keen (1989), reviewing Jacques Le Goff's book *The Medieval Imagination* (1988), described that mood and its consequences this way:

Le Goff evokes the way in which men of the Middle Ages who did not question the spatial continuity of earth to heaven felt themselves . . . watched at all points by angels and by demons bent on ensnaring the wayward. He clearly explains the patterns of hope and fear that this sense of constantly being under surveillance stamped on their mentality. . . . The conception of Christian society as composed of "orders" or "conditions" of man, each with its own God-given function, was used to justify social repression. The idea of orders, and the related emphasis on group membership as the key factor in defining the rights and freedoms of the individual, promoted multiple struggles between different classes and groups. The loner, the stranger, and the heterodox were not just distrusted but persecuted. Women, who, because of Eve, were seen as responsible for the Fall, were for the most part restricted to an unenviable and underprivileged place; perhaps, Le Goff muses, that was why women were so prominent in heretical movements. In this society riven with tensions the efforts of the Church to uphold the unity of Christianity through forceful temporal and spiritual authority only succeeded in precipitating further quarrels, first between popes and emperors and then between popes and kings.

The Codes of the Dark Ages preserved the spirit of enforced orthodoxy. The Visigothic Code (the adjective "gothic" initially meant "barbarian") contained provisions prohibiting the practice of fundamental Jewish rites of circumcision, celebration of Passover, and Jewish marriage, and it contained such rhetoric as:

> The blessed apostle Paul said, "To the pure all things are pure," but nothing is pure to those who are defiled, because they are unbelievers; and, for this reason, the execrable life of the Jews and the vileness of their horrible belief, which is more foul than any other detestable error, must be destroyed and cast out. Therefore, no Jew shall make a distinction between food which is clean and unclean. . . .

The High Middle Ages

Christianity's spread did promote the idea that one great unity, one God, governed all. People naturally concluded that they should unify earthly rule, that church and state could not peacefully coexist if both tried to govern separately. Inevitably a pope would declare that, in a unitary spiritual world (a "Monist" rather than "dualist" world), the Church must have final political authority. Gregory the Great accomplished just that when he declared what modern historians call the "papal revolution" in 1075. The logic seems difficult to refute. Otto von Gierke (1900, 1968) wrote:

> [If] mankind be only one, and if there can be but one State that comprises all Mankind, that State can be no other than the Church that God Himself has founded, and all temporal lordship can be valid only in so far as it is part and parcel of the Church.

Earthly princes did not tolerate this threat to their power for long. They forced the Church to accept what became known as the "two swords" theory of jurisdiction. The king's forces would adjudicate violations of earthly law and the Church would decide spiritual matters. The theory, of course, did not work in practice. Who, for example, had jurisdiction to try a priest who sexually assaulted a member of the king's family? And could a bishop excommunicate a king? Thomas Becket's much dramatized martyrdom in the cathedral of Canterbury in 1170 resulted from the conflicting loyalties between pope and king.

And so, from the beginning of the twelfth century to the Reformation, kings, feudal lords, and popes jockeyed, in slow motion by today's standards, for power. Their jockeying extended the cycle of persecution at the same time that it helped create the modern world. This period included the major Crusades and the fall of Constantinople to the Muslims; the Hundred Years' War between England and France, during which Joan of Arc was burned at the stake for heresy; recurring and devastating sweeps of bubonic plague, the Black Death; and the collapse of the Papacy itself into warring factions which regularly aligned themselves with secular princes in deadly contests over territory.

This period marks the beginning of the discovery that orthodoxy in religion and politics produced disastrous practical consequences. Barbara Tuchman's *A Distant Mirror: The Calamitous Fourteenth Century* (1978) described this undoing of form for form's sake. In religious matters it became increasingly difficult to reconcile the Church's insistence on obedience to its formal teachings when the Church itself was so corrupted by the quest for political power. In political matters themselves the unquestioned adherence to distinctions of rank and status regularly thwarted men's hopes. The French lost battle after battle in the Hundred Years' War because, unlike the less formal English, they insisted that knights, being ordained by God to a higher status than that of ordinary archers, must lead the lower-status archers into battle. Time after time the archer peasants who manned the English front lines with cross-bows mowed down the knights in the French front lines.

The failure of the papal revolution to create absolute earthly supremacy brought some formal doctrinal relaxation of strictures on Jewish life. After all, Jews were in no sense under the spiritual power of the Church. These relaxations did not in practice change the habit, which Tuchman repeatedly documents, of slaughtering Jews as scapegoats for a variety of reasons, such as causing plagues. The Church's weakened authority was in no position to protect non-Christians. Still we find stern regulations of Jewish life. In 1254, for example, the Council of Albi decreed a Jewish dress code:

> [S]ince by reason of the round capes which Jews generally wear, the respect due the clergy is seriously impaired, for they (the Clergy) use round capes habitually, we decree . . . that in the future Jews shall not dare to wear round capes. They may, however, in the future wear capes with long sleeves, . . . but in these sleeves there must be no folds or creases. . . . They shall, moreover, continually and publicly wear a circular sign upon their chest. The width of the oval shall be one digit and half a palm its height.

The standard justification of such regulations rested on scripture and Christian tradition. The Siete Partidas of Alfonso the Wise of Castile in 1265 barred Jews from holding any public office or employment in which the Jew might oppress Christians. They reasoned that Jews had "instead of showing [Jesus] reverence humiliated Him by shamefully putting Him to death on the cross. . . ."

Note how foreign the concept of individualism was to medieval thought. The categories and forms that Le Goff described prevailed. Jews, not individuals, put Christ (a Jew) to death, therefore Jews, the same form or category, deserve punishment today. Individualism is the only antidote to the categorical thinking that leads man to kill so wantonly members of his own species.

At that time, as Joseph Lecler (1960) wrote, official policy repressed dissident Christians more absolutely than it did Jews:

> If it is possible to speak of some genuine tolerance toward Jews and Moslems, the intolerance of the medieval Church toward heretics can only be called absolute. It went much further than the hardships of early Christianity. The death penalty, which horrified St. Augustine, spread during the 11th and 12th centuries and became regular practice in the 13th with the establishment of the monastic inquisition. . . . [T]he decisive factor which sealed the fate of the heretic lay in the sociological structure of the medieval world. Faced with the power of Islam, Christendom had to rely on the unity of its faith for its strength and cohesion. Any attempt at corrupting the faith brought with it a seriously divisive element in the social setup. Like the apostate in Islam, the heretic became an outlaw in Christendom.

The obvious inconsistency between Christian teachings and religious persecution in God's name, like other gross failings to practice church teachings, helped provoke the final collapse of the Church as a political power in secular affairs.

The Protestant Reformation

Imagine now a single lifetime during which occurred numerous events that produced the modern political world. Imagine a life lived from roughly 1465 to 1545. During such a lifetime Gutenberg's movable type printing process became widely used, the Italian Renaissance reached its peak in the works of Raphael and Michelangelo, Columbus discovered a New World, Martin Luther nailed his 95 Theses to a church door and began the Protestant Reformation, England's Henry VIII married six times in violation of Church law and divorced the English Church from Rome, and Nicholas Copernicus suggested quietly that the Earth, seemingly immobile, spun its way around the sun and not the sun around the earth. Also, in 1532, Machiavelli published *The Prince*. All these events, as we shall see, led to the emergence of liberalism. In fact, less than a hundred years after this lifetime, Puritans, claiming the right of religious freedom, began settling America.

Since the time of the First Crusade and Gregory's attempted revolution in the late eleventh century, the Church claimed to hold total power over at the very least the governance of spiritual affairs on earth. It followed logically that the Pope, St. Peter's heir and God's representative on earth, controlled the keys to heaven and could, in his infallibility, grant or sell indulgences (forgiveness for sins and hence promises of heavenly admission) at his will. Against this practice Martin Luther, a monk in Germany, rebelled. In his view, the Apostle Paul had declared the Church to be Christ's "spotless bride"; it also followed that no spotless bride of Christ could possibly behave as did the medieval Church. In this rebellion, Luther was committing a capital heresy and the Church excommunicated him. Luther published and circulated among many sympathetic Germans a defense in which he added criticisms of the doctrines of confession, transubstantiation in the Eucharist, priestly celibacy (so widely honored in the breach), and the like. In effect he proposed to abandon the two-swords doctrine of earthly power, with its inevitable jurisdictional conflicts, in favor of a two-kingdoms theory in which the Church would abandon responsibility for earthly affairs altogether. The Church would need no legal system of its own, no canon law and ecclesiastical courts to determine a person's salvation. God's grace, not institutionalized bureaucracies, would save us.

Neither Luther's reforms nor Henry VIII's establishment of the Church of England, nor the growing Calvinist community in Geneva, advocated what we today call separation of church and state. Puritan sects came to America precisely because they wanted to live in communities governed purely and completely by Christ. Henry's establishment, interrupted by Mary's bloody attempt to reunite with Rome, became under Elizabeth I a permanent arm of the administration of the government of England. In Germany, the Church tried to execute its death sentence, but Luther sought and received protection from secular powers. Thus the 1555 Peace of Augsburg, which declared the resolution of the conflict with Rome, allowed every German prince to choose Catholicism or Lutheranism for himself and his subjects. Lutheranism thus produced not the separation of religion and politics but, to Luther's chagrin, the supremacy of the state over the church.

Nevertheless the Reformation achieved at least embryonic visions of both religious liberty and separation. Luther was the most extreme advocate, for he denied that the Church could properly proceed by legal and political means against the faithful. Neither canon law nor the sacraments of the church mediated between man and God. Man and God make direct contact. The Spirit, not temporal powers, judges us, said Luther:

> No law, whether of men or of angels, may rightfully be imposed upon Christians without their consent, for we are free of all laws. . . . Neither pope nor bishop nor any other man has the right to impose a single syllable of law upon a Christian man; if he does, it is done in the spirit of tyranny.

Martin Luther's vision certainly did not come true in his lifetime. Indeed Luther, embittered by his failure, lashed out in 1543 against Jews, and thus against the principles of individualism he had earlier embraced:

> What then shall we Christians do with this damned, rejected race of Jews: Since they live among us and we know about their lying and blasphemy and cursing, we can not tolerate them if we do not wish to share in their lies, curses and blasphemy. . . . We must prayerfully and reverentially practice a merciful severity. . . . First, their synagogues or churches should be set on fire, and whatever does not burn up should be covered or spread over with dirt so that no one may ever be able to see a cinder or stone of it.

It took another century before people could begin the serious practice of toleration.

The Reformation in England engineered by Henry VIII contained not even the glimpse of religious freedom that Luther envisioned. It too put religion at the service of the State, and so followed the familiar pattern of killing nonconformists. In 1530 Henry's Parliament enacted the Proclamation Against Erroneous Books, which banned certain books deemed heretical and imposed strict censorship on the printing of "any book or books in the English tongue concerning Holy Scripture." Worse, following Rome's rejection of Henry's divorce from Catherine of Aragon, Parliament in 1534 ratified as complete a religious tyranny as our millennium has seen. The Act of Supremacy declared that the king was "the only supreme head on earth of the Church of England." He had "full power and authority over all such errors, heresies, abuses, offences, contempts, and enormities, whatsoever they be. . . ." Parliament required all adults to take an oath of loyalty "only to the king." Catholics who remained loyal to Rome were deemed traitors to their country, and thus began the hundreds of beheadings in the Tower of London, including that of Thomas More. Henry's defense of his absolute rule was simple: If he claimed more than was fair or just, God would punish him, and God's punishment would suffice.

Following Henry's death came an equally bloody struggle for power in England. After a period of toleration, Mary Tudor (Bloody Mary), who sought reunification with Rome, earned her nickname by aggressively enforcing the Supremacy Acts against the increasing numbers of Protestant dissenters. Elizabeth I took the throne in 1558 and promptly returned to Protestantism, though, like her father, for largely political reasons. She too rejected any official sanction of religious toleration. As Lecler put it:

> Little religious by nature, she was as much opposed to the radical forms of Protestantism as to the demands of Catholicism. She founded Anglicanism as a compromise solution, the one most compatible with the entirely profane and secular nature of her political ideals. For the same reason she demanded of her subjects that they should conform outwardly; she imposed this conformity not out of zeal for religion, but because she thought, with William Cecil, "that the State could never be in Safety, where there was a Tolleration of two religions."

Executions for religious crimes began again in England in 1570. In 1583 the Archbishop of Canterbury required all clergy to agree that the Queen held supreme power in the Church of England and that the Book of Common Prayer contained nothing contrary to the Word of God. Over 200 Protestant clergy refused to sign this declaration, whereupon the church initiated an inquisition of its own. Those who refused to answer all questions put to them by this Ecclesiastical Commission were bound over to the Star Chamber for punishment.

Here began the first serious move, initiated by the Dutch Anabaptists and the English Puritans, to create a genuine separation of church and state. Many of the Protestant sects we recognize today, especially those we recognize as "fundamentalist," such as the Mennonites and Amish (followers of Menno Simons), the Baptists, and the Quakers, originated at that time. They stood in most cases for a radical rejection of worldly politics, and especially of warfare and persecution, as the work of the Devil whose kingdom on earth is opposed by Christ's heavenly kingdom. The Anabaptists in particular refused to hold office, to take loyalty oaths, and, above all, to bear arms. Their "coherent system" depended on the authority of the loving and nonviolent character of the New Testament's Christ, not on the edicts of earthly authority. Such views, of course, marked one as politically disloyal, either to the Catholic Church or to the official Protestant religion as adopted at the discretion of the secular German princes. As early as 1529 in Europe, Zwingli and the Zurich town council ordered that "every Anabaptist and rebaptized person, of whatever age or sex, be put to death by sword, or fire, or otherwise. All preachers and those who abet and conceal them, all who persist in Anabaptism or relapse after retraction, must be put to death."

Modern Liberalism

I trust that by now my sprint through Western history has revealed a deeply ingrained pattern in political life. James Madison stated the pattern this way: "During almost fifteen centuries has the legal establishment of religion been on trial. What have been its fruits? More or less in all places, pride and indolence in the Clergy; ignorance and servility in the laity; in both, superstition, bigotry, and persecution. . . ." Regimes, particularly under stress, need to compel orthodoxy. This might be justified if states did so only to defend against external attacks. Sadly, the pattern shows that persecution protects the power of individual rulers themselves. Rulers need scapegoats to avoid responsibility for their own shortcomings, and they need to compel compliance from unwilling subjects through fear.

Even though the liberal alternative began to take root in the seventeenth century, we could trace the story of persecution from then to our own day beginning with the seventeenth-century persecution of Anne Hutchinson by the Massachusetts Calvinists, who escaped European persecution only to initiate persecutions of their own. In the eighteenth century, in spite of the fact that Virginia had incorporated the English Act of Toleration in 1689, Virginia sheriffs imprisoned Baptist ministers for preaching without a license. (In 1771 a sheriff in Caroline County interrupted a minister in the middle of a sermon by taking him out and flogging him.) In the late nineteenth century the Supreme Court upheld Congress's power to require that, as a condition of voting, monogamous citizens of the territories, especially Mormons, swear an oath that they do not advocate or belong to a sect that advocated polygamy. (Imagine being granted the right to vote today on the condition that you swear not to belong to a group advocating abortion rights!) In our own century the Nazi regime conducted the West's most hideous persecution of all. Also the U.S. Army imprisoned Americans of Japanese ancestry, and the state of Indiana sentenced two female Jehovah's Witnesses to 2- to 10-year prison terms for "flag desecration" after the women had distributed pamphlets opposing the compulsory flag salute.

Nevertheless, back in the seventeenth century men had begun to recognize both the pervasiveness and the destructiveness of this pattern. They recognized that breaking out of the pattern required an entirely new philosophy of both government and the individual. Man can know God individually only through acts of conscience, and these neither the religion nor the state can compel. As John Locke and Roger Williams so clearly saw, the state must govern only with respect to those things that influence common safety of individuals and their property. Government must abandon the orthodoxy business altogether. Such ideas were, of course, central to our founding. The Restoration of both the English monarchy and the Church of England in 1660 led to the Toleration Act of 1689, which eliminated most of the restrictions on the civil liberties of Protestants. John Locke, the moderate Anglican, of course influenced this shift in England, but Roger Williams, the founder of Rhode Island, anticipated Locke by several decades. In 1655, urging a philosophy of liberal toleration in his letter to the Town of Providence, he used this metaphor:

> There goes many ship to sea, with many hundred souls in one ship, whose weal and woe is common, and is a true picture of a commonwealth, or a human combination or society. It hath fallen out sometimes that both papists and protestants, Jews and Turks, may be embarked in one ship; upon which supposal I affirm, that all the liberty of conscience, that ever I pleaded for, turns upon these two hinges—that none of the papists, protestants, Jews, or Turks be forced to come to the ship's prayers or worship, nor compelled from their own particular prayers or worship, if they practice any. I further add, that I never denied that, notwithstanding this liberty, the commander of this ship ought to command the ship's course, yea, and also command that justice, peace, and sobriety, be kept and practiced, both among the seamen and all the passengers. If any of the seamen refuse to perform their services, or passengers to pay their freight; if any refuse to help, in person or purse, toward the common charges or defence; if any refuse to obey the common laws and orders of the ship, concerning their common peace or preservation; . . . the commander or commanders may judge, resist, compel and punish such transgressors, according to their deserts and merits.

This metaphor captures the essence of liberal government. It regulates only for the common good. It avoids interference with both religious beliefs and religious practices unless such is shown to conflict with common defense and peace.

How, then, does this history help the Supreme Court make sense of the First Amendment today? Despite the superficial tensions between the clauses, both the free-exercise and establishment clauses move in the same direction, toward extinguishing, as James Madison put it, "for ever the ambitious hope of making laws for the human mind." Only in this way can we overcome the most pervasive patterns historians find in all of history, those of scapegoating and persecution. Liberalism offsets that pattern by requiring government to regulate only when our collective experience gives us confidence that the actions it regulates hurt common interests. The burden must always rest on the government to demonstrate this need. To do otherwise inevitably leaves the door open for government to give in to the tendency history so strongly confirms.

Hence discharging Goldman from the service in the absence of any proof that wearing orderly religious garb threatened military operations comes too close for comfort to the reasoning in the World War II cases that affirmed the Japanese relocation plan. Two millennia of history confirm that this country was founded on the political hope that we would avoid precisely that evil. The essence of the Jewish religious experience is to keep the covenants with God. Goldman's yarmulke was not a daily routine. It was his symbol of his personal place in the entire Jewish story. Our military exists to protect our freedom to place ourselves in our own story.

For essentially the same reason, the Court wrongly decided the creation-science case. Fundamentalist Christians deserve a place in their story, too. Justice Scalia in his dissent makes much of the obscurities of the legislature's actual intent. He is right, but he does not go nearly far enough. The Louisiana legislature passed a law endorsing the teaching of unorthodox beliefs alongside more orthodox ones. In principle I can think of no better educational policy for promoting respect for individual differences than this kind of teaching. Doing so reinforces the positive spirit of the Constitution. In fact, though we tend to forget it, Clarence Darrow defended Scopes's right to teach evolution in the famous 1925 trial on just this ground. Justice Scalia should have said so, clearly and forcefully. We can have no basis for concluding that creation science is a Trojan Horse for indoctrinating fundamentalist Christianity in the schools until the state implements the law. To prejudge this case on the basis of forms and categories rather than on what individual teachers actually do in the classroom only reverts to the medieval thinking that liberalism and our country exist to overcome.

Although doubt may sometimes seem unpatriotic, we must learn to respect it. The respect for doubt is just another way of respecting human differences. Political processes must constantly reinforce tolerance for human differences. They can do so only by constantly practicing neutrality on ideologically divisive matters. We did so in the Amish education case, and we could do so in the creation-science case as well.

Thank you.

LECTURE II: ON THE NEED FOR COMMUNITARIAN VALUES

Keynote Address to the 1991 Annual Meeting of the National Bar Association

Dr. Walter Kindles, Professor of History, U.S. University

Good evening. I want tonight to describe what I think history has to teach us about the meaning of the Constitution, particularly with respect to religious matters. I focus on religion because history confirms that religion or something comparable to it serves an essential political function. When polities lose their common core of moral aspirations, their citizens lose both trust and hope, and they are doomed. Modern political rhetoric fails badly to keep our aspirations alive. History teaches that we must restore such values, and restoring them in constitutional interpretation may be the best place to start.

I know my approach will provoke controversy, but let me try to anticipate and forestall two possible misunderstandings at the outset. First, when I speak of religion, I by no means advocate returning to a formal religious foundation, Christian or otherwise, for the modern state. The Court quite rightly decided the recent creation-science case when it prevented teaching creation science in the schools. Formal religion is much too personal and ideologically divisive to provide common aspirations in a pluralist polity such as ours.

Second, when I speak of history and law, I do not mean anything so simple-minded as a return to the intent of the framers. I know we have recently seen a president nominate to the Court a judge and former law professor because of the political appeal of that position. As Robert Bork put his obligation to the Constitution in an interview with Bill Moyers, "I don't see how we can treat it as law if we don't apply it as it was intended." If by that position he means anything like a calculus by which to generate "the correct answers" to modern constitutional issues, I reject it entirely. We have no records adequate enough to tell what the majority of those who wrote and voted to adopt the Constitution felt about specific issues of their own day, let alone issues two hundred years later and separated by a scientific and technological revolution. And it will do no good to appeal to the more general principles of the Framers, the mood of their time, because those moods contradict each other.

To illustrate what I mean by contradictory moods, consider on one hand that neither the original authors nor the authors of the Fourteenth Amendment in all probability intended the Bill of Rights to apply to the states. But on the other hand, as H. Jefferson Powell (1985) has shown, principles of interpretation common at the time held that the intent of the author of a document did not count in its interpretation. And the historical evidence shows even James Madison, "the father of our Constitution," waffling on interpretive matters, waffling on the degree of separation of church and state, and waffling on the question of whether the Constitution can change with experience. Madison, a deeply conservative thinker, sometimes advocated orderly legislative reinterpretation of the Constitution and sometimes urged change only by amendment, but in each case, as Drew McCoy explains, Madison sought to preserve social order by maintaining a common respect for the Constitution as the source of our political morality. At this level of generality— preserving respect for the Constitution—we may find no disagreement among the Framers or among today's Supreme Court Justices. But this mood is of course far too general to help in any way to decide concrete cases.

It is of course plausible to read Western history as a deliberate rejection of my proposition. My friend and colleague Janet Taylor and I have had many delightful debates on the subject. She argues that centuries of efforts, by both churches and kings, to rule by compelling common orthodox beliefs led to continuous persecution and warfare, and therefore liberalism from John Locke forward has worked to retool government in an essentially utilitarian fashion. In this model, government may rule to achieve not ideological ends but protection of things we all share, protection of our property and our safety so that we can realize our personal hopes, goals, and faiths. The recent shifts in Central and Eastern Europe away from the pretense of ruling in the name of a Marxist-Leninist ideology certainly seem to confirm liberalism's wisdom.

Liberalism rightly moves away from government by ideology, but tonight I want to suggest that it is a mistake to read liberalism as divorcing politics from values and aspirations. To dismiss public values inevitably means dismissing justice itself, but polities, especially liberal ones, must maintain a commitment to justice or die. In other words I want to suggest that the persistence of political support for religion, from ancient Greek democracy to democracy in a scientific age, and indeed the yearning for a "religion" of constitutional interpretation of a Robert Borkish sort, reveal a permanent condition of political life. People need to share such common value systems or their communities sooner or later fall apart.

The Historical Pattern

The bulk of the political history of Western civilization tells a story of regimes in which religion and politics were virtually one and the same. The Greeks had their Pantheon of gods, and Socrates's irreverence toward them, and therefore his simultaneous threat to the state, led to his death sentence. Rome, though in many ways a secular state, integrated religion and politics. Its emperors held divine status. Indeed, cultural anthropologists find that in most primitive societies ritual observances comparable to today's religiously orthodox practices are the very political glue that gives tribes and groups their identity. Such rituals seem to give groups the cohesiveness they need to defend themselves and survive. A political life that addresses the problems of group identity and self defense—a politics that creates standards of justice in the economic distribution of wealth and in the way people treat one another—*without* incorporating and appealing to religious teachings and the rituals to keep them alive is a very modern concept. But even this modern concept abandons only formal religion, not the political function it has always served.

Liberalism's Religious Foundation

The secularization of First Amendment law since 1940 tended to blind us to the religious origins of our justice system. As Harold Berman recently pointed out, all modern legal systems in the West descend directly from the creation of canon law after the power struggle that the papal revolution initiated over 900 years ago. From the Church, secular law inherited systematic organization and also the sense that law embodies the moral values and speaks with the moral authority of those who make it.

It should not surprise us that statements of liberal teachings come from men with devout religious beliefs. Liberalism is the product of devout Christians, like Menno Simons, Martin Luther, Roger Williams, and other sixteenth-century Protestants who so earnestly sought ways to practice Christ's teaching of toleration on earth. Modern jurisprudence has led us to misinterpret the role of values and virtue in the polities that Locke, Madison, and Jefferson envisioned. None of these three thought the way a modern utilitarian or policy rationalist does. Locke, a trained theologian, wrote extensively in support of the reasonableness of Christianity and firmly believed that Christ's moral teachings bound Christians. He served as Lord Shaftesbury's secretary for ecclesiastical matters for many years. During Shaftesbury's tenure as Lord Chancellor he vigorously opposed toleration or political participation for Catholics and lobbied to have the king's Catholic brother, James, removed from the line of succession to the throne on that ground.

Locke completed his famous "Letter Concerning Toleration" in early 1686 during his self-imposed exile in Holland. From its first paragraph the letter makes clear Locke's conviction that political tolerance among Protestants follows directly from Christ's teaching of charity and goodwill.

> "The kings of the Gentiles exercise lordship over them," said our Savior to His disciples, "but ye shall not be so." The business of true religion is quite another thing. It is not instituted in order to the erecting of an external pomp, nor to the obtaining of ecclesiastical dominion, nor to the exercising of compulsive force, but to the regulating of men's lives, according to the rules of virtue and piety.

By its third paragraph Locke's famous letter urges civil leaders to "follow the perfect example of that Prince of Peace, who sent out his soldiers . . . not armed with the sword . . . but prepared with the Gospel of peace. . . ."

Locke limits the scope of government to the impartial execution of equal laws concerning such "civil interests" as life, liberty, health, money, and real and personal property. The state may use force effectively against such matters because they are "outward things," visible for all to see. The state may not use force to compel belief because belief must come from within, "for everyone is orthodox to himself." The goal is the salvation of a soul and this requires the inner work of reason and conscience. The very act of compelling belief makes salvation impossible. Thus civil authorities may compel washing children to cure or prevent disease, but they may not compel baptism for the saving of souls.

Locke thus proposed not a secular state but a version of a Christian nation that would, by encouraging a conscious inner journey to Christ, succeed where force had failed. His concluding paragraph regarding atheists mirrors the religious impulse of his first:

> Lastly, those are not at all to be tolerated who deny the being of a God. Promises, covenants, and oaths, which are the bonds of human society, can have no hold upon an atheist. The taking away of God, though but even in thought, dissolves all; besides also, those that by their atheism undermine and destroy all religion, can have no pretence of religion whereupon to challenge the privilege of a toleration.

To take away God dissolves all. My thesis this evening holds that our polity will dissolve unless we profess some equally powerful alternative to God. Our heritage specifies that alternative: justice and individual virtue.

Religion and the American Founding

Let us turn now to the American founding. I won't rehash the familiar events that shaped James Madison's writings except to note that he was fully aware of the jailing in Virginia of Separate Baptists for refusing to obtain permits to preach, and of how 4,000 Baptists massed to protest when the Orange County, Virginia, sheriff seized a Baptist minister in the middle of his sermon and flogged him. For the most part Madison's published views—written both in 1776 during the preparation of revolutionary Virginia's first declaration of rights and again in 1785 in opposition to a Virginia bill to impose a tax to pay "Teachers of the Christian Religion"—echoed Locke. In 1776 he wrote:

> That religion, or the duty which we owe to our Creator, and the manner of discharging it, can be directed only by reason and conviction, not by force or violence; and therefore all men are equally entitled to the free exercise of religion, according to the dictates of conscience; and that it is the mutual duty of all to practise Christian forbearance, love, and charity, towards each other.

Madison's famous Memorial and Remonstrance to the Virginia legislature in 1785, our most eloquent early justification for the strict separation of church and state, hardly promotes a secular or utilitarian society:

> The Religion then of every man must be left to the conviction and conscience of every man; and it is the right of every man to exercise it as these may dictate. This right is in its nature an unalienable right. It is unalienable, because the opinions of men, depending only on the evidence contemplated by their own minds cannot follow the dictates of other men: It is unalienable also, because what is here a right towards men, is a duty towards the Creator. It is the duty of every man to render to the Creator such homage and such only as he believes to be acceptable to him. This duty is precedent, both in order of time and degree of obligation, to the claims of Civil Society. Before any man can be considered as a member of Civil Society, he must be considered as a subject of the Governor of the Universe. . . .

Jefferson, whose bill on religious toleration the Virginia legislature passed in place of the tax in support of Christianity, was more openly tolerant of atheism than Madison, but of course the first paragraph of his Declaration of Independence refers to "Nature's God" and our endowment by our "Creator" with unalienable rights to life, liberty, and the pursuit of happiness. Madison's own support of the establishment and free-exercise clauses of the First Amendment arose not from any doubts about Christian morality but purely from the political premise that "it is proper to take alarm at the first experiment on our liberties" and "Wherever the real power in a government lies, there is the danger of oppression." The Congress of 1789, which passed the Bill of Rights, urged President Washington to proclaim a day of "public thanksgiving and prayer, to be observed by acknowledging with grateful hearts the many and signal favors of Almighty God." Washington complied.

The founding fathers distinguished not between a religious and a secular state but between voluntary and mandatory methods of achieving virtue. This distinction had from the start an anti-legal character. The Quakers, for example, forbade anyone from practicing law at all for Pennsylvania's first 70 years as a colony. We were, culturally speaking, a Protestant republic, in contrast to the Catholic democracy of bloody revolutionary France, which pursued and liquidated heretics from the new social order much as it had earlier persecuted religious dissidents. But we were a Christian nation, unabashedly so in New England, where the Connecticut constitution declared "the duty of all men to worship the Supreme being" and where Massachusetts required all public officials to "believe the Christian religion." In the 1811 *Ruggles* case the New York courts affirmed a conviction for the common law crime of blasphemy, saying, "whatever strikes at the root of Christianity tends manifestly to the dissolution of civil government."

Thus it is fair to characterize the prevailing understanding at the founding as varying on the following continuum: on the one end an explicit endorsement of Christianity and on the other the belief that all religions promote a common morality without which the United States could not survive, but that men would achieve not by the compulsion of law but from personal growth toward God.

The second approach, which struck framers such as Jefferson and Madison as the riskiest aspect of our constitutional experiment, seemed to Tocqueville to have paid off handsomely. In 1830 America, Tocqueville found a successful unification of morality and liberty. Here are his most notable comments:

> The sects which exist in the United States are innumerable. They all differ in respect to the worship which is due from man to his Creator, but they all agree in respect to the duties which are due from man to man. . . . Christian morality is everywhere the same. . . .
>
> In the United States religion exercises but little influence upon the laws and upon the details of public opinion, but it directs the manners of the community, and by regulating domestic life it regulates the State. . . .
>
> Religion is much more necessary in the republic which they set forth in glowing colors than in the monarchy which they attack; and it is more needed in democratic republics than in any others. How is it possible that society should escape destruction if the moral tie be not strengthened in proportion as the political tie is relaxed?

Tocqueville attributed the beneficial social effects of religion on the separation of church and state:

> . . . [I]n America one of the freest and most enlightened nations in the world fulfills all the outward duties of religious fervor. . . . In France I had almost always seen the spirit of religion and the spirit of freedom pursuing courses diametrically

opposed to each other; but in America I found that they were intimately united. . . .
I questioned the members of all the different sects. . . . To each of these I
expressed my astonishment and explained my doubts; I found that they differed
upon matters of detail alone; and that they mainly attributed the peaceful dominion
of religion in their country to the separation of Church and State. I do not hesitate to
affirm that during my stay in America I did not meet with a single individual, of the
clergy or of the laity, who was not of the same opinion upon this point.
    . . . Man alone, of all created beings, displays a natural contempt of existence,
and yet a boundless desire to exist; he scorns life, but he dreads annihilation. These
different feelings incessantly urge his soul to the contemplation of a future state,
and religion directs his musings thither. Religion, then, is simply another form of
hope; and it is no less natural to the human heart than hope itself. . . . As long as a
religion rests upon those sentiments which are the consolation of all affliction, it
may attract the affections of mankind. But if it be mixed up with the bitter passions
of the world, it may be constrained to defend allies whom its interests, and not the
principle of love, have given to it. . . . The Church cannot share the temporal
power of the State without being the object of a portion of that animosity which the
latter excites.

Looked at whole, the history of the founding confirms two essential truths about the
Constitution. First, as Stephen Conrad (1988) noted, the common law system the
founders worked within was not for them a method of synthesizing correct under-
standings and legal solutions. It was always understood as a quasi-religious activity
that preserved a reverence for the polity and its traditions. Second, the Constitution
did not create merely a political system based on checks and balances and representative responsibility to the voters. Self-government meant more than electoral
politics, it meant just what Madison prescribed and Tocqueville found: the individual learns moral rules and disciplines himself, governs his self, to follow them. He
does so not because he is coerced but because he is taught their wisdom. Religion—
and Protestant Christianity specifically—provided both the moral code and the
teaching process.

Modern First Amendment Law

But what of today? The common morality of religion no longer regulates private life
and hence the state. And there is no point in trying to reconstruct such a past. In the
loss of that past, however, we have lost Tocqueville's "form of hope." The bulk of
modern establishment and free-exercise cases merely trivializes the religious impulse. The crèche ceases to symbolize a great religion and instead merely reminds
us of a common holiday, a time to buy. A yarmulke becomes "headgear." A
legislature may open its own sessions with a prayer but cannot so much as authorize
a voluntary moment of silent prayer in schools. These public attitudes indeed
suggest we have lost something the founders valued.
    I come at last to my central point. From the perspective I've just sketched,
modern constitutional interpretation, especially in the First Amendment area, com-

pletely fails to perform the political function we need. It fails to link us to our traditions. I do not call here for a traditionalist jurisprudence, what Jaroslav Pelikan (1984) has rejected as a slavish and mechanistic preservation of the past. In contrast I speak of Pelikan's "vindication of tradition," in which leaders give fresh meaning to the past, where leaders teach us both how our past creates us and also how we may fulfill anew who we are in our own actions.

To vindicate our tradition we must first identify it and possess it. That tradition, as I have already suggested, is undeniably Judeo-Christian. The Old Testament tells a story of a persecuted people wandering in search of land in which to dwell with God. The New Testament adds to that yearning for place and space the Greek aspiration to respect human dignity, to transcend racial and ethnic boundaries, for a Jew to love a Samaritan. The founding of North America unquestionably continues that same story, the seeking of a new land in which we may dwell in peace and justice and in which we both preach and practice genuine respect for each other's dignity. The Constitution quite rightly tells us how to do so, by paradoxically setting aside medieval contests for religious supremacy and practicing the same kind of respect for others that Jesus showed for prostitutes and tax collectors. As Emerson put it in his sermon, "The Lord's Supper," Christ sought to "redeem us from formal religion."

Please don't mistake me for a fundamentalist. I claim no absolute truth for this position, I only claim that it is *our* tradition and we must not lose it. We must recover what Emerson (and William James) so clearly understood a century ago: Faith does not lock us into a historic past. Rather it makes change possible by giving us an ideal to seek, a past to perfect.

But how can we maintain this tradition in our constitutional rhetoric without falling back into some kind of establishment trap? We must start by recognizing that modern legal rhetoric blocks the path. This rhetoric speaks only to the legal profession. The *Lemon* test is a perfect example. It seeks to craft technical rules that will mask over the inconsistencies among precedents and the tension between free exercise and establishment. Legal rhetoric is the product of our love of technology. It has moved away from the poetry of Frankfurter and Jackson disagreeing vehemently with each other in the second flag salute case. Why not abandon the pretense that lawyers have a technical lock on justice, a pretense of special institutional competence that itself descends from the Catholic origins of our legal system that our Protestant founders rejected?

More concretely, why not return to the concept that establishment prohibits official state endorsement of a particular religious position. Given the record in the Arkansas and Louisiana creation-science cases, the Court should have no difficulty concluding that this statutory scheme was an official endorsement of a particular religious belief, the Genesis version of creation. Why not, conversely, read free-exercise, free-speech, and free-press clauses as endorsing the widest possible toleration for individual differences? In short, why not reclaim and vindicate the constitutional tradition of justice? Why not in Goldman's case teach both the Armed Services and the rest of us that if we properly understood and put faith in our traditions, the case would never have arisen. The base commandant would have done either of two things, both of them consistent with our traditions. He could have enforced the headgear rule from the outset; he could have explained that the military exists to defend a religiously plural nation and that he cannot make exceptions to normal regulations for members of any one religion. Or he could have defended Goldman's religious liberty, at least in the absence of any threat to effective military operations, by claiming that the military exists to defend precisely what Goldman wanted to practice. I prefer the second course, but either keeps alive the sense that our traditions give us a hopeful ethical basis for acting.

The young Thomas Jefferson wrote in 1774, "The whole art of government consists of being honest." In 1989 the tremendous popularity of Mikhail Gorbachev seemed attributable directly to Gorbachev's practice of Jefferson's art. But one can be honest about one's beliefs only if one has beliefs to be honest about, something not unlike a faith which one can profess. Lawyers' talk denies this political reality, and this is why it fails us. We must recover that force which connects personal lives to collective political life. Without that connection we lose the motivation to care for others and act competently. Our public rhetoric must reclaim the possibility of virtue through justice in public life, or we will fail to learn the negative lesson of religious persecution, and the positive lesson of liberalism, that communities must keep common hopes alive.

Thank you.

CONCLUSION

Both lecturers believe that Western history confirms a truth that American constitutional law must honor. Professor Taylor concludes that the Court must aggressively protect individual rights while Professor Kindles would have the Court model virtue. These positions have several common elements. Both approaches are dignitarian. Both respect the individual, either as an autonomous actor or as a creature capable of learning the good without coercion. Both aspire to a coherent theory by which we can integrate our historical experience and our law. Of the two approaches, Taylor's is more scientific. She claims to have discovered a pattern, a law of politics, that requires protecting the unorthodox to avoid totalitarian persecution. Kindles poses a more explicitly moral theory. The next chapter examines whether modern scientific and moral philosophy supports either of these aspirations.

BIBLIOGRAPHIC NOTES

The primary sources for the history of church state relations from Rome to the liberal enlightenment are: Harold Berman, *Law and Revolution: The Formation of the Western Legal Tradition* (1983); Sidney Z. Ehler, *Twenty Centuries of Church and State: A Survey of Their Relations Past and Present* (1957); Otto von Gierke,

Political Theories of the Middle Ages (1900, 1968, Frederick Maitland, trans. and ed.); Maurice Keen, "A Master of the Middle Ages," *New York Review of Books*, May 18, 1989; Joseph Lecler, *Toleration and the Reformation* (1960, Westow, trans.); Jacob R. Marcus, *The Jew in the Medieval World: A Source Book 315–1791* (1938); Jaroslav Pelikan, *Spirit Versus Structure: Luther and the Institutions of the Church* (1968); Carl Stephenson and Frederick Marcham, eds., *Sources of English Constitutional History* (1937); Barbara Tuchman, *A Distant Mirror: The Calamitous Fourteenth Century* (1978); see also her essay, "A Nation in Decline," *New York Times Magazine,* September 20, 1987, p. 52.

From liberalism forward see: Thomas Buckley, S.J., *Church and State in Revolutionary Virginia* (1977); Stephen Conrad, "The Constitutionalism of the Common-Law Mind," (1988); Mark DeWolfe Howe, *The Garden and the Wilderness: Religion and Government in American Constitutional History* (1965); Thomas Jefferson, *Autobiography, Writings,* Albert E. Bergh, ed., (1907); John Locke, *Epistola de Tolerantia (Letter on Toleration),* Raymond Klibansky, ed. (1968); James Madison, *Papers,* William Hutchison and William Rachal, eds. (1962); Michael Malbin, *Religion and Politics: The Intentions of the Authors of the First Amendment* (1978); Drew McCoy, *The Last of the Fathers: James Madison and the Republican Legacy* (1989); William G. McLoughlin, *New England Dissent, 1630–1833: The Baptists and Separation of Church and State* (1971); Perry Miller, *Nature's Nation* (1967); Jaroslav Pelikan, *The Vindication of Tradition* (1984); H. Jefferson Powell, "The Original Understanding of Original Intent," (1985); and "Rules for Originalists," (1987); Suzanna Sherry, "The Founders' Unwritten Constitution," (1987); Alexis de Tocqueville, *Democracy in America,* Henry Reeves, trans. (1875).

Sotirios Barber has defended the aspirational approach to constitutional interpretation in *On What the Constitution Means* (1984). For the most persuasive argument that the Judeo-Christian heritage deeply shapes our aspirations and that we aspire to extend the Judeo-Christian story, see Milner Ball, *The Promise of American Law* (1981). L. H. LaRue's *Political Discourse* (1988) brilliantly explains and models why the technical talk of lawyers cannot generate political trust. The prolific Leonard Levy addresses and rejects interpretive theories based on the framers' intent in *Original Intent and the Framers' Constitution* (1988).

CHAPTER 5

From Correspondence to Coherence: Trends in Natural Philosophy

What a thing really is depends on the fictions I surround it with.
—*Ludwig von Wittgenstein*

One of the interpretive theories introduced in Chapter 1 suggests that we can answer constitutional questions by deducing solutions from what used to be called natural law. Today we can think of natural law as truths about the human condition so universal and fundamental that government must conform to them. If such principles objectively exist in nature, then scientists presumably discover them. Legal philosophers in turn would presumably know how to convert these scientific truths into specific solutions to legal cases. This chapter explores why neither modern philosophy nor modern science can do so. The short reason is this: Modern science does not claim to describe accurately what nature is. Modern science is skeptical. Though it strives for it, science constantly denies that it has in fact found any natural law of the universe. In this chapter we shall see that modern science and its norms emerged out of the same Reformation forces that rejected the Church's natural-law claim to hold power. We shall then meet two more conversationalists, a minister and a scientist, who discuss how to interpret the Constitution if we can't agree on any moral or scientific natural law.

We can put this another way. The Court has ruled that we may teach the facts and theories of religion in the same way we teach the facts and theories of science; as an academic subject. But we may not teach religion as faith; doing so would violate the establishment clause, and maybe the free-exercise clause as well. But what is this difference between science and religion? If science, religion, and folklore are one and the same in primitive cultures, how has our culture come to distinguish science and religion so that science is politically safe and religion is not? Is one somehow truer than the other?

Perhaps science is politically safer than religion because it *does not* claim to be true. It is faith's claim of truth that leads to bloodshed. To explain how this distinction has come about, we will review briefly some 2,500 years of "natural philosophy." This history directly shapes how constitutional interpretation itself operates in our culture. Court decisions are not true or correct in any absolute sense, and this book's goal is to show how decisions may be good even when they are not demonstrably true or correct.

CLASSICAL PHILOSOPHY: TRUTH AS CORRESPONDENCE WITH NATURE

The story begins with Aristotle, for the Greek understanding of reality heavily dominated the Catholic Church, and hence all Western religion, for the better part of the last two thousand years. Aristotle (and Ptolemy, who formalized the conception that the sun and the planets revolve around the earth) believed that nature fully reveals itself to us. Nature in all its forms, from biology to politics, waits for men to describe and catalog it accurately and fully. The Greeks did so by combining observation and logical argumentation. We observe the sun to revolve around the earth. We feel no earthly motion. We observe that bodies in motion soon cease their motion. And bodies seem often to change when put into motion. If we posit that the earth is a body and observe that its does not change motion, it follows that it does not move around the sun. In this Greek worldview, good science accurately describes an objective world. Good science *corresponds* to reality, and once it does, there is no reason for compromising that reality by subjecting it to political debate or vote. Once the experts get the right answer, the debate ends.

This way of thinking suited the needs of the Catholic Church as it rose to a position of political power and had the consequent need to judge the fate of the people it controlled. The Church, of course, assumed that the Bible, and primarily the New Testament, described God's creation. It was up to the Church to reconcile our experience of nature, of life and death, of cruelty and beauty, with the Bible. Since few people could read, and since before the invention of the printing press copies of religious materials were scarce, the Church had a virtual monopoly on the process. The Church's expert judgment left no room for open debate or compromise. The debates occurred behind the closed doors of the universities.

At the time of the Reformation, nearly all formal education, particularly in the universities, was an intimate part of the Church's ruling apparatus, and the scholastics patterned what they knew, and how they could communicate it, from Aristotle. This was particularly true of the legal positions and rulings the Church's authority forced it to take on political affairs. (Combatants in the Hundred Years' War often called a halt to their warfare for months while waiting for a ruling from the University of Paris.) This Aristotelian form of argument reached the height of elegance in the writing of Thomas Aquinas in the thirteenth century. Here, for example, is Thomas's prescription, in the *Summa Theologiae* 2–2, for the legal treatment of infidels (i.e., those, like Jews and Muslims, who subscribe to another religion).

> Are infidels to be forced to the Faith? I proceed to the eighth article:
>
> 1. It appears that infidels are in no way to be forced to the faith. For it is said in Matthew that the slaves asked the householder in whose field the tares were sown, "Shall we go and gather them?" and he replied, "No, lest in gathering up the tares, you eradicate the wheat with them." On this Chrysostom says: "The Lord says these things to forbid killings. For it is necessary not to kill the heretics, because if you kill them you must kill many of the saints at the same time." Therefore it seems by a parallel reason that other infidels are not to be forced to the faith. . . .
> 3. Further, Augustine says: A man can do other things unwillingly, but "he cannot believe except willingly." But the will cannot be forced. Therefore it appears that infidels are not to be forced to the faith.

Thomas's logic led to conclusions not unlike Locke's, but the main point for our purposes is that the medieval church assumed the merger of science and religion and therefore stated authoritatively, and compelled obedience to, a complete and formal code governing all religious affairs. Formal logic and the syllogism expressed official, final truths. The natural-law habits of scholastic thought were so strong that practically until Locke's writing, English scholars seriously debated the possibility of a universal language, in which the sound of every word would correspond to its natural essence so obviously that all humans would understand the language without any training.

From our perspective the formal statement of official truths by the Church looks like a cover for exercising corrupt political power. Indeed it looked that way from Martin Luther's perspective, too. But within the Aristotelian framework, the Church's scholasticism—and even the search for a universal language—did make logical sense. Since one nature, and one best logic by which to describe it truly, can exist, there can be only one natural truth. If God made this nature and described it in the Bible, then the Bible must contain that natural truth. Biblical doctrine can have but one meaning. If so, there is no reason to encourage or allow open and free political debate and disagreement about such matters, and no reason to distinguish the sacred church from secular politics.

THE MODERN SCIENTIFIC REVOLUTION: TRUTH AS COHERENCE

If ancient notions of science and truth prevailed today, our attitudes toward law and the Supreme Court would be radically different. Indeed, I would probably be treated as a heretic for writing this book. In the old view, the Court as final authority and expert would, like the old church, claim the authority to pronounce unquestionable constitutional truths. Anyone challenging the announced truths would necessarily threaten the system.

Fortunately for writers like me, twentieth-century standards of truth and of science have abandoned the correspondence model. Modern science does not presume to know nature truly and completely. Scientific inquiry today more modestly measures that part of nature it thinks it observes. It measures changes in the things it observes, expresses these changes in statistical and mathematical expressions, and then toys with theories and hypotheses that fit the data. It is a trial-and-error method in which what we think about the world is always provisional, always subject to change when new measurements fail to fit in existing theories. This attitude is just what made the launching of the Hubble space telescope in 1990 so exciting, and its failure so newsworthy. Today a good theory is one whose parts fit together coherently with each other and with what we observe. The modern scientist is free to disagree with and to rewrite accepted theory by showing better ways of fitting together theory and experience. The modern scientist is also free to say, as did those who first encountered the "cold fusion" process in the spring of 1989, that they can't explain what they observe at all, and that the event is a "mystery." Modern science, in other words, is inherently skeptical.

We need to study the origins of this shift, a nearly 180 degree reversal of ancient natural philosophy, because its history is tied so closely to the Protestant Reformation and the origins of modern liberalism. We do not "do" modern science because a few geniuses invented it. We do it because over centuries it came to fit better with the pluralism of beliefs begun in the Protestant Reformation and with the invention of the printing press and the rapid growth of literacy and education (motivated in part by the hope that better educated people would behave in less rebellious and destructive ways toward their superiors). Above all, this shift toward skepticism and away from conformity to orthodoxy worked. It yielded practical results for cloth dyers, winemakers, stonecutters, weavers, and all the other bourgeois mercantilists who rose to power in place of feudal landlords and the Church. Skeptical science promised to tame nature, and hence God, for man's benefit.

As Margaret Jacob tells it in her book, *The Cultural Meaning of the Scientific Revolution* (1987), the story of the separation of Church and state is very much a story of the separation of the church and science. In Galileo's time, all scholarship was done within the Church, for the Church had a virtual monopoly on the language and the resources to think abstractly about anything. Galileo, of course, observed through his telescope mountains on the moon, and this observation suggested a universe less perfect than the official Church explanation decreed. Combined with Copernicus's conclusion that the sun, not the earth, occupied the center of the universe, Galileo's position suggested the inevitability of movement, of the spinning and revolving of the seemingly still earth and, by implication, movement of official Church doctrine as well. The threat of doctrinal movement forced upon it from outside threatened the Church. Galileo responded to hostility from the Church with a curiously elitist strategy. He claimed that his ideas could become the source of a reunification of all educated elites, of elite Catholic and Protestant clergy as well as elite political and mercantile laity. He tried to reassure the Church that the superstitious masses would never understand the new science and that traditional, unchanged doctrines would maintain the Church's power over the masses.

Galileo's strategy backfired. When the Church brought Galileo before the Inquisition, Protestant opponents of the Church could not resist the temptation to criticize Rome by popularizing Galileo's case. Science, a language of change, became part of low, or popular, culture in spite of Galileo. Within a hundred years of Galileo's 1616 confrontation with the Church we find secular elites, especially in Protestant countries, deliberately promoting the study of nature by the general population. Science offered the immediate advantage of promising to make labor and capital more productive, but in political affairs it also empowered secular forces to resist the dogmatism on which the political power of both Protestant and Catholic hierarchies depended.

The promise of science to master nature displaced the Church's primary reason for being; by mastering nature through observation and practical calculation, people no longer needed a church whose main role was to justify a cruel and unpredictable universe and nasty, short, and brutish lives. More important, science did so not by substituting one objective truth for another but by tilting science toward practical invention to improve the here and now. Open investigation, free inquiry into the nature of things, played a crucial role in the political triumph of secular institutions over sacred ones. Science became a series of incremental and provisional steps whose value depended on whether its applications made at least some people's lives easier. People began to see payoffs in discarding one truth when a better one came along.

Thus science joined the Protestant Reformation and liberalism in making the modern age. Of the three, the shift of scientific truth from correspondence with nature to coherence with immediate practical experience most forcefully overthrew the power of the Church to tell us what nature and truth are. It was absolutely essential in the Protestant reordering of things that each person read the Bible and come to his own truth in his own way, free of coercion and subject only to the test of reason, which is to say of coherence.

This history bears on this book's subject in two ways. I have already mentioned the first: we are empowered to challenge freely and openly the Supreme Court's constitutional interpretations. We are free to read the Constitution for ourselves. The Court's authority does not guarantee the goodness of its decisions any more than did the authority of the Church. Second, we begin to see the reason for keeping formal, organized religion separate from politics. If religion insists on being absolute and beyond discussion, then it does not fit into skeptical, practical, and discursive political life. But do these developments make constitutional interpretation impossible? Not if we recognize that interpretation is itself no longer an authoritarian pronouncement of a religious truth. Interpretation has become part of this skeptical, practical, and conversational world that modern science and the Reformation helped create. We can judge its goodness on the same coherence terms we use for other modern issues. Since the coherence test boils down to a test of the goodness of discourse, communication, and conversation, I turn again to the conversational form to make this chapter's next point, that science has a faith of its own, and that religion can meet the coherence test too.

THE PROFESSOR AND THE REVEREND

Imagine that two friends, Amy, a biochemistry professor, and Ron, a minister at a local "mainline" Protestant church in Amy's town, have gotten together for dinner. Neither is an extremist, but each naturally sympathizes with the basic perspective of his/her profession. At the same each sees obvious truth in the other's position and aspires to harmonize the two.

AMY: Ron, I read the other day some poll data showing that about 38 percent of Americans still believe that the creation story of Genesis is literally true. That scares the hell out of me, if you'll pardon the expression.

RON: Pardon granted, though that's a strange expression, since we'd all be better off rid of our internal hells by whatever means. Let's say it scares the heaven out of you, but why? We all need a faith of some kind to live by, and it's hardly surprising that the Bible, which has been the main moral and educational force in our civilization for many centuries, should still have some followers.

AMY: It makes me feel as if I'm living in a primitive and dangerous world, where uneducated and superstitious savages lurk behind trees to ambush us with crazy absolutist ideologies. Thank God the Supreme Court has stopped the teaching of religious faith in the schools dead in its tracks.

RON: Whoa! What makes you say that science depends any less on a faith or ideology than religion does? Doesn't science have its own secular faith, a faith in observation and experimentation and so on? How can you say science is any truer than religion without becoming just as dogmatic as the people who say the reverse?

AMY: That's just it. Science does not claim to be true. It's only a method of knowing that has certain rules. One of these rules defines a scientific theory or hypothesis as a prediction or explanation of observable conditions and events in the world, like natural forces or human actions, in terms of other observable (or potentially observable) conditions and events. You can't by definition appeal to supernatural forces, because then you can explain anything, like Flip Wilson's character Geraldine, who took no responsibility for her actions because "The Devil made me do it." Another rule requires that scientific theories must originate in observations and experiments and must always be tested against further evidence. It legitimates ways for people to disagree and debate peacefully, sort of like the adversary system in law. Science is one of the most important ways we avoid the pattern of ideologically driven bloodshed, which we saw in June of 1989 when the old-line Chinese Stalinists mowed down student protesters in Beijing.

RON: Sure, that's the official line about science, and in principle I agree. But in reality the scientific culture has a different faith, which is just as unshakable as a religious faith. I mean, don't you scientists believe deep down that there are no limits to what science can know, that you can unlock the secrets of the universe in some grand unified theory? Worse, I think scientists believe that the only reality is matter in motion and that anything else we claim to know is "not real" at all.

AMY: Well, a lot of scientists, myself included, do claim to believe in God.

RON: Bless you, but your God has become the ultimate mystery behind the Big Bang, right? That's hardly the Bible's personal God. You treat the Bible as poetry, an early human struggle to know the human condition and improve it. No problem. But you also deny that the Bible is an alternative way of knowing, which is just what threatens the creationists.

AMY: But scientific evidence is coherent.

RON: Yes, but only in terms of your faith, which is no less a faith than a religious faith. All the creationists and the opponents of secular humanism want is equal recognition for another possible way of looking at the world. In fact, I'll make that view just as coherent in their terms as you can make yours: There are all sorts of good religiously based reasons to oppose evolution. The survival of the fittest glorifies a struggle for survival that turns in a wink into a justification for war and killing anyone who gets in your way. There's nothing that frightens me more in our culture than these self-help books that advise you to look out for number one, swim with the sharks, and so on, and they have a direct connection to Darwin. The greedy hunt for material success and the competitiveness of the industrial world put great stress on us and deny our spiritual and ideal side. Without that we have no hope for community. William Jennings Bryan back in the Scopes trial wasn't a flaming rabble-rousing know-nothing. The fundamentalists today can point to drugs and drift and dispiritedness among our youth and say, very coherently, "See, we told you so." Any society that loses its connection with ideals and other things we call spiritual is sick. When we look, aren't we forced to admit that this very sickness surrounds us?

AMY: Of course you're right about the political necessity that we maintain hope, but you miss the point I wanted to make about science. Science doesn't worry about achieving fairness. I have no objection to teaching religion as an academic subject in the schools and contrasting it with other moral systems and other ways of knowing. I object to the claim that anything remotely like a Genesis version of creation can be scientific at all. It just doesn't play by the rules.

RON: You know I'm playing devil's advocate. I and most mainstream clergy I know do oppose teaching fundamentalism in the schools because it's bad religion. But why is it bad science? There are tremendous gaps in the fossil records. We have only a small handful of possible examples of actual changes in species. The fossil records show tremendous stability where Darwin would predict constant mutation.

AMY: That's part of the point I tried to make about science not claiming to state what's true. We do what the creationists refuse to do; we modify our theory to fit the data, just as we now work on models of sudden mutation influenced by cataclysmic events to explain the fossil record better.

RON: But why not admit other possibilities, like sudden creation? Why isn't that part of the free competition of ideas in science you applauded?

AMY: Because it doesn't fit coherently within our faith, as you call it. If the creation scientists would stop calling it science, I'd trust them more. Let me catalog the basic evidence. First we have the consistent radioactive isotope decay in rocks, both on earth, Mars, and the moon, that all point to the age of the solar system at about 4.5 billion years. Then there's the consistent finding that, even though the fossils are stable, they get simpler and more primitive the deeper one goes in the sedimentary layers. And we just don't find any confusion within single layers. We never find human bones together with dinosaur bones. (I once saw a Creationist on television claim that that was because during the Flood dinosaurs were heavier and poorer swimmers than humans, so they sank first.) And then there's the completely consistent pattern of amino acid analysis, that shows virtual identity among animals in the same species, slight variations among members of the same genus, slightly larger differences among families, and so on up the biological chain. So human genetic material is more like that of chimpanzees than of dogs, and more like that of chickens than of fish, and so on. It's just not possible to harmonize all this data within the rubric of an earth that's only a few thousand years old.

RON: So coherence is your ultimate scientific test?

AMY: No. I admit religion can meet a coherence test. There's something deeper than coherence, something I can't fully put my finger on that has to do with the morality of communication. Insisting on coherence is the way we keep the lines of communication open, the way we discipline ourselves to stay honest with each other. Only by doing that can we trust each other. It creates democratic community by insisting that no one can ever claim to hold power because he or she is right and the rest of us aren't.

RON: But that deeper honesty you describe is what coherence is all about, and deeper honesty is exactly what the Bible and religion help us achieve. They provide a discipline and a method for persuading others and thereby forming communities without resorting to the use of raw power.

AMY: Yes, but the two don't mix. Actually I believe religious fundamentalism is very much a product of modern science. Wasn't it in the mid-seventeenth century, in the beginnings of the enlightenment, when scholars began to calculate things like man was created on September 17, 3928 B.C., at nine in the morning? To the extent that we push the faith you rightly accused us of, to the extent that we promote the idea that only science is neutral and rational, we feed the forces that want to mix them up. I'd rather stick to the ground rules. Science isn't any more neutral than religion, it's just different. Science produced the Holocaust as much as religion did, maybe more so. We ought to admit that creationists *can* interpret the evidence just as rationally and neutrally and coherently as we can, but they have to assume a supernatural premise to do so, and that's just not playing by our particular rules. Their theory becomes coherent only by relating it to God and the Bible, and that makes it a religious theory, not a scientific one. We'd say the same thing of a lawyer who tried to get his client off by claiming that God or the devil performed the crime through him. We'd say that was a religious theory, not a legal theory.

RON: I agree with you completely about that. And I think we really agree that creation science fails us because it is dishonest, it fakes being science and destroys its good coherence claim, which is that we need to preserve our moral heritage. But I'm still worried that we haven't solved the 38 percent problem you started with. I don't think science possesses any way of proving what you and I believe to your 38 percent. To them, science and religion do not deal with separate cultures or ways of knowing. For them religion *is* a picture of reality, a way of knowing and making safe the world around them. The anthropologist Clifford Geertz (1973) concluded that religion is not the theory that beyond the visible world there lies an invisible one; . . . not even the more diffident opinion that there are things in heaven and earth undreamt of in our philosophies. Rather it is the conviction that the values one holds are grounded in the inherent structure of reality.

If he's right, then science and religion are practically one and the same. After all, you just said the ultimate test of science rests on the morality of communication. Science turns out to be a value system, too!

AMY: As long as teachers teach it dialogically and openly, it would be ideal to teach evolution and creation science "competitively." We do wrestle with difficult questions. The second law of thermodynamics, which says the universe moves from order to disorder (entropy) seems to contradict the rise of more complex animal species. The geological record does not contradict the possibility of a worldwide flood. Indeed we know the heating of the earth could melt enough of Antarctica to cause sudden flooding. And how far from biblical descriptions of the Apocalypse would a global nuclear war be? Not very. But we wrestle honestly with those problems. I don't find creation scientists wrestling as honestly as scientists do with the problems their own perspective creates, such as why the loving and merciful God they preach would create a world with so much data that trick us into thinking it just evolved.

RON: But that's easy for them to answer. God created the misleading data to remind people that they can relate to God only by faith.

AMY: I do think that debating these issues openly in school, and showing how science rejects some theories in favor of others, would give the ideal science education. Students would find in the process that creationists in fact do not have a coherent position because they do not agree among themselves, such as on whether complex amino acids can or cannot form spontaneously. You see, science is uncertain, and we're honest about it. We change our minds. Einstein in his original relativity theory could not accept the possibility of an infinite universe. So, to explain why gravity hadn't caused the universe to collapse, and to make his theory coherent, he created a cosmic force that counteracted gravity. But after the discovery of the red shift and the expansion of the observable universe, he cheerfully abandoned it. Those stories, set before the students in contrast to the inflexibility of the creationists, would show science at its best.

RON: But, at least in public schools, the Supreme Court won't let that happen. And maybe the Court is right precisely because the line between science and religion is so paper-thin. Charles Krauthammer (1981) wrote, in the context of Reagan's supply-side economics, "A study can be found to prop up any social theory, however cranky." What I really fear is corrupting the religious mystery by pretending that we can solve it with computers, money, and time.

THE MORALITY OF SCIENCE AND RELIGION

Amy and Ron agree that we live in a pluralistic world, and this means a world in which people's moral views vary widely. Labels such as liberal and conservative that divide us into either/ors do not tell us very much. It seems more accurate to think of people, of us, as living in various communities that give us our sense of what we believe and how we should act. Ron is a mainline Protestant minister. He has no trouble accepting that the Bible is a literary record of a people shaping their history and therefore their identity. He experiences no conflict between science and religion. But Amy, the professor, and fundamentalist creation scientists belong to different communities. They are trained in different ways. They have different friends who value different ways of talking. The scientist does have difficulty shaking the belief that observable and predictable events are the only reality, just as the creationist has difficulty shaking the belief that the Bible is the ultimate reality.

It is common philosophical practice these days to refer to these communities as "interpretive communities" or "communities of discourse." Can people bridge from one to the other? Do we share across our culture a deeper morality that allows members of one group to talk to another trustingly? If we can do so, it would seem that the constitutional work of the Supreme Court should try to do so, since the law is precisely where the different communities clash within the larger community we try to maintain.

People who share similar moral ideas and ideals, people who belong to the same moral community, presumably can resolve specific problems and cases in ways that seem to follow from and reaffirm their community's moral foundation. The history of religion and politics in the West is so bloody precisely because neither Church nor kings could conceive of their moral community as anything less than universal. The liberal political state is designed to prevent authoritarian oppression in the name of universal moral truth. And so we and the justices disagree about what the Constitution means in specific cases. William Brennan's interpretive community defends civil liberties and plainly differs from Justice Rehnquist's more conservative community, which defends the power of the state from judicial intrusion.

If we live in a morally plural world where people won't agree on moral standards, how is justice possible at all? We know it is not possible to follow rules laid down, for rules laid down, particularly constitutional rules, are too ambiguous, too general, and too likely to conflict with each other, just as the free-exercise and establishment clauses do. And the liberal state forecloses the authoritarian alternative, that justice is whatever the powerful declare. To preserve the ideal of doing justice, we must find a moral basis for it. To entitle a judge to rule for one party and against another by interpreting the law, the judge must be able to claim that a moral principle applicable to winner and loser alike justifies the result. How is that possible in a pluralist system where no one moral system can or should prevail?

The answer to this question depends on rethinking what we mean by a moral system. If we seek a system that dictates correct results in specific cases, we won't find it in moral theory any more than we will find it in law, and for the same reasons. But if by morality we mean something about the integrity of the justification for the decision, if morality refers to the quality, the honesty, and the trustworthiness by which judges explain their results, modern moral theory keeps the idea of justice alive.

I shall use Michael Perry's (1988) analytical categories as a starting point to explain how. Of course there is no more a single right moral theory than there is a single right way of interpreting the law. I mean here only to describe how *I* solve the problem just outlined. You may want to solve it another way. However, if your solution opts for the authoritarian route, you will have to reject, I think, the lessons of the last 1,500 years.

Does morality exist at all? Yes, moral knowledge does exist. Let us define morality as ideas about ways of living with others that contribute to human flourishing. Defined this way, morality excludes purely personal decisions. Suppose I have an embarrassing skin condition on my face that is exacerbated by shaving. I may choose to grow a beard as a means to my own social flourishing, but I would not be making a moral decision; I would not claim to generalize it to other men in the same circumstances. That is up to them. Not everything, however, is a matter of personal taste. People do believe that some standards ought to govern groups. People think they have moral knowledge about ways of living that do and do not contribute to human flourishing. I know that genocide, the killing of American Indians or of Jews in the Holocaust, prevents human flourishing. Even if someone were to disagree, to defend genocide because it's a dog-eat-dog world out there and for one person to flourish another must perish, the fact remains that moral knowledge exists. Both I and my opponent think of ourselves as having moral knowledge.

Acknowledging that people possess moral knowledge, however, does not get us anywhere, for knowledge is relative. We all believe and know in relation to other things we believe and know. Our beliefs exist as webs of belief and of experience. Our interpretive communities create webs of belief for us. Hence a fundamentalist within his framework may be just as honest as an atheist is in hers. Primitives may know that the sun goes around the earth just as surely as I know that the earth goes around the sun. We cannot prove what is true from observing nature. We have seen that modern science differs from ancient science for just this reason.

I cannot demonstrate to another that I am correct without coercing the other to change his or her web of beliefs, but I can do something. I can make clear how and why *my* conclusion fits into and follows from my web of beliefs, and I can invite my opponent to do likewise. In doing so I can seek to demonstrate my integrity, my honesty, and my virtue, and I can invite my opponent to do the same, and this process itself is what leads to flourishing in pluralistic politics. I cannot demonstrate that my position on the abortion issue is the correct position to take (except to people who already share my web of beliefs), but I can demonstrate my integrity as a fellow citizen by showing that my views fit my web of beliefs.

I might, in fact I do, make such a claim this way: I believe that all human beings need affection, the caring and cooperation of others, and help when they are in trouble. I believe that for government to dictate that no woman may have an abortion except in life-threatening circumstances cuts the woman off from the kind of affectionate caring help she needs in facing the difficult decision whether to terminate a pregnancy. I also believe it is impossible to distinguish between a fetus before it is viable and the sperm and egg before they connect, and I find no historical justification in law or practice for such a distinction. In fact, I find the opposite. I believe that the principle of liberty itself allows the government to dictate fundamental life choices only when such choices, like the choice whether to have a vaccination to prevent the spread of a serious disease, will have serious effects on other people.

In making such a claim, I do not actually prove that any one thing I say is true, but I do two other things that build community. I show that I care about the issue that divides me from my opponent, that I could not have concocted my position on the spur of the moment simply to exert power over him or her. I also invite my opponent to respond, to acknowledge the assumptions we share and to educate me about something I may have missed. I acknowledge that my position might be wrong when I agree to shift it to make it more coherent. Either way, I demonstrate that my opponent can trust that I am committed to flourishing in community with him or her. I do so by meeting as best I can a standard of coherence in my communication, with myself and with my opponent.

In other words, modern moral theory does offer a solution to the age-old problems of Western civilization. It begins by recognizing that in our political life, our lives together, what matters is not "the truth" or "what we can prove," but rather the goodness of our justifications for our actions and beliefs. The test of a good justification is not whether it proves that it corresponds to an objective world. It thus avoids, just as modern science does, the Aristotelian assumption that the world can be only what correct logic deduces from observation. It recognizes instead that the world is what our language makes of it. We test good justifications by whether their elements correspond to our languages, whether they cohere. The morality of science, as Philip Kitcher (1982) points out, takes seriously the language of scientific coherence: "independent testability" (can we test a proposition both in the real world and in the lab), "unification" (does a small group of predictive theories and techniques explain a broad class of seemingly unrelated problems), and "fecundity" (does a theory open up new lines of inquiry that effectively solve previously unsolved problems).

Biblical creation justifications frame themselves in a different way. Their frame is unquestioning faith in Genesis instead of the frame of faith in "the data," but each can be coherent. The creationist who speculates why we find no dinosaur and human bones together—perhaps because we would not expect humans to want to live near dinosaurs—struggles for coherence just as the scientist struggles to explain the gaps in the fossil record.

Within each system, "knowing" describes not a proven truth but a reaction to the arrangement of symbols in any form of communication—a sermon, a scientific paper, a poem, a painting, a musical composition, or a legal opinion. The actions and the events that matter in political life are our words. Language is action. We cannot verify that this symbolic language is correct, because in order to do that we would need another, deeper language in which to express that correctness, and then would need some way of verifying that *that* language was correct. Logically, arguments inevitably get stuck in one of two traps. Either they are circular or they fall into the infinite regress, the endless search for deeper languages in which to prove the correctness of the language above. We can, however, respect the honesty, the commitment to the morality of justification, of someone from a radically different interpretive community if we sense her fidelity to her own sense of what symbols must mean. And the communities can overlap; their members can find some common ground. Thus the physicist Stephen Hawking (1988), who seeks the final grand unified theory of the universe, seems unable to avoid God talk. Both modern religion and science may thus have escaped the Aristotelian world, with its authoritarian tendencies, because both know that we understand the world imperfectly and that the world reveals itself to our imperfect minds slowly and incompletely.

What, then, about justice? John Rawls has written:

> What justifies a conception of justice is not its being true to an order antecedent and given to us, but its congruence with our deeper understanding of ourselves and our aspirations, and our realization that, given our history and the traditions embedded in our public lives, it is the most reasonable doctrine for us.

It may seem paradoxical, but Rawls really advocates an optimistic message. By abandoning the search for objectively and logically correct statements of absolute justice, we free ourselves to talk democratically and openly about values and hopes for ourselves and our communities. If both we and judges know that our value judgments really drive our political choices, we become freer to debate moral alternatives for our lives. Paradoxically, moral relativism gives us no choice but to take our moral knowledge, though relative, seriously. We have no choice because science and technology give us no objective, logically correct solutions to the political problems communities must solve. When judges struggle imperfectly to justify their decisions in cases by fitting the decision to a "deeper understanding of ourselves and our aspirations," we can confidently say they do justice. They do justice not because they solve the case correctly but because they keep the struggle to know ourselves and our traditions and hopes alive.

BIBLIOGRAPHIC NOTES

Two particularly useful treatments of the distinctions between religion and science, with specific reference to creation science, are Philip Kitcher's *Abusing Science* (1982) and the essays collected by Robert Hanson in *Science and Creation* (1986). Dorothy Nelkin's essay (Hanson, Chapter 3) cites and reinforces Clifford Geertz's (1973) conclusion that science and religion are equally grounded in a socially constructed reality. William Thwaites, in Hanson, Chapter 7, shows how creation science fails to meet coherence tests. Much of the material for the conversation in this chapter comes from these two books. A complete version of the trial court's opinion in the *McLean* case discussed at the end of my Chapter 3 appears in an appendix in Hanson.

Michael Perry's *Morality, Politics and Law* (1988), Chapters 1 and 2, lays out a theory of moral knowledge from which I borrow. Michael Moore is one of the best-known exponents of the moral realist position. See, for example, his ''Precedent, Induction, and Ethical Generalization,'' in Laurence Goldstein, ed., *Precedent in Law* (1987). This chapter has also referred to:

Thomas Aquinas, *Summa Theologiae* (1964). Stephen Hawking, *A Brief History of Time* (1988). Richard Rorty, ''That Old-Time Philosophy,'' *The New Republic,* April 4, 1988, pp. 28–33, quotes Rawls. See more generally Rorty's *Philosophy and the Mirror of Nature* for a discussion of the twin traps of the vicious circle and infinite regress. Charles Krauthammer, ''Science ex Machina,'' *The New Republic,* June 6, 1981, pp. 19–25.   .

CHAPTER 6

Religion and Constitutional Interpretation

In tribal times, there were the medicine-men. In the Middle Ages, there were the priests. Today there are the lawyers. For every age, a group of bright boys, learned in their trade and jealous of their learning, who blend technical competence with plain and fancy hocus-pocus to make themselves masters of their fellow men. For every age, a pseudo-intellectual autocracy, guarding the tricks of its trade from the uninitiated, and running, after its own pattern, the civilization of its day.

—*Fred Rodell*

In the preceding chapter the distinctions in practice between science and religion, and between law and morality, began to blur. Of course the dictionary, in rather academic fashion, defines each differently: Science observes, describes, and explains natural phenomena; religion is the organized expression of beliefs about and worship of supernatural powers that govern the universe. Law is an official code of rules governing the conduct of men in communities; morality is a set of customs and beliefs that distinguish between right and wrong. In practice, however, they interweave completely. Science depends on a faith in certain conventions about what it means to know something. Religion, as Geertz pointed out, depends on faith in different conventions, but they are just as structured and coherent and "real" as those of science. Our law grows out of a history dominated by religion, and its justice depends on preserving faith and commitment to the moral goodness of communities.

This chapter speculates on how constitutional interpretation might appear if we accept these blurrings. More specifically, how can we imagine constitutional interpretation as an extension of the Judeo-Christian heritage without running afoul of the establishment and free-exercise clauses? Perhaps two hundred years of Supreme Court constitutional lawmaking *do* extend that tradition. In fact, if modern cultures express what they have become through formal law, constitutional interpretation can't help but extend that tradition, including its religious component.

The political role of the Supreme Court has much in common with the biblical story. We become pure, or at least better, by arguing it out, Isaiah 1:18 says. I, for one, can make the constitutional extension of the biblical story coherent only by finding in it a message about the sinfulness and imperfection of people. By acknowledging our imperfections, our tradition necessarily admits that we will never get religion, or law, "right" in any final sense. Instead we aspire to become better than we are. We cannot aspire to what is better unless we test our aspirations against other people's aspirations in open conversation. And to do that we must respect the dignity of all people, including those with whom we disagree. As Judge Learned Hand put it, "The spirit of liberty is the spirit which is not too sure that it is right." Both lecturers in Chapter 4 drew this dignitarian lesson from Western history. We may also draw the same lesson from the politics of religion itself.

RELIGION AND RIGHT ANSWERS

We know we live in a world of many different religions and many different sects within a single religion. Islam contains the Shiite and Sunni sects. Orthodox and Reform Judaism have sects within themselves. Christianity in the United States encompasses everything from Roman Catholicism to the Quakers to the Church of Latter Day Saints to Christian Science. Many such sects seem ready in the late twentieth century to split once again; Episcopalians over the ordination of women to the priesthood and Southern Baptists over the moral meaning of scripture. For some reason religion does not seem capable of generating collective agreement on answers to basic spiritual and theological questions. The religious quest seems to lead people down plural paths. The more a sect takes itself seriously, the more authoritarian it becomes, and the more likely will dissenters find no option but rebellion.

More to the point, a single religious tradition does not offer right answers. A person who begins the serious study of the Bible as a text, as I did as part of preparing this book, finds a startling pattern. Religious texts turn out to be unclear in just the ways the Constitution is. Neither the Bible nor the Constitution offers a blueprint of a spiritual and social order. Part of this pattern is due to the uncertainties of history and the problems of translating from past to present. Biblical stories reach back into an oral tradition nearly 3,000 years old. Yet not even the Old Testament was systematically written down before about 500 B.C., and Jewish religious leaders did not select the texts we know today as the sacred texts of the Old Testament until 100 A.D.!

Scholars cannot conclusively discern the "intent of the framer(s)" of either the Bible or the Constitution. Many early Hebrew texts contain neither vowels nor even separation of words. In the translations from Hebrew to Greek to Hebrew to

English, considerable doubt about the original meaning inevitably arises. In some versions, deriving from the prophesy of Isaiah, Mary is a "virgin," in others merely a "young woman." Indeed the very first words of the Old Testament can translate out of the Hebrew equally well to mean either that God created the universe from nothing or that God imposed form on preexisting matter.

The Bible was compiled by a variety of authors over an extended time. Differences in word usages and writing styles have allowed biblical scholars to identify at least four different primary sources of material in the Old Testament. As a result, just as the free-exercise and establishment clauses contradict each other, the Bible contradicts itself. Richard John Neuhaus points out such a contradiction at the beginning of his book, *The Naked Public Square* (1984), whose message, despite its confused metaphor, calls clearly for a reintegration of religious values in political and public life:

> What has been is what will be, and what has been done is what will be done; and there is nothing new under the sun. Is there a thing of which it is said, "See, this is new"? It has been already, in the ages before us. (Ecclesiastes 1:9–10)

but

> Remember not the former things, nor consider the things of old. Behold, I am doing a new thing; now it springs forth, do you not perceive it? (Isaiah 43:18–19)

The contradictions begin "In the beginning . . ." and extend through the New Testament. Genesis chapter 1 tells a creation story that seems only remotely connected at best to the Adam and Eve creation story of chapter 2. The Bible introduces the young David in two contradictory ways, first as the musical shepherd identified by Samuel as Saul's successor, but later as the young man who slays Goliath. The New Testament reflects and does not resolve the tension in Mediterranean thought of its time, that is, the tension between a Greek concept of an impersonal god, rational, unchanging, and absolute, and the personal god, creator, father, and actor in history of the Old Testament.

Some biblical stories, for example the story of the Red Heifer in Numbers, chapter 19, have defied any coherent interpretation. Their inclusion in the Bible and Torah seems to demand reverence for the stories in themselves. They beseech us to give up making sense and instead simply to have faith.

THE BIBLE AS NARRATIVE

Obviously the Bible maintains its hold on millions despite these tensions and contradictions. It does so because it is a work of narrative art in which the contradictions enhance the story by allowing us to see various sides of an immensely complex whole. Robert Alter's *The Art of Biblical Narrative* (1981) explains the creation contradiction in the first two chapters of Genesis this way:

> The decision to place in sequence two ostensibly contradictory accounts of the same event is an approximate narrative equivalent to the technique of post-Cubist painting which gives us, for example, juxtaposed or superimposed, a profile and a frontal perspective of the same face. The ordinary eye could never see these two at once, but it is the painter's prerogative to represent them as a simultaneous perception . . . to provide an encompassing representation of his subject. Analogously, the Hebrew writer takes advantage of the composite nature of his art to give us a tension of views that will govern most of the biblical stories—first, woman as man's equal sharer in dominion, standing exactly in the same relation to God as he; then, woman as man's subservient helpmate, whose weakness and blandishments will bring such woe into the world.

With respect to the David story, Alter suggests:

> [T]he two introductions of David correspond to two different aspects of the future king which are reflected in his relationship with Saul and which will remain in tension throughout his story—the private person and the public figure.

As a purely descriptive matter, constitutional interpretation seems to follow the same pattern. Each case decision becomes a precedent we add to our narrative. Each case tells a real story about the justness with which government treats citizens. If both the Constitution and the Bible try to paint a picture of an extremely complex yet immensely important vision of human relationships, contradictions and imperfections in law may be not merely inevitable but desirable, because they acknowledge and teach the complexity honestly. In fact the parallel is even stronger, for the substance of the most central biblical stories shows us that law itself does not "get it right." The contradictory lines of cases that Ben and Mary debated in Chapter 2 don't get it right, but the contradictions confirm our aspiration to achieve justice and fairness.

WHAT BIBLICAL STORIES TEACH

While, like Court precedents, individual biblical stories often contradict one another, we may learn from them. At least we may learn common themes and threads of ideas that repeat throughout. In the New Testament, behind the superficial contradictions (the "Prince of Peace" says "I bring not peace but a sword"), we find the common theme of sacrifice of self for others and for a greater good, of love defined as giving rather than receiving, of caring for and acceptance of the unorthodox as a unique and dignified person. Locke drew on that story in his Letter on Toleration when he wrote, "[T]hat the Church of Christ should persecute others, and force others by fire and sword to embrace her faith and doctrine, I could never yet find in any of the books of the New Testament."

But for an understanding of our constitutional experience, the core story of the Old Testament is, I think, more telling. The Old Testament tells of an endless cycle in human affairs: creation, sin, judgment, and redemption. Adam and Eve are created, sin, are judged, and then given another chance. Man again sins against God but is redeemed through the flood. Moses' followers cannot keep the peace, but they come nevertheless to the promised land, where they sin again and are driven again into exile. They returned to their promised land in 1948, and their treatment of Palestinians since then strike some as another swing of the cycle.

And now we come to the constitutional analogy directly. The Old Testament narratives have such power because they describe modern experiences, both in our personal and our communal lives. The Old Testament tells a story of creation and covenant, not unlike the founding through our Constitution, and the covenant endures despite the fact that men do not and cannot consistently keep it. Only God through redemption can keep it. Frank Alexander (1986) describes the fundamental pattern this way:

> The covenant is a promise in which humans are charged with responsibility, responsibility to respond to this promise. The covenant stands as a call to action; together with creation it describes the purposive quality of human nature.
> Precisely because it points to human responsibility, the biblical tradition is also the story of failure to fulfill the covenant, and redemption notwithstanding that failure. The creation narrative contains a story of forbidden fruit, of breach of promise and disobedience, that is a metaphor for the inability of humanity to do that which it is called to do. The sin is the selfish pride of human nature by which the individual declares his ultimate independence both from God and from other persons. . . . The biblical tradition is thus the story of the brokenness of humanity, of injustice, isolation, and suffering.

Please do not mistake what I am attempting here. I am not taking a plunge into fundamentalism, trying to convert you in a fit of evangelical fervor. I merely explore parallels that seem too obvious to ignore. Assuming for the sake of argument that the U.S. constitutional experience extends the Judeo-Christian tradition, that tradition does teach that constitutional interpretation will inevitably be imperfect. We cannot expect to keep the constitutional covenant consistently. We can, however, say it calls us to responsible action. In Alexander's words:

> Creation and covenant . . . focus on the issues within the element of individuality which concern human reason and responsibility. The covenant tradition points to the existence of responsibility for our actions and stands as a call for the greatest degree of human responsibility in all relationships. It indicates a role for human rationality in the experience of personal relationships, and places emphasis upon the exercise of individual and collective reason. . . .
> As the story of a covenant being worked out through history, the covenant tradition is a dynamic movement through time. It is never static or precisely

quantifiable. It is always in the process of discovery and response, of confusion and new responses.

The final chapter explores how the idea of a covenant working out in history may translate into a standard for judging the goodness of constitutional interpretation. However, this chapter must plant one more seed first. Our constitutional story contains many examples of the same sin and redemption cycle. A nation that declared its independent existence by invoking the proposition that all men are created equal has come to see *Dred Scott*'s and *Plessy*'s rejection of racial equality as wrong—wrong not as a technical error in constitutional interpretation but as sin. We accept as sin the stripping of Japanese-American citizens of their liberty and property and "relocating" them because of their race. Modern constitutional law has acknowledged this sin and given racial equality another chance. A nation founded in part on the principle of no taxation without representation found it increasingly difficult to deny women the vote after it started taxing them. A nation pledged to the free expression of unpopular ideas no longer denies the vote to someone simply for belonging to a group that advocates changing the law. These constitutional allegories seem deeply consistent with a biblical pattern stretching back thousands of years. Something deep in our political experience accepts that we will, in the name of the law, make moral mistakes, but that we can renounce these errors and aspire to improving our polity.

CONCLUSION

Law as a code of rules for governing behavior in communities does not fare well in the Bible. The Old Testament describes man as a creature who cannot keep the law and who therefore must depend on God's redemption. The New Testament seems deliberately to downplay law. The Prodigal Son seems to receive better treatment than did the Type A law-abiding dutiful son. As John Sanford put it in his book *The Kingdom Within* (1987), "The kingdom, however, is dynamically creative, and the ethic of the kingdom is a creative ethic based on consciousness and love, not legalism" (p. 48). Perhaps we should therefore redefine law, think of it not as a list of commands but rather as a series of stories that helps us identify ourselves, just as biblical stories created Judaism, and that thus keep alive models of personal and collective growth. If American law continues this religious tradition, may we then conclude that law should not take itself too reverentially, that law is not an end but a means to the end in which individuals flourish?

BIBLIOGRAPHIC NOTES

Milner Ball has drawn the connection between the narrative essence of our religious tradition and the narrative quality of American law. See *The Promise of American Law* (1981) and *Lying Down Together: Law, Metaphor, and Theology* (1985).

Robert Alter's classic work on the subject is *The Art of Biblical Narrative* (1981). Other sources in this chapter are Frank Alexander, "Beyond Positivism: A Theological Perspective," (1986); Richard John Neuhaus, *The Naked Public Square* (1984); John Sanford, *The Kingdom Within* (1987). You might also review Martin Buber, *The Prophetic Faith* (1960), and David Daube, *Studies in Biblical Law* (1969).

CHAPTER 7

Good Law

[T]here is no ultimate meaning to convey and no final truth to discover, let alone any canon of texts to master. Learning is at once the creation of ourselves and the re-creation of our civilization, and both of these could go anywhere and be anything. . . . We engage in a "conversation" that leads somewhere and nowhere at the same time, a conversation that it is impossible to avoid but easy to forget. And to enter into the conversation is the point of education: concluding it would be fatal to our humanity.

—*Andrew Sullivan*

And so, to the end of history, murder shall breed murder, always in the name of right and honor and peace, until the gods are tired of blood and create a race that can understand.

—*George Bernard Shaw,* Caesar and Cleopatra

WHERE ARE WE?

At this point some readers may conclude that this book proposes radically new ways of thinking, not only about law and religion, but about how we know anything at all. This book may unintentionally send unnerving or scary messages; leaping into the unknown is always scary. In this closing chapter, I want to defuse these fears by making a case for this book's ordinariness. I actually began to do so when I urged in the previous chapter that we accept some strong parallels between religious and legal experiences, including the widespread experience that the letter killeth but the spirit giveth life. I now want to extend the effort to reassure by describing a way of seeing the materialistic, stressful, and dehumanizing conditions of modern political and legal life as capable of changing into a more harmonious and satisfying kind of politics. Indeed, the relaxation of ideological international tensions and the growing popular support for environmental protection suggest we may already have taken the first step toward becoming, in Shaw's words, "a race that can understand."

In 1975 Peter d'Errico began an essay with these words:

> We are living in a time of changing consciousness about the meaning and function of authority. Law, which is often taken to be the backbone of authority structures in society, has come increasingly under scrutiny, both for its role in maintaining oppressive social conditions and for the exceeding narrowness of legalism as a world-view.

D'Errico titled his essay, "The Law Is Terror Put into Words." This image of law descends directly from the medieval experience, where both religious and secular authority used law to coerce obedience.

Since Locke, the liberal political tradition in the West has tried to tame the law in three kinds of ways, none of which works today. The first of these, election of lawmakers, sought to insure that legal decisions met the preferences of at least most of the people most of the time. Electoral representation fails to stop law from being terror put in words because the arbitrariness that makes law terrible still resides in the daily decisions of policemen, judges, and members of the legal profession itself who implement and enforce law without any direct connection to popular opinion. The second solution turned to science. It fails because its key assumption—that technicians could by policy analysis and technocratic examination of data discover optimal social policy—cannot accommodate the reality that every perception of fact is colored by values and ideologies that cannot be quantified and compared. The third, and the most recent, is to turn the whole problem over to the legal profession on the assumption that its internal codes of ethics, rigorous professional training, and commitment to fairness and justice, will somehow work things out. The legal profession has yet to accept that responsibility, however, and shows no sign of doing so soon. And if it did, the history of the Church's misuse of its unique priestly power gives us reason to fear that the law would, for similar reasons, in time use its special professional authority to govern oppressively.

Hence for the moment we seem to be in a kind of legal desert. We have discovered that equating justice with protecting constitutional rights doesn't work. If we claim a right as an absolute, we are right back in the Middle Ages, for we can only make that assertion stick by backing it up with the threat of force. If we see rights as flexible and contingent, rights quickly lose their moral appeal, for the right to religious liberty quickly converts into questions such as whether the Constitution protects women who have sex for pay from prosecution for prostitution because they belong to the Church of the Most High Goddess, whose credo requires that women sleep with at least 1000 men before qualifying for the priesthood. And the right to personal liberty quickly turns into whether a smoker has a right to smoke in public places. Besides, as Rogers Smith pointed out in 1988, "American identity has *never* in fact rested on allegiance or even full adherence to liberal democratic values." The slogan "A government of laws, not of men" has failed us.

But we are now experimenting with a fourth solution, and its main feature is that it distinguishes between governing on the basis of theories, truth claims, policies and ideologies on one hand, and governing that depends on the quality of relationships that our ways of community-making encourage. This solution in effect returns us to the constructive parts of our religious past, returns us to what Charles Taylor calls a love of that which is "incomparably higher." This love in turn makes all other loves meaningful. Just now "the earth" or "the life force" seems the leading candidates for the office of incomparably high, but the point is that by mutually acknowledging something that is itself so unknowable as to be beyond debate, we can then learn to channel our talk about what is debatable in ways that build trust, respect, and connections. We recognize, with Martha Nussbaum (1990), that the abstractions of all philosophical talk, including formal law talk—the theories and the generalized truth claims, including rights—impoverish us because they do not seem "to connect with anything that really matters when we make judgments in ordinary life."

The fourth solution thus converts our image of law from being a declarer of truth to being a language by which we can learn to talk in more trusting and bonding ways. The rest of the book fleshes out what this image might look like, and then encourages you to practice it yourself. But as you begin, ask yourselves whether this fourth solution is, if not ordinary, at least quite old and familiar. Ask whether it may not restore some of the wisdom of Greek drama—say *Antigone*—or of such biblical stories as the Good Samaritan, or of American folk heros like Abraham Lincoln.

NARRATIVE AND CONVERSATION IN LAW AND RELIGION

The Supreme Court makes decisions that have important consequences, both symbolic and practical, for political life in the United States. We know the practical consequences of permitting abortions, for example, but the abortion decision is equally important as a symbol. To some the abortion issue symbolizes reverence for life and creation, for others the meaning of liberty. In April 1990, as the nation debated the immensely practical problem of drug use, the Court decided another case with strong symbolic and practical dimensions. A divided Court upheld Oregon's denial of unemployment compensation to two men who were fired from jobs in a private drug rehabilitation organization for using peyote in a Native American Church ceremony. The decision will presumably have little immediate impact on more than a handful of lives, but its treatment of religious and legal symbols defines who we are. Justices on both sides passionately argued their positions.

This book has suggested a reason why people take a practically insignificant case so seriously. People need to feel connected to their polities, and they do so by keeping common political symbols and values alive. The Constitution provides such symbols. The Court by interpretation seeks to preserve the Constitution as a positive, politically unifying force. For the Court to succeed in doing so, citizens who are not trained as lawyers and constitutional scholars must feel able to judge the quality of a Supreme Court interpretation. This process of citizen judgment turns out to be less challenging than we first thought. The Court does not consistently follow a technology of interpretation. Rather, interpretation is a communicative act, a process in which a writer tries peacefully to persuade a reader that the writer has identified a desirable vision of the community they share.

This chapter's epigraph describes this process of community-making as essentially conversational. This book has urged that the ways we evaluate constitutional interpretations are the same as those we use to evaluate good conversations. This conversational quality is built into our law from the bottom up. Law students used to learn law by studying treatises and codes. Now they spend three years in law school reading stories, cases that follow the narrative the judge has learned and that add a new chapter to it. Students study this way because their own practice will extend the narrative further. Trials and appeals operate according to the principles of the adversary system, in which truth comes not from investigation and experiment but from the quality of the conversations the lawyers have with other lawyers, and the quality of the stories they tell in court on their client's behalf to judges and jurors. And judges write opinions to explain and justify their results; their opinions converse with each other.

As the previous chapter indicated, this conversational and narrative quality in our law descends in part from the conversational and storytelling quality of the biblical tradition. Our legal system rejects authoritarian pronouncements of right answers because our Protestant-based culture has rejected centralized authority, embodied by the claim to power of the old monolithic Church in Rome. Our political traditions have struggled hard to encourage the use of political power through influence, persuasion, and justification. As Philip Soper (1986) put it:

> Dissenting individuals must be assured of the right to discourse, a right to insist on the bona fides of belief in the only form in which sincerity can be tested: communication, dialogue, exchange, debate.

This chapter summarizes how I judge the goodness of constitutional conversations. This solution to the problem of constitutional interpretation prevents me from claiming that I have found the correct solution. The message prior chapters have taught about law, history, science, religion, morality, and politics tells me that correct answers are not possible but that good answers are, and that a good answer is that which encourages us to talk further about the goodness of our polity. Having summarized this perspective, I conclude by reprinting the opinions in the 1990 peyote case. I hope the concepts this book has developed work for you. I hope, as you apply these concepts to the peyote opinions, these opinions become more interesting than they otherwise would. I hope these concepts help you see that the real constitutional question is not whether the First Amendment defends using peyote in a religious ceremony: The real question is whether we trust the integrity and impartiality of those who decide as they do.

COHERENCE, TRUST, AND JUSTICE

If justice does not happen when a judge proves she got the right answer, when does it happen? From the conversational perspective, it happens when we trust that the judge has decided, not to achieve personal gain, in money or advancement or prestige, but because the judge believes the result follows from a vision or model of a community that judge, winner, loser, and outside reader share. Even if we disagree with the vision, we may trust that the honest effort to state it keeps our aspiration of a shared community alive. The effort we trust makes our commitment to the continuing conversation worthwhile.

A writer or speaker builds trust by following the criteria of coherence. Coherence, in my experience, always contains some mystery. A full and complete analytical dissection of a message kills it, or rather treats it as already dead, for we only dissect the dead. I cannot fully explain why I find so powerful the argument in the second flag salute case that compelling the flag salute during war with Nazi Germany for national security reasons violates a basic reason for fighting that war. I cannot explain fully why Locke's appeal to the New Testament to support an argument against religious persecution seems so powerful, or why the fact that Jesus was a Jew seems so important to the case against anti-Semitism. But these positions seem good in the deepest possible way.

For the same reason that I cannot perfectly capture, I found some of Ronald Reagan's rhetoric incoherent. For example, his farewell address from the Oval office includes this advice better suited to Hitler's youth corps:

> And children, if your parents haven't been teaching you what it means to be an American, let 'em know and nail 'em on it. That would be a very American thing to do.

While I cannot completely specify coherence, coherent messages and positions do seem to meet two criteria. First, they exist within a frame the author creates. All messages must have frames, fictional limits that arbitrarily stop the argument from plunging into the infinite regress of analyzing assumptions. Simultaneously this frame is the faith the author professes but cannot prove. The coherent message makes those limits plain, either by describing them outright or, through dramatic and poetic devices, encouraging us to create the limits ourselves. By the strict rules of logic, the framed argument is circular.

Second, the coherent message fits together the parts of an argument defined as inside the argument frame. If patriotism provides the frame in the second flag case, if we fight to preserve *our* constitution as opposed to Hitler's, then oppressing persecuted religious minorities does not fit with the First Amendment. If a Protestant model of community frames Locke's politics, then religious persecution does not fit the New Testament. I trust that both Justice Jackson and John Locke sought not personal gain but a just decision because they seem committed to practicing what they preach.

But obviously a professional hit man or an avowed racist may also practice what he preaches. Creation science meets within (but only within) the framework of a faith in the literal truth of Genesis the same criteria of coherence that astronomical, biological, and geological explanations meet within conventional scientific frameworks. Hence constitutional law must require some specific kind of frame. Not any frame will do. The constitutional frame does specify certain parts that the judge must fit together. The constitutional frame requires fitting together the rules and precedents themselves, the political and social history from which they and our polity grow, a common moral sensibility, and some pragmatic experience of the way we think the world works. Above all, the constitutional frame includes the obligation to tell a new chapter in a story, to fit law, history, morality, and experience together in a narrative way. The only reason to prefer courts to legislatures to make decisions on constitutional matters is that court decisions tell such stories, as does the Bible, while rules and statutes do not. I judge the yarmulke and creation science opinions in terms of how well they seem to fit those things together and thus continue a story.

EVALUATING GOLDMAN AND EDWARDS

The political, legal, religious, philosophical, and scientific histories of the last two thousand years all point in one direction: There are only two ways to generate agreement that a given solution to a problem is *the* correct one. Either the problem becomes entirely technological, that is, devoid of any moral or economic consequences, so that groups can develop rules for solving problems which, like the rules of arithmetic, threaten no one, or those within the group who hold political power declare that one solution is ideologically correct and coerce agreement by punishing dissenters. Historically, as we have seen, this leads to fighting those who resist enforcement and killing dissenters when the fight escalates. Modern science, philosophy, and religion solve that problem by discarding altogether the notion that one right way correctly solves the problem. In science, theories are tentative. We do not prove them, and we agree to modify or abandon them at the point where they no longer fit the data. Christianity's many sects live, relative to our history and to the strife of the Middle East, in peace. Each sect offers its vision of religious truth and limits its tactics for winning new converts to no more than aggressive evangelism, which is itself a form of political persuasion.

Of the seven opinions you have read in these two cases, Justice Rehnquist's is in my judgment the worst, but not because it reaches the wrong result. I do not conclude that the Constitution guarantees a right to Jews to wear yarmulkes in the military. He does not fit the parts of the argument together in a way I can find coherent because he does not converse honestly with us about the following matters.

1. The Law. As we saw in Ben and Mary's debate about this case, the specific case law about civil liberties in the military gives the military wide latitude. The civil liberties claim usually loses. Nevertheless, in virtually every modern free exercise case the Court has insisted on some showing some fact-based reason to believe that the sacrifice of civil liberties is necessary to the efficient and effective operation of the military. Justice Rehnquist's decision in *Goldman* to defer to the expert professional judgment of the military changes that law. The Supreme Court can and occasionally does change its law, its own constitutional story. But when it does so, as it did in the flag salute cases, it must admit that it is doing so and give reasons for doing so. The Rehnquist opinion wants instead to change the law behind our backs and without a justification.

If we turn to the civilian free exercise cases, the recent cases, particularly the Amish and unemployment compensation cases, stand clearly for the proposition that the government can impede a person's free exercise only on a showing of compelling state interest. On what ground are we to exempt the military from that requirement? On what legal basis does the conclusion rest that the military is so much more essential to our survival than, say, good education, that the military can deny a person from exercising a fundamental religious practice without any proof, while the state may not insist that a person complete an education. The opinion gives us no basis for that conclusion.

2. History. We have seen that our entire political system from its inception in liberalism onward has striven to correct the political evils that come when religious authority uses brute force to compel belief. As Charles Cochrane (1957) has shown, the recognition of individual dignity in Western thought began not with John Locke but with St. Augustine, who lived and wrote around 400 A.D. The horror of the potential of institutions to do violence to individuals "because we say so and you must agree or die" lies at the very core of democracy. Our system avoids that horror through the twin principles of accountability and justification. This is what the rule of law means. Elections and judicial opinions alike force those who rule to justify their actions. The military, together with the police agencies, are the analogues to the medieval power of church and king to torture and kill. They above all must meet the democratic principles of accountability. Justice Rehnquist's opinion exempts the military from that obligation. In doing so he belies the very authority on which he himself, who does not face the voters, has the power to decide, namely by giving a reasoned justification for his result.

3. Morality and Religion. The military's unproven claim to require Goldman to conform to the headgear regulation rests on the assumption that uniformity creates a disciplined morality on which the military must depend in combat and other times of stress. The military requires unthinking obedience. Yet on what basis does an

Orthodox Jew observe his religious faith by wearing an odd little hat every day? What kind of morality and discipline do we think Goldman possesses? Do we not want to believe that the military exists to defend a country in which people are free to worship their god in such disciplined ways? Do we not suspect, since we have no proof of the matter, that Goldman's role model enhances the very qualities that *both* the nation and its military stand for? Does not the history of the Jewish people's struggle to keep a covenant explain why, from Goldman's perspective, keeping faith with the requirement to cover his head places him squarely in the covenantal relationship with God?

4. Facts and Experience. I can imagine situations in the Air Force in which it might be necessary to prohibit wearing yarmulkes. We need not risk the damage if they are sucked into jet engines, for example. But my experience does not equip me to see what risks we face if a doctor wears a yarmulke in a hospital. Furthermore, my every experience with the drafting skills of lawyers tells me that the Air Force could, and as Congress indeed did, draft a rule that distinguishes between yarmulkes on one hand and flowing robes on the other. The former does not destroy the appearance of a uniform, the latter does.

Is it possible for another person with a different framework to find Justice Rehnquist's opinion coherent? Of course. That is my point. Such an argument might go this way: The law is one place where the buck must stop. It is precisely because we *can* go on forever arguing all sides of issues that we need institutions that declare what we must do. The role of the Supreme Court is to tell us to stop talking and get on with being what we are. The Court *is* just like the military when it insists that it is final because it has the final say, not because it is right. Justice Rehnquist thus captures just the right message when he practices what the military practices, by not pretending to prove that the result is correct.

To this argument I would of course reply that if Rehnquist believed that position, he should have said so. We cannot trust that he means that, given his words. And of course if this authoritarian position is accurate, why do we persist in the custom of requiring judicial justifications for their results? At this point my opponent and I might find ourselves deep in a conversation about just what our Constitution and the law and political trust are all about. So much the better. That conversation, if it is honestly done, will do more to connect me with my opponent in community than anything the Supreme Court might do. But if that proves true, I would still insist that Rehnquist wrote a bad opinion because he did not seem to care to converse with us in this way. And I would say that simply because I cannot make politics and law coherent and therefore just any other way.

The opinions in *Edwards* for me nearly succeed in modeling an ideal constitutional conversation. With respect to the law, Justice Brennan leaves little doubt that the purpose of *this* law could only have promoted a religious theory, which establishment clause precedents clearly prohibit. Justice Scalia, however, makes a cogent case for dumping the purpose prong of the *Lemon* test, and unlike Justice Rehnquist in *Goldman,* he speaks clearly of his willingness to change the law. Each opinion explicitly integrates deeper political values, in Brennan's case that we respect religion's essential privateness and in Scalia's that we do not prejudge people without first getting the facts. We should not, Scalia argued, judge the motives of the legislators or effects of the law until a full trial reveals that creation science in fact puts God back in the classroom.

But it is Justice Powell's opinion that seems most coherent to me. I trust it more because it brings us closer to the completely religious character of creation science discussed fully in *McLean* and it acknowledges more honestly the competing values that our history and law support equally well.

"TO ENTER INTO THE CONVERSATION IS THE POINT OF EDUCATION"

This book has done little more than refine a set of questions people may or may not choose to ask about the Constitution and the Court. It makes no pretense at arriving at final answers, particularly to the most important questions. For example, Mark Tushnet's epigraph that set the tone of this book seeks a culture in which civic virtue may flourish. But what is civic virtue? Openness, honesty, and trustworthiness? Or is it Michael Oakeshott's "patience, accuracy, economy, elegance, and style?" The frames we create within which we dare to speak and write coherently are always fictions. The epigraphs that I extracted from the majority opinions in *Goldman* and *Edwards* at the beginnings of Chapters 2 and 3 indicate central framing fictions in Rehnquist's and Brennan's opinions. But how we can distinguish those fictions that help frame and clarify a message from those fictions that distort and mislead? Indeed the previous chapters do not even seriously attempt to define law, religion, morality, or science. I have opted not to try to define such things in any final way, partly because to do so would put me back in the Aristotelian mode I wish to avoid. Perhaps how I define those things should not matter to you. You will do them differently, and your only political obligation is to do so coherently if you wish to persuade others to follow you. Whether this book's approach seems coherent to you will matter only in an academic sense. The book will have persuaded you only if you find you want to use it in judging cases for yourself. Hence this book ends with another case and another potential source of conversation.

I do, however, want to get in a penultimate word. *All* the elements I have tried to weave together in this book for me fit together coherently to support one conclusion about politics and human affairs. This conclusion is much too general to provide an easy guide to who wins and loses in constitutional cases, but it shapes deeply how we think about the Constitution and about the community that our talk about the Constitution continuously creates: Rules by themselves are not a proper object of worship, nor do they deserve deeper respect than do other aspects of political life. We learn this from the New Testament lesson that the letter killeth but the spirit giveth life. We learn it from modern science, which freely accepts that a law or principle governs only as long as it works better than other laws and principles. We learn it when we realize that we may have full and complete moral knowledge but that others who disagree with us may have different but equally real moral knowledge. And above all we learn it from the Supreme Court itself, which often respects the Constitution best when it is not too sure that it is right. My general point is that we find meaning in the world not by classifying our experiences according to general rules but, as Martha Nussbaum (1986) put it, "by burrowing down into the depths of the particular, finding images and connections that will permit us to see it more truly, describe it more richly." Good interpretation burrows into the depths of the particular and enriches us in the process. How well do the opinions in the concluding case empower us to see ourselves more truly and richly? How well do they build our trust in the virtue of these deciding justices? How well do they encourage us to converse and debate our character with each other? You be the judge.

THE LAST CASE

EMPLOYMENT DIVISION, DEPARTMENT OF HUMAN RESOURCES OF OREGON, ET AL., PETITIONERS v. ALFRED L. SMITH ET AL.

108 L. Ed. 2d 876 (1990)

SCALIA J., delivered the opinion of the Court, in which REHNQUIST, C. J., and WHITE, STEVENS, and KENNEDY, JJ., joined. O'CONNOR, J., filed an opinion concurring in the judgment, in Parts I and II of which BRENNAN, MARSHALL, and BLACKMUN, JJ., joined without concurring in the judgment. BLACKMUN, J., filed a dissenting opinion, in which BRENNAN and MARSHALL, JJ., joined.

JUSTICE SCALIA delivered the opinion of the Court.

This case requires us to decide whether the Free Exercise Clause of the First Amendment permits the State of Oregon to include religiously inspired peyote use within the reach of its general criminal prohibition on use of that drug, and thus permits the State to deny unemployment benefits to persons dismissed from their jobs because of such religiously inspired use.

I

Oregon law prohibits the knowing or intentional possession of a "controlled substance" unless the substance has been prescribed by a medical practitioner. Ore. Rev. Stat. § 475.992(4) (1987). The law defines "controlled substance" as a drug classified in Schedules I through V of the Federal Controlled Substances Act, 21 U.S.C. §§ 811–812 (1982 ed. and Supp. V), as modified by the State Board of Pharmacy. Ore. Rev. Stat. § 475.005(6) (1987). Persons who violate this provision by possessing a controlled substance listed on Schedule I are "guilty of a Class B felony." § 475.992(4)(a). As compiled by the State Board of Pharmacy under its statutory authority, see Ore. Rev. Stat. § 475.035 (1987), Schedule I contains the drug peyote, a hallucinogen derived from the plant *Lophophorawilliamsii Lemaire*. Ore. Admin. Rule 855–80–021(3)(s) (1988).

Respondents Alfred Smith and Galen Black were fired from their jobs with a private drug rehabilitation organization because they ingested peyote for sacramental purposes at a ceremony of the Native American Church, of which both are members. When respondents applied to petitioner Employment Division for unemployment compensation, they were determined to be ineligible for benefits because they had been discharged for work-related "misconduct." The Oregon Court of Appeals reversed that determination, holding that the denial of benefits violated respondents' free exercise rights under the First Amendment.

On appeal to the Oregon Supreme Court, petitioner argued that the denial of benefits was permissible because respondents' consumption of peyote was a crime under Oregon law. The Oregon Supreme Court reasoned, however, that the criminality of respondents' peyote use was irrelevant to resolution of their constitutional claim—since the purpose of the "misconduct" provision under which respondents had been disqualified was not to enforce the State's criminal laws but to preserve the financial integrity of the compensation fund, and since that purpose was inadequate to justify the burden that disqualification imposed on respondents' religious practice. Citing our decisions in *Sherbert v. Verner*, 374 U.S. 398 (1963), and *Thomas v. Review Board, Indiana Employment Security Div.*, 450 U.S. 707 (1981), the court concluded that respondents were entitled to payment of unemployment benefits. *Smith v. Employment Div., Dept. of Human Resources* 721 P. 2d 445, 449–450 (1986). We granted certiorari.

Before this Court in 1987, petitioner continued to maintain that the illegality of respondents' peyote consumption was relevant to their constitutional claim. We agreed, concluding that "if a State has prohibited through its criminal laws certain kinds of religiously motivated conduct without violating the First Amendment, it certainly follows that it may impose the lesser burden of denying unemployment compensation benefits to persons who engage in that conduct." *Employment Div., Dept. of Human Resources of Oregon v. Smith*, 485 U.S. 660, 670 (1988) (*Smith I*). We noted, however, that the Oregon Supreme Court had not decided whether respondents' sacramental use of peyote was in fact proscribed by Oregon's controlled substance law, and that this issue was a matter of dispute between the parties. Being "uncertain about the legality of the religious use of peyote in Oregon," we determined that it would not be "appropriate for us to decide whether the practice is protected by the Federal Constitution." *Id.*, at 673. Accordingly, we vacated the judgment of the Oregon Supreme Court and remanded for further proceedings. *Id.*, at 674.

On remand, the Oregon Supreme Court held that respondents' religiously inspired use of peyote fell within the prohibition of the Oregon statute, which "makes no exception for the sacramental use" of the drug. 763 P. 2d 146, 148 (1988). It then considered whether that prohibition was valid under the Free Exercise Clause, and concluded that it was not. The court therefore reaffirmed its previous ruling that the State could not deny unemployment benefits to respondents for having engaged in that practice.

We again granted certiorari.

II

Respondents' claim for relief rests on our decisions in *Sherbert v. Verner, supra*, *Thomas v. Review Board, Indiana Employment Security Div., supra*, and *Hobbie v. Unemployment Appeals Comm'n of Florida*, 480 U.S. 136 (1987), in which we held that a State could not condition the availability of unemployment insurance on an individual's willingness to forego conduct required by his religion. As we observed in *Smith I*, however, the conduct at issue in those cases was not prohibited by law. We held that distinction to be critical, for "if Oregon does prohibit the religious use of peyote, and if that prohibition is consistent with the Federal Constitution, there is no federal right to engage in that conduct in Oregon," and "the State is free to withhold unemployment compensation from respondents for engaging in work-related misconduct, despite its religious motivation." 485 U.S., at 672. Now that the Oregon Supreme Court has confirmed that Oregon does prohibit the religious use of peyote, we proceed to consider whether that prohibition is permissible under the Free Exercise Clause.

A

The Free Exercise Clause of the First Amendment, which has been made applicable to the States by incorporation into the Fourteenth Amendment, see *Cantwell v. Connecticut*, 310 U.S. 296, 303 (1940), provides that "Congress shall make no law respecting an establishment of religion, or *prohibiting the free exercise thereof*. . . ." U.S. Const. Am. I (emphasis added). The free exercise of religion means, first and foremost, the right to believe and profess whatever religious doctrine one desires. Thus, the First Amendment obviously excludes all "governmental regulation of religious *beliefs* as such." *Sherbert v. Verner, supra,* at 402. The government may not compel affirmation of religious belief, see *Torcaso v. Watkins,* 367 U.S. 488 (1961), punish the expression of religious doctrines it believes to be false, *United States v. Ballard,* 322 U.S. 78, 86–88 (1944), impose special disabilities on the basis of religious views or religious status, see *McDaniel v. Paty,* 435 U.S. 618 (1978); *Fowler v. Rhode Island,* 345 U.S. 67, 69 (1953); cf. *Larson v. Valente,* 456 U.S. 228, 245 (1982), or lend its power to one or the other side in controversies over religious authority or dogma, see *Presbyterian Church v. Hull Church,* 393 U.S. 440, 445–452 (1969); *Kedroff v. St. Nicholas Cathedral,* 344 U.S. 94, 95–119 (1952); *Serbian Eastern Orthodox Diocese v. Milivojevich,* 426 U.S. 696, 708–725 (1976).

But the "exercise of religion" often involves not only belief and profession but the performance of (or abstention from) physical acts: assembling with others for a worship service, participating in sacramental use of bread and wine, proselytizing, abstaining from certain foods or certain modes of transportation. It would be true, we think (though no case of ours has involved the point), that a state would be "prohibiting the free exercise [of religion]" if it sought to ban such acts or abstentions only when they are engaged in for religious reasons, or only because of the religious belief that they display. It would doubtless be unconstitutional, for example, to ban the casting of "statues that are to be used for worship purposes," or to prohibit bowing down before a golden calf.

Respondents in the present case, however, seek to carry the meaning of "prohibiting the free exercise [of religion]" one large step further. They contend that their religious motivation for using peyote places them beyond the reach of a criminal law that is not specifically directed at their religious practice, and that is concededly constitutional as applied to those who use the drug for other reasons. They assert, in other words, that "prohibiting the free exercise [of religion]" includes requiring any individual to observe a generally applicable law that requires (or forbids) the performance of an act that his religious belief forbids (or requires). As a textual matter, we do not think the words must be given that meaning. It is no more necessary to regard the collection of a general tax, for example, as "prohibiting the free exercise [of religion]" by those citizens who believe support of organized government to be sinful, than it is to regard the same tax as "abridging the freedom . . . of the press" of those publishing companies that must pay the tax as a condition of staying in business. It is a permissible reading of the text, in the one case as in the other, to say that if prohibiting the exercise of religion (or burdening the activity of printing) is not the object of the tax but merely the incidental effect of a generally applicable and otherwise valid provision, the First Amendment has not been offended. Compare *Citizen Publishing Co. v. United States,* 394 U.S. 131, 139 (1969) (upholding application of antitrust laws to press), with *Grosjean v. American Press Co.,* 297 U.S. 233, 250–251 (1936) (striking down license tax applied only to newspapers with weekly circulation above a specified level); see generally *Minneapolis Star & Tribune Co. v. Minnesota Commissioner of Revenue,* 460 U.S. 575, 581 (1983).

Our decisions reveal that the latter reading is the correct one. We have never held that an individual's religious beliefs excuse him from compliance with an otherwise valid law prohibiting conduct that the State is free to regulate. On the contrary, the record of more than a century of our free exercise jurisprudence contradicts that proposition. As described succinctly by Justice Frankfurter in *Minersville School Dist. Bd. of Educ. v. Gobitis*, 310 U.S. 586, 594–595 (1940): "Conscientious scruples have not, in the course of the long struggle for religious toleration, relieved the individual from obedience to a general law not aimed at the promotion or restriction of religious beliefs. The mere possession of religious convictions which contradict the relevant concerns of a political society does not relieve the citizen from the discharge of political responsibilities (footnote omitted)." We first had occasion to assert that principle in *Reynolds v. United States*, 98 U.S. 145 (1879), where we rejected the claim that criminal laws against polygamy could not be constitutionally applied to those whose religion commanded the practice. "Laws," we said, "are made for the government of actions, and while they cannot interfere with mere religious belief and opinions, they may with practices. . . . Can a man excuse his practices to the contrary because of his religious belief? To permit this would be to make the professed doctrines of religious belief superior to the law of the land, and in effect to permit every citizen to become a law unto himself." *Id.*, at 166–167.

Subsequent decisions have consistently held that the right of free exercise does not relieve an individual of the obligation to comply with a "valid and neutral law of general applicability on the ground that the law proscribes (or prescribes) conduct that his religion prescribes (or proscribes)." *United States v. Lee*, 455 U.S. 252, 263, n. 3 (1982) (STEVENS, J., concurring in judgment); see *Minersville School Dist. Bd. of Educ. v. Gobitis, supra*, at 595 (collecting cases). In *Prince v. Massachusetts*, 321 U.S. 158 (1944), we held that a mother could be prosecuted under the child labor laws for using her children to dispense literature in the streets, her religious motivation notwithstanding. We found no constitutional infirmity in "excluding [these children] from doing there what no other children may do." *Id.*, at 171. In *Braunfield v. Brown*, 366 U.S. 599 (1961) (plurality opinion), we upheld Sunday-closing laws against the claim that they burdened the religious practices of persons whose religions compelled them to refrain from work on other days. In *Gillette v. United States*, 401 U.S. 437, 461 (1971), we sustained the military selective service system against the claim that it violated free exercise by conscripting persons who opposed a particular war on religious grounds.

Our most recent decision involving a neutral, generally applicable regulatory law that compelled activity forbidden by an individual's religion was *United States v. Lee*, 455 U.S. at 258–261. There, an Amish employer, on the behalf of himself and his employees, sought exemption from collection and payment of Social Security taxes on the ground that the Amish faith prohibited participation in governmental support programs. We rejected the claim that an exemption was constitutionally required. There would be no way, we observed, to distinguish the Amish believer's objection to Social Security taxes from the religious objections that others might have to the collection or use of other taxes. "If, for example, a religious adherent believes war is a sin, and if a certain percentage of the federal budget can be identified as devoted to war-related activities, such individuals would have a similarly valid claim to be exempt from paying that percentage of the income tax. The tax system could not function if denominations were allowed to challenge the tax system because tax payments were spent in a manner that violates their religious belief." *Id.*, at 260. Cf. *Hernandez v. Commissioner*, 490 U.S. ——— (1989) (rejecting free exercise challenge to payment of income taxes alleged to make religious activities more difficult).

The only decisions in which we have held that the First Amendment bars application of a neutral, generally applicable law to religiously motivated action have involved not the Free Exercise Clause alone, but the Free Exercise Clause in conjunction with other constitutional protections, such as freedom of speech and of the press, see *Cantwell v. Connecticut*, 310 U.S. at 304–307 (invalidating a licensing system for religious and charitable solicitations under which the administrator had discretion to deny a license to any cause he deemed nonreligious); *Murdock v. Pennsylvania*, 319 U.S. 105 (1943) (invalidating a flat tax on solicitation as applied to the dissemination of religious ideas); *Follet v. McCormick,* 321 U.S. 573 (1944) (same), or the right of parents, acknowledged in *Pierce v. Society of Sisters,* 286 U.S. 510 (1925), to direct the education of their children, see *Wisconsin v. Yoder,* 406 U.S. 205 (1972) (invalidating compulsory school-attendance laws as applied to Amish parents who refused on religious grounds to send their children to school).[1] Some of our cases prohibiting compelled expression, decided exclusively upon free speech grounds, have also involved freedom of religion, cf. *Wooley v. Maynard,* 430 U.S. 705 (1977) (invalidating compelled display of a license plate slogan that offended individual religious beliefs); *West Virginia Board of Education v. Barnette,* 319 U.S. 624 (1943) (invalidating compulsory flag salute statute challenged by religious objectors). And it is easy to envision a case in which a challenge on freedom of association grounds would likewise be reinforced by Free Exercise Clause concerns. *Cf. Roberts v. United States Jaycees,* 468 U.S. 609, 622 (1983) ("An individual's freedom to speak, to worship, and to petition the government for the redress of grievances could not be vigorously protected from interference by the State [if] a correlative freedom to engage in group effort toward those ends were not also guaranteed.").

The present case does not present such a hybrid situation, but a free exercise claim unconnected with any communicative activity or parental right. Respondents urge us to hold, quite simply, that when otherwise prohibitable conduct is accompanied by religious convictions, not only the convictions but the conduct itself must be free from governmental regulation. We have never held that, and decline to do so now. There being no contention that Oregon's drug law represents an attempt to regulate religious beliefs, the communication of religious beliefs, or the raising of one's children in those beliefs, the rule to which we have adhered ever since *Reynolds* plainly controls. "Our cases do not at their farthest reach support the proposition that a stance of conscientious opposition relieves an objector from any colliding duty fixed by a democratic government." *Gillette v. United States, supra,* at 461.

B

Respondents argue that even though exemption from generally applicable criminal laws need not automatically be extended to religiously motivated actors, at least the claim for a religious exemption must be evaluated under the balancing test set forth in *Sherbert v.*

---

[1] Both lines of cases have specifically adverted to the non–free exercise principle involved. *Cantwell,* for example, observed that "[t]he fundamental law declares the interest of the United States that the free exercise of religion be not prohibited and that freedom to communicate information and opinion be not abridged." 310 U.S., at 307. *Murdock* said:

"We do not mean to say that religious groups and the press are free from all financial burdens of government. . . . We have here something quite different, for example, from a tax on the income of one who engages in religious activities or a tax on property used or employed in connection with those activities. It is one thing to impose a tax on the income or property of a preacher. It is quite another thing to exact a tax from him for the privilege of delivering a sermon. . . . Those who can deprive religious groups of their colporteurs can take from them a part of the vital power of the press which has survived from the Reformation." 319 U.S., at 112.

Yoder said that "the Court's holding in *Pierce* stands as a charter of the rights of parents to direct the religious upbringing of their children. And, when the interests of parenthood are combined with a free exercise claim of the nature revealed by this record, more than merely a 'reasonable relation to some purpose within the competency of the State' is required to sustain the validity of the State's requirement under the First Amendment." 406 U.S., at 233.

Verner, 374 U.S. 398 (1963). Under the *Sherbert* test, governmental actions that substantially burden a religious practice must be justified by a compelling governmental interest. See *id.*, at 402–403; see also *Hernandez v. Commissioner, supra* at ———. Applying that test we have, on three occasions, invalidated state unemployment compensation rules that conditioned the availability of benefits upon an applicant's willingness to work under conditions forbidden by his religion. See *Sherbert v. Verner, supra; Thomas v. Review Board, Indiana Employment Div.*, 450 U.S. 707 (1981); *Hobbie v. Unemployment Appeals Comm'n of Florida*, 480 U.S. 136 (1987). We have never invalidated any governmental action on the basis of the *Sherbert* test except the denial of unemployment compensation. Although we have sometimes purported to apply the *Sherbert* test in contexts other than that, we have always found the test satisfied, see *United States v. Lee*, 455 U.S. 252 (1982); *Gillette v. United States*, 401 U.S. 437 (1971). In recent years we have abstained from applying the *Sherbert* test (outside the unemployment compensation field) at all. In *Bowen v. Roy*, 476 U.S. 693 (1986), we declined to apply *Sherbert* analysis to a federal statutory scheme that required benefit applicants and recipients to provide their Social Security numbers. The plaintiffs in that case asserted that it would violate their religious beliefs to obtain and provide a Social Security number for their daughter. We held the statute's application to the plaintiffs valid regardless of whether it was necessary to effectuate a compelling interest. See *id.*, at 699–701. In *Lyng v. Northwest Indian Cemetery Protective Assn.*, 485 U.S. 439 (1988), we declined to apply *Sherbert* analysis to the Government's logging and road construction activities on lands used for religious purposes by several Native American Tribes, even though it was undisputed that the activities "could have devastating effects on traditional Indian religious practices," 485 U.S., at 451. In *Goldman v. Weinberger*, 475 U.S. 503 (1986), we rejected application of the *Sherbert* test to military dress regulations that forbade the wearing of yarmulkes. In *O'Lone v. Estate of Shabazz*, 482 U.S. 342 (1987), we sustained, without mentioning the *Sherbert* test, a prison's refusal to excuse inmates from work requirements to attend worship services.

Even if we were inclined to breathe into *Sherbert* some life beyond the unemployment compensation field, we would not apply it to require exemptions from a generally applicable criminal law. The *Sherbert* test, it must be recalled, was developed in a context that lent itself to individualized governmental assessment of the reasons for the relevant conduct. As a plurality of the Court noted in *Roy*, a distinctive feature of unemployment compensation programs is that their eligibility criteria invite consideration of the particular circumstances behind an applicant's unemployment: "The statutory conditions [in *Sherbert* and *Thomas*] provided that a person was not eligible for unemployment compensation benefits if, 'without good cause,' he had quit work or refused available work. The 'good cause' standard created a mechanism for individualized exemptions." *Bowen v. Roy, supra*, at 708 (opinion of BURGER, C. J., joined by POWELL and REHNQUIST, JJ.). See also *Sherbert, supra*, at 401 n. 4 (reading state unemployment compensation law as allowing benefits for unemployment caused by at least some "personal reasons"). As the plurality pointed out in *Roy*, our decisions in the unemployment cases stand for the proposition that where the State has in place a system of individual exemptions, it may not refuse to extend that system to cases of "religious hardship" without compelling reason. *Bowen v. Roy, supra*, at 708.

Whether or not the decisions are that limited, they at least have nothing to do with an across-the-board criminal prohibition on a particular form of conduct. Although, as noted earlier, we have sometimes used the *Sherbert* test to analyze free exercise challenges to such laws, see *United States v. Lee, supra*, at 257–260; *Gillette v. United States, supra*, at 462, we have never applied the test to invalidate one. We conclude today that the sounder approach, and the approach in accord with the vast majority of our precedents, is to hold the test inapplicable to such challenges. The government's ability to enforce generally applicable prohibitions of socially harmful conduct, like its ability to carry out other aspects of public policy, "cannot depend on measuring the effects of a governmental action on a religious objector's spiritual development." *Lyng, supra,* at 451. To make an individual's obligation to obey such a law contingent upon the law's coincidence with his religious beliefs, except where the State's interest is "compelling"—permitting him, by virtue of his beliefs, "to become a law unto himself," *Reynolds v. United States,* 98 U.S., at 167—contradicts both constitutional tradition and common sense.[2]

The "compelling government interest" requirement seems benign, because it is familiar from other fields. But using it as the standard that must be met before the government may accord different treatment on the basis of race, see, *e. g., Palmore v. Sidoti,* 466 U.S. 429, 432 (1984), or before the government may regulate the content of speech, see, *e. g. Sable Communications of California v. FCC,* 492 U.S. ——, —— (1989), is not remotely comparable to using it for the purpose asserted here. What it produces in those other fields—equality of treatment, and an unrestricted flow of contending speech—are constitutional norms; what it would produce here—a private right to ignore generally applicable laws—is a constitutional anomaly.[3]

---

[2] JUSTICE O'CONNOR seeks to distinguish *Lyng v. Northwest Indian Cemetery Protection Assn., supra,* and *Bowen v. Roy, supra,* on the ground that those cases involved the government's conduct of "its own internal affairs," which is different because, as JUSTICE DOUGLAS said in *Sherbert,* "the Free Exercise Clause is written in terms of what the government cannot do to the individual, not in terms of what the individual can exact from the government." *Post,* at 10 (O'CONNOR, J., concurring), quoting *Sherbert, supra,* at 412 (DOUGLAS, J., concurring). But since JUSTICE DOUGLAS voted with the majority in *Sherbert,* that quote obviously envisioned that what "the government cannot do to the individual" includes not just the prohibition of an individual's freedom of action through criminal laws but also the running of its programs (in *Sherbert,* state unemployment compensation) in such fashion as to harm the individual's religious interests. Moreover, it is hard to see any reason in principle or practicality why the government should have to tailor its health and safety laws to conform to the diversity of religious belief, but should not have to tailor its management of public lands. *Lyng, supra,* or its administration of welfare programs, *Roy, supra.*

[3] JUSTICE O'CONNOR suggests that "[t]here is nothing talismanic about neutral laws of general applicability," and that all laws burdening religious practices should be subject to compelling-interest scrutiny because "the First Amendment unequivocally makes freedom of religion, like freedom from race discrimination and freedom of speech, a 'constitutional norm,' not an 'anomaly.' " *Post,* at 11 (O'CONNOR, J., concurring). But this comparison with other fields supports, rather than undermines, the conclusion we draw today. Just as we subject to the most exacting scrutiny laws that make classifications based on race, see *Palmore v. Sidoti, supra,* or on the content of speech, see *Sable Communications, supra,* so too we strictly scrutinize governmental classifications based on religion, see *McDaniel v. Paty,* 435 U.S. 618 (1978); see also *Torcaso v. Watkins,* 367 U.S. 488 (1961). But we have held that race-neutral laws that have the *effect* of disproportionately disadvantaging a particular racial group do not thereby become subject to compelling-interest analysis under the Equal Protection Clause, see *Washington v. Davis,* 426 U.S. 229 (1976) (police employment examination); and we have held that generally applicable laws unconcerned with regulating speech that have the *effect* of interfering with speech do not thereby become subject to compelling-interest analysis under the First Amendment, see *Citizen Publishing Co. v. United States,* 394 U.S. 131, 139 (1969) (antitrust laws). Our conclusion that generally applicable, religion-neutral laws that have the effect of burdening a particular religious practice need not be justified by a compelling governmental interest is the only approach compatible with these precedents.

Nor is it possible to limit the impact of respondents' proposal by requiring a "compelling state interest" only when the conduct prohibited is "central" to the individual's religion. Cf. *Lyng v. Northwest Indian Cemetery Protective Assn., supra,* at ———— (BRENNAN, J., dissenting). It is no more appropriate for judges to determine the "centrality" of religious beliefs before applying a "compelling interest" test in the free exercise field, than it would be for them to determine the "importance" of ideas before applying the "compelling interest" test in the free speech field. What principle of law or logic can be brought to bear to contradict a believer's assertion that a particular act is "central" to his personal faith? Judging the centrality of different religious practices is akin to the unacceptable "business of evaluating the relative merits of differing religious claims." *United States v. Lee,* 455 U.S., at 263 n. 2 (STEVENS J., concurring). As we reaffirmed only last Term, "[i]t is not within the judicial ken to question the centrality of particular beliefs or practices to a faith, or the validity of particular litigants' interpretation of those creeds." *Hernandez v. Commissioner,* 490 U.S., at ————. Repeatedly and in many different contexts, we have warned that courts must not presume to determine the place of a particular belief in a religion or the plausibility of a religious claim. See, *e.g., Thomas v. Review Board, Indiana Employment Security Div.,* 450 U.S., at 716; *Presbyterian Church v. Hull Church,* 393 U.S., at 450; *Jones v. Wolf,* 443 U.S. 595, 602–606 (1979); *United States v. Ballard,* 322 U.S. 78, 85–87 (1944).[4]

If the "compelling interest" test is to be applied at all, then, it must be applied across the board, to all actions thought to be religiously commanded. Moreover, if "compelling interest" really means what it says (and watering it down here would subvert its rigor in the other fields where it is applied), many laws will not meet the test. Any society adopting such a system would be courting anarchy, but that danger increases in direct proportion to the society's diversity of religious beliefs, and its determination to coerce or suppress none of them. Precisely because "we are a cosmopolitan nation made

---

[4] While arguing that we should apply the compelling interest test in this case, JUSTICE O'CONNOR nonetheless agrees that "our determination of the constitutionality of Oregon's general criminal prohibition cannot, and should not, turn on the centrality of the particular religious practice at issue," *post,* at 15 (O'CONNOR, J., concurring). This means, presumably, that compelling interest scrutiny must be applied to generally applicable laws that regulate or prohibit *any* religiously motivated activity, no matter how unimportant to the claimant's religion. Earlier in her opinion, however, JUSTICE O'CONNOR appears to contradict this, saying that the proper approach is "to determine whether the burden on the specific plaintiffs before us is constitutionally significant and whether the particular criminal interest asserted by the State before us is compelling." *Post,* at 9. "Constitutionally significant burden" would seem to be "centrality" under another name. In any case, dispensing with a "centrality" inquiry is utterly unworkable. It would require, for example, the same degree of "compelling state interest" to impede the practice of throwing rice at church weddings as to impede the practice of getting married in church. There is no way out of the difficulty that, if general laws are to be subjected to a "religious practice" exception, *both* the importance of the law at issue *and* the centrality of the practice at issue must reasonably be considered.

Nor is this difficulty avoided by JUSTICE BLACKMUN'S assertion that "although courts should refrain from delving into questions of whether, as a matter of religious doctrine, a particular practice is 'central' to the religion, I do not think this means that the courts must turn a blind eye to the severe impact of a State's restrictions on the adherents of a minority religion." *Post,* at 13 (BLACKMUN, J. dissenting). As JUSTICE BLACKMUN'S opinion proceeds to make clear, inquiry into "severe impact" is no different from inquiry into centrality. He has merely substituted for the question "How important is X to the religious adherent?" the question "How great will be the harm to the religious adherent if X is taken away?" There is no material difference.

up of people of almost every conceivable religious preference," *Braunfield v. Brown,* 366 U.S., at 606, and precisely because we value and protect that religious divergence, we cannot afford the luxury of deeming *presumptively invalid,* as applied to the religious objector, every regulation of conduct that does not protect an interest of the highest order. The rule respondents favor would open the prospect of constitutionally required religious exemptions from civic obligations of almost every conceivable kind—ranging from compulsory military service, see, *e. g., Gillette v. United States,* 401 U.S. 437 (1971), to the payment of taxes, see, *e. g., United States v. Lee, supra;* to health and safety regulation such as manslaughter and child neglect laws, see, *e.g., Funkhouser v. State,* 763 P. 2d 695 (Okla. Crim. App. 1988), compulsory vaccination laws, see, *e. g., Cude v. State,* 237 Ark. 927, 377 S. W. 2d 816 (1964), drug laws, see, *e. g., Olsen v. Drug Enforcement Administration,* ——— U.S. App. D.C. ———, 878 F. 2d 1458 (1989), and traffic laws, see *Cox v. New Hampshire,* 312 U.S. 569 (1941); to social welfare legislation such as minimum wage laws, see *Susan and Tony Alamo Foundation v. Secretary of Labor,* 471 U.S. 290 (1985), child labor laws, see *Prince v. Massachusetts,* 321 U.S. 158 (1944), animal cruelty laws, see, *e. g., Church of the Lukumi Babalu Aye Inc. v. City of Hialeah,* 723 F. Supp. 1467 (S. D. Fla. 1989), cf. *State v. Massey,* 229 N.C. 734, 51 S. E. 2d 179, appeal dism'd, 336 U.S. 942 (1949), environmental protection laws, see *United States v. Little,* 638 F. Supp. 337 (Mont. 1986), and laws providing for equality of opportunity for the races, see, *e. g., Bob Jones University v. United States,* 461 U.S. 574, 603–604 (1983). The First Amendment's protection of religious liberty does not require this.[5]

Values that are protected against government interference through enshrinement in the Bill of Rights are not thereby banished from the political process. Just as a society that believes in the negative protection accorded to the press by the First Amendment is likely to enact laws that affirmatively foster the dissemination of the printed word, so also a society that believes in the negative protection accorded to religious belief can be expected to be solicitous of that value in its legislation as well. It is therefore not surprising that a number of States have made an exception to their drug laws for sacramental peyote use. See, *e. g.,* Ariz. Rev. Stat. Ann. § 13–3402(b)(1)–(3) (1989); Colo. Rev. Stat. § 12–22–317(3) (1985); N. M. Stat. Ann. § 30–31–6(D) (Supp. 1989). But to say that a nondiscriminatory religious-practice exemption is permitted, or even that it is desirable, is not to say that it is constitutionally required, and that the appropriate occasions for its creation can be discerned by the courts. It may fairly be said that leaving accommodation to the political process will place at a relative disadvantage those religious practices that are not widely engaged in; but that unavoidable consequence of democratic government must be preferred to a system in which each conscience is a law unto itself or in which judges weigh the social importance of all laws against the centrality of all religious beliefs. . . .

---

[5] JUSTICE O'CONNOR contends that the "parade of horribles" in the text only "demonstrates . . . that courts have been quite capable of strik[ing] sensible balances between religious liberty and competing state interests." *Post,* at 11 (O'CONNOR, J., concurring). But the cases we cite have struck "sensible balances" only because they have all applied the general laws, despite the claims for religious exemption. In any event, JUSTICE O'CONNOR mistakes the purpose of our parade: it is not to suggest that courts would necessarily permit harmful exemptions from these laws (though they might), but to suggest that courts would constantly be in the business of determining whether the "severe impact" of various laws on religious practice (to use JUSTICE BLACKMUN's terminology) or the "constitutiona[l] significan[ce]" of the "burden on the particular plaintiffs" (to use JUSTICE O'CONNOR's terminology) suffices to permit us to confer an exemption. It is a parade of horribles because it is horrible to contemplate that federal judges will regularly balance against the importance of general laws the significance of religious practice.

Because respondents' ingestion of peyote was prohibited under Oregon law, and because that prohibition is constitutional, Oregon may, consistent with the Free Exercise Clause, deny respondents unemployment compensation when their dismissal results from use of the drug. The decision of the Oregon Supreme Court is accordingly reversed.

It is so ordered.

JUSTICE O'CONNOR, with whom JUSTICE BRENNAN, JUSTICE MARSHALL, and JUSTICE BLACKMUN join as to Parts I and II, concurring in the judgment.*

Although I agree with the result the Court reaches in this case, I cannot join its opinion. In my view, today's holding dramatically departs from well-settled First Amendment jurisprudence, appears unnecessary to resolve the question presented, and is incompatible with our Nation's fundamental commitment to individual religious liberty.

I

At the outset, I note that I agree with the Court's implicit determination that the constitutional question upon which we granted review—whether the Free Exercise Clause protects a person's religiously motivated use of peyote from the reach of a State's general criminal law prohibition—is properly presented in this case. As the Court recounts, respondents Alfred Smith and Galen Black were denied unemployment compensation benefits because their sacramental use of peyote constituted work-related "misconduct," not because they violated Oregon's general criminal prohibition against possession of peyote. We held, however, in *Employment Div., Dept. of Human Resources of Oregon v. Smith*, 485 U.S. 660 (1988) *(Smith I)*, that whether a State may, consistent with federal law, deny unemployment compensation benefits to persons for their religious use of peyote depends on whether the State, as a matter of state law, has criminalized the underlying conduct. See *id.*, at 670–672. The Oregon Supreme Court, on remand from this Court, concluded that "the Oregon statute against possession of controlled substances, which include peyote, makes no exception for the sacramental use of peyote." 307 Ore. 68, 72–73, 763 P. 2d 146, 148 (1988) (footnote omitted).

Respondents contend that, because the Oregon Supreme Court declined to decide whether the Oregon Constitution prohibits criminal prosecution for the religious use of peyote, see *id.*, at 73, n. 3, 763 P. 2d, at 148, n. 3, any ruling on the federal constitutional question would be premature. Respondents are of course correct that the Oregon Supreme Court may eventually decide that the Oregon Constitution requires the State to provide an exemption from its general criminal prohibition for the religious use of peyote. Such a decision would then reopen the question whether a State may nevertheless deny unemployment compensation benefits to claimants who are discharged for engaging in such conduct. As the case comes to us today, however, the Oregon Supreme Court has plainly ruled that Oregon's prohibition against possession of controlled substances does not contain an exemption for the religious use of peyote. In light of our decision in *Smith I*, which makes this finding a "necessary predicate to a correct evaluation of respondents' federal claim," 485 U.S., at 672, the question presented and addressed is properly before the Court.

---

* Although JUSTICE BRENNAN, JUSTICE MARSHALL, and JUSTICE BLACKMUN join Parts I and II of this opinion, they do not concur in the judgment.

II

The Court today extracts from our long history of free exercise precedents the single categorical rule that "if prohibiting the exercise of religion . . . is . . . merely the incidental effect of a generally applicable and otherwise valid provision, the First Amendment has not been offended." *Ante,* at 5–6 (citations omitted). Indeed, the Court holds that where the law is a generally applicable criminal prohibition, our usual free exercise jurisprudence does not even apply. *Ante,* at 11. To reach this sweeping result, however, the Court must not only give a strained reading of the First Amendment but must also disregard our consistent application of free exercise doctrine to cases involving generally applicable regulations that burden religious conduct.

A

The Free Exercise Clause of the First Amendment commands that "Congress shall make no law . . . prohibiting the free exercise [of religion]." In *Cantwell v. Connecticut,* 310 U.S. 296 (1940), we held that this prohibition applies to the States by incorporation into the Fourteenth Amendment and that it categorically forbids government regulation of religious beliefs. *Id.,* at 303. As the Court recognizes, however, the "free *exercise*" of religion often, if not invariably, requires the performance of (or abstention from) certain acts. *Ante,* at 5; cf. 3 A New English Dictionary on Historical Principles 401402 (J. Murray, ed. 1897) (defining "exercise" to include "[t]he practice and performance of rites and ceremonies, worship, etc.; the right or permission to celebrate the observances (of a religion)" and religious observances such as acts of public and private worship, preaching, and prophesying). "[B]elief and action cannot be neatly confined in logic-tight compartments." *Wisconsin v. Yoder,* 406 U.S. 205, 220 (1972). Because the First Amendment does not distinguish between religious belief and religious conduct, conduct motivated by sincere religious belief, like the belief itself, must therefore be at least presumptively protected by the Free Exercise Clause.

The Court today, however, interprets the Clause to permit the government to prohibit, without justification, conduct mandated by an individual's religious beliefs, so long as that prohibition is generally applicable. *Ante,* at 5. But a law that prohibits certain conduct—conduct that happens to be an act of worship for someone—manifestly does prohibit that person's free exercise of his religion. A person who is barred from engaging in religiously motivated conduct is barred from freely exercising his religion. Moreover, that person is barred from freely exercising his religion regardless of whether the law prohibits the conduct only when engaged in for religious reasons, only by members of that religion, or by all persons. It is difficult to deny that a law that prohibits religiously motivated conduct, even if the law is generally applicable, does not at least implicate First Amendment concerns.

The Court responds that generally applicable laws are "one large step" removed from laws aimed at specific religious practices. *Ante,* at 5. The First Amendment, however, does not distinguish between laws that are generally applicable and laws that target particular religious practices. Indeed, few States would be so naive as to enact a law directly prohibiting or burdening a religious practice as such. Our free exercise cases have all concerned generally applicable laws that had the effect of significantly burdening a religious practice. If the First Amendment is to have any vitality, it ought not be construed to cover only the extreme and hypothetical situation in which a State directly targets a religious practice. As we have noted in a slightly different context, " '[s]uch a test has no basis in precedent and relegates a serious First Amendment value to the barest level of minimum scrutiny that the Equal Protection Clause already provides.' " *Hobbie v. Unemployment Appeals Comm'n of Florida,* 480 U.S. 136, 141–142 (1987) (quoting

Bowen v. Roy, 476 U.S. 693, 727 [1986] [opinion concurring in part and dissenting in part]).

To say that a person's right to free exercise has been burdened, of course, does not mean that he has an absolute right to engage in the conduct. Under our established First Amendment jurisprudence, we have recognized that the freedom to act, unlike the freedom to believe, cannot be absolute. See, e. g., *Cantwell, supra,* at 304; *Reynolds v. United States,* 98 U.S. 145, 161–167 (1879). Instead, we have respected both the First Amendment's express textual mandate and the governmental interest in regulation of conduct by requiring the Government to justify any substantial burden on religiously motivated conduct by a compelling state interest and by means narrowly tailored to achieve that interest. See *Hernandez v. Commissioner,* 490 U.S. ——, —— (1989); *Hobbie, supra,* at 141; *United States v. Lee,* 455 U.S. 252, 257–258 (1982); *Thomas v. Review Bd., Indiana Employment Security Div.* 450 U.S. 707, 718 (1981); *McDaniel* v. *Paty,* 435 U. S. 618, 626–629 (1978) (plurality opinion); *Yoder, supra,* at 215; *Gillette v. United States,* 401 U.S. 437, 462 (1971); *Sherbert v. Verner,* 374 U.S. 398, 403 (1963); see also *Bowen v. Roy, supra,* at 732 (opinion concurring in part and dissenting in part); *West Virginia State Bd. of Educ. v. Barnette,* 319 U.S. 624, 639 (1943). The compelling interest test effectuates the First Amendment's command that religious liberty is an independent liberty, that it occupies a preferred position, and that the Court will not permit encroachments upon this liberty, whether direct or indirect, unless required by clear and compelling governmental interests "of the highest order," *Yoder, supra,* at 215. "Only an especially important governmental interest pursued by narrowly tailored means can justify exacting a sacrifice of First Amendment freedoms as the price for an equal share of the rights, benefits, and privileges enjoyed by other citizens." *Roy, supra,* at 728 (opinion concurring in part and dissenting in part).

The Court attempts to support its narrow reading of the Clause by claiming that "[w]e have never held that an individual's religious beliefs excuse him from compliance with an otherwise valid law prohibiting conduct that the State is free to regulate." *Ante,* at 6. But as the Court later notes, as it must, in cases such as *Cantwell* and *Yoder* we have in fact interpreted the Free Exercise Clause to forbid application of a generally applicable prohibition to religiously motivated conduct. See *Cantwell, supra,* at 304–307; *Yoder, supra,* at 214–234. Indeed, in *Yoder* we expressly rejected the interpretation the Court now adopts:

> "[O]ur decisions have rejected the idea that religiously grounded conduct is always outside the protection of the Free Exercise Clause. It is true that activities of individuals, even when religiously based, are often subject to regulation by the States in the exercise of their undoubted power to promote the health, safety, and general welfare, or the Federal Government in the exercise of its delegated powers. But to agree that religiously grounded conduct must often be subject to the broad police power of the State is not to deny that there are areas of conduct protected by the Free Exercise Clause of the First Amendment and thus beyond the power of the State to control, *even under regulations of general applicability.* . . .
>
> ". . . A regulation neutral on its face may, in its application, nonetheless offend the constitutional requirement for government neutrality if it unduly burdens the free exercise of religion." 406 U.S., at 219–220 (emphasis added; citations omitted).

The Court endeavors to escape from our decisions in *Cantwell* and *Yoder* by labeling them "hybrid" decisions, *ante,* at 9, but there is no denying that both cases expressly relied on the Free Exercise Clause, see *Cantwell,* 310 U.S., at 303–307; *Yoder,* 406

U.S., at 219–229, and that we have consistently regarded those cases as part of the mainstream of our free exercise jurisprudence. Moreover, in each of the other cases cited by the Court to support its categorical rule, *ante,* at 7–8, we rejected the particular constitutional claims before us only after carefully weighing the competing interests. See *Prince v. Massachusetts,* 321 U.S. 158, 168–170 (1944) (state interest in regulating children's activities justifies denial of religious exemption from child labor laws); *Braunfield v. Brown,* 366 U.S. 599, 608–609 (1961) (plurality opinion) (state interest in uniform day of rest justifies denial of religious exemption from Sunday closing law); *Gillette, supra,* at 462 (state interest in military affairs justifies denial of religious exemption from conscription laws); *Lee, supra,* at 258–259 (state interest in comprehensive social security system justifies denial of religious exemption from mandatory participation requirement). That we rejected the free exercise claims in those cases hardly calls into question the applicability of First Amendment doctrine in the first place. Indeed, it is surely unusual to judge the vitality of a constitutional doctrine by looking to the winloss record of the plaintiffs who happen to come before us.

B

Respondents, of course, do not contend that their conduct is automatically immune from all governmental regulation simply because it is motivated by their sincere religious beliefs. The Court's rejection of that argument, *ante,* at 9, might therefore be regarded as merely harmless dictum. Rather, respondents invoke our traditional compelling interest test to argue that the Free Exercise Clause requires the State to grant them a limited exemption from its general criminal prohibition against the possession of peyote. The Court today, however, denies them even the opportunity to make that argument, concluding that "the sounder approach, and the approach in accord with the vast majority of our precedents, is to hold the [compelling interest] test inapplicable to" challenges to general criminal prohibitions. *Ante,* at 12.

In my view, however, the essence of a free exercise claim is relief from a burden imposed by government on religious practices or beliefs, whether the burden is imposed directly through laws that prohibit or compel specific religious practices, or indirectly through laws that, in effect, make abandonment of one's own religion or conformity to the religious beliefs of others the price of an equal place in the civil community. As we explained in *Thomas:*

> "Where the state conditions receipt of an important benefit upon conduct proscribed by a religious faith, or where it denies such a benefit because of conduct mandated by religious belief, thereby putting substantial pressure on an adherent to modify his behavior and to violate his beliefs, a burden upon religion exists." 450 U.S., at 717–718.

A State that makes criminal an individual's religiously motivated conduct burdens that individual's free exercise of religion in the severest manner possible, for it "results in the choice to the individual of either abandoning his religious principle or facing criminal prosecution." *Braunfield, supra,* at 605. I would have thought it beyond argument that such laws implicate free exercise concerns.

Indeed, we have never distinguished between cases in which a State conditions receipt of a benefit on conduct prohibited by religious beliefs and cases in which a State affirmatively prohibits such conduct. The *Sherbert* compelling interest test applies in both kinds of cases. See, e.g., *Lee,* 455 U.S., at 257–260 (applying *Sherbert* to uphold social security tax liability); *Gillette,* 401 U.S., at 462 (applying *Sherbert* to uphold military conscription requirement); *Yoder, supra,* at 215–234 (applying *Sherbert* to strike down criminal convictions for violation of compulsory school attendance law). As I noted in *Roy v. Bowen:*

"The fact that the underlying dispute involves an award of benefits rather than an exaction of penalties does not grant the Government license to apply a different version of the Constitution. . . .

". . . The fact that appellees seek exemption from a precondition that the Government attaches to an award of benefits does not, therefore, generate a meaningful distinction between this case and one where appellees seek an exemption from the Government's imposition of penalties upon them." 476 U.S., at 731–732 (opinion concurring in part and dissenting in part).

See also *Hobbie, supra,* at 141–142; *Sherbert,* 374 U.S., at 404. I would reaffirm that principle today: a neutral criminal law prohibiting conduct that a State may legitimately regulate is, if anything, *more* burdensome than a neutral civil statute placing legitimate conditions on the award of a state benefit.

Legislatures, of course, have always been "left free to reach actions which were in violation of social duties or subversive of good order." *Reynolds,* 98 U.S., at 164; see also *Yoder,* 406 U.S., at 219–220; *Braunfield,* 366 U.S., at 603604. Yet because of the close relationship between conduct and religious belief, "[i]n every case the power to regulate must be so exercised as not, in attaining a permissible end, unduly to infringe the protected freedom." *Cantwell,* 310 U.S., at 304. Once it has been shown that a government regulation or criminal prohibition burdens the free exercise of religion, we have consistently asked the Government to demonstrate that unbending application of its regulation to the religious objector "is essential to accomplish an overriding governmental interest," *Lee, supra,* at 257–258, or represents "the least restrictive means of achieving some compelling state interest," *Thomas,* 450 U.S., at 718. See, *e.g., Braunfield, supra,* at 607; *Sherbert, supra,* at 406; *Yoder, supra,* at 214–215; *Roy,* 476 U.S., at 728–732 (opinion concurring in part and dissenting in part). To me, the sounder approach—the approach more consistent with our role as judges to decide each case on its individual merits—is to apply this test in each case to determine whether the burden on the specific plaintiffs before us is constitutionally significant and whether the particular criminal interest asserted by the State before us is compelling. Even if, as an empirical matter, a government's criminal laws might usually serve a compelling interest in health, safety, or public order, the First Amendment at least requires a case-by-case determination of the question, sensitive to the facts of each particular claim. Cf. *McDaniel,* 435 U.S., at 628, n. 8 (plurality opinion) (noting application of *Sherbert* to general criminal prohibitions and the "delicate balancing required by our decisions in" *Sherbert* and *Yoder*). Given the range of conduct that a State might legitimately make criminal, we cannot assume, merely because a law carries criminal sanctions and is generally applicable, that the First Amendment *never* requires the State to grant a limited exemption for religiously motivated conduct.

Moreover, we have not "rejected" or "declined to apply" the compelling interest test in our recent cases. *Ante,* at 10–11. Recent cases have instead reaffirmed that test as a fundamental part of our First Amendment doctrine. See, *e.g., Hernandez,* 490 U.S., at———; *Hobbie, supra,* at 141–142 (rejecting CHIEF JUSTICE BURGER's suggestion in *Roy, supra,* at 707–708, that free exercise claims be assessed under a less rigorous "reasonable means" standard). The cases cited by the Court signal no retreat from our consistent adherence to the compelling interest test. In both *Bowen v. Roy, supra,* and *Lyng v. Northwest Indian Cemetery Protective Assn.,* 485 U.S. 439 (1988), for example, we expressly distinguished *Sherbert* on the ground that the First Amendment does not "require the Government *itself* to behave in ways that the individual believes will further his or her spiritual development. . . . The Free Exercise Clause simply cannot be understood to require the Government to conduct its own internal affairs in ways that comport with the religious beliefs of particular citizens." *Roy, supra,* at 609; see *Lyng, supra,* at 449. This distinction makes sense because "the Free Exercise Clause is written in terms of what the government cannot do to the individual, not in terms of what the individual can exact from the government." *Sherbert, supra,* at 412 (DOUGLAS, J., concurring). Because the case *sub judice,* like the other cases in which we have applied *Sherbert,* plainly falls into the former category, I would apply those established precedents to the facts of this case.

Similarly, the other cases cited by the Court for the proposition that we have rejected application of the *Sherbert* test outside the unemployment compensation field, *ante,* at 11, are distinguishable because they arose in the narrow, specialized contexts in which we have not traditionally required the government to justify a burden on religious conduct by articulating a compelling interest. See *Goldman v. Weinberger,* 475 U.S. 503, 507 (1986) ("Our review of military regulations challenged on First Amendment grounds is far more deferential than constitutional review of similar laws or regulations designed for civilian society"); *O'Lone v. Estate of Shabazz,* 482 U.S. 342, 349 (1987) ("[P]rison regulations alleged to infringe constitutional rights are judged under a 'reasonableness' test less restrictive than that ordinarily applied to alleged infringements of fundamental constitutional rights") (citation omitted). That we did not apply the compelling interest test in these cases says nothing about whether the test should continue to apply in paradigm free exercise cases such as the one presented here.

The Court today gives no convincing reason to depart from settled First Amendment jurisprudence. There is nothing talismanic about neutral laws of general applicability or general criminal prohibitions, for laws neutral toward religion can coerce a person to violate his religious conscience or intrude upon his religious duties just as effectively as laws aimed at religion. Although the Court suggests that the compelling interest test, as applied to generally applicable laws, would result in a "constitutional anomaly," *ante,* at 13, the First Amendment unequivocally makes freedom of religion, like freedom from race discrimination and freedom of speech, a "constitutional nor[m]," not an "anomaly." *Ibid.* Nor would application of our established free exercise doctrine to this case necessarily be incompatible with our equal protection cases. Cf. *Rogers v. Lodge,* 458 U.S. 613, 618 (1982) (race-neutral law that " 'bears more heavily on one race than another' " may violate equal protection) (citation omitted); *Castaneda v. Partida,* 430 U.S. 482, 492–495 (1977) (grand jury selection). We have in any event recognized that the Free Exercise Clause protects values distinct from those protected by the Equal Protection Clause. See *Hobbie,* 480 U.S., at 141–142. As the language of the Clause itself makes clear, an individual's free exercise of religion is a preferred constitutional activity. See, *e.g.,* McConnell, Accommodation of Religion, 1985 Sup. Ct. Rev. 1, 9 ("[T]he text of the First Amendment itself 'singles out' religion for special protections"); P. Kauper, Religion and the Constitution 17 (1964). A law that makes criminal such an activity therefore triggers constitutional concern—and heightened judicial scrutiny—even if it does not target the particular religious conduct at issue. Our free speech cases similarly recognize that neutral regulations that affect free speech values are subject to a balancing, rather than categorical, approach. See, *e.g., United States v. O'Brien,* 391 U.S. 367, 377 (1968); *City of Renton v. Playtime Theatres, Inc.,* 475 U.S. 41, 46–47 (1986); cf. *Anderson v. Celebrezze,* 460 U.S. 780, 792794 (1983) (generally applicable laws may impinge on free association concerns). The Court's parade of horribles, *ante,* at 1516, not only fails as a reason for discarding the compelling interest test, it instead demonstrates just the opposite: that courts have been quite capable of applying our free exercise jurisprudence to strike sensible balances between religious liberty and competing state interests.

Finally, the Court today suggests that the disfavoring of minority religions is an "unavoidable consequence" under our system of government and that accommodation of such religions must be left to the political process. *Ante,* at 17. In my view, however, the First Amendment was enacted precisely to protect the rights of those whose religious practices are not shared by the majority and may be viewed with hostility. The history of our free exercise doctrine amply demonstrates the harsh impact majoritarian rule has had on unpopular or emerging religious groups such as the Jehovah's Witnesses and the Amish. Indeed, the words of JUSTICE JACKSON in *West Virginia Board of Education v. Barnette* (overruling *Minersville School District v. Gobitis*, 310 U.S. 586 (1940)) are apt:

> "The very purpose of a Bill of Rights was to withdraw certain subjects from the vicissitudes of political controversy, to place them beyond the reach of majorities and officials and to establish them as legal principles to be applied by the courts. One's right to life, liberty, and property, to free speech, a free press, freedom of worship and assembly, and other fundamental rights may not be submitted to vote; they depend on the outcome of no elections." 319 U.S., at 638.

See also *United States v. Ballard*, 322 U.S. 78, 87 (1944) ("The Fathers of the Constitution were not unaware of the varied and extreme views of religious sects, of the violence of disagreement among them, and of the lack of any one religious creed on which all men would agree. They fashioned a charter of government which envisaged the widest possible toleration of conflicting views"). The compelling interest test reflects the First Amendment's mandate of preserving religious liberty to the fullest extent possible in a pluralistic society. For the Court to deem this command a "luxury," *ante*, at 15, is to denigrate "[t]he very purpose of a Bill of Rights."

III

The Court's holding today not only misreads settled First Amendment precedent; it appears to be unnecessary to this case. I would reach the same result applying our established free exercise jurisprudence.

A

There is no dispute that Oregon's criminal prohibition of peyote places a severe burden on the ability of respondents to freely exercise their religion. Peyote is a sacrament of the Native American Church and is regarded as vital to respondents' ability to practice their religion. See O. Stewart, Peyote Religion: A History 327–336 (1987) (describing modern status of peyotism); E. Anderson, Peyote: The Divine Cactus 41–65 (1980) (describing peyote ceremonies); Teachings from the American Earth: Indian religion and Philosophy 96–104 (D. Tedlock & B. Tedlock eds. 1975) (same); see also *People v. Woody*, 61 Cal. 2d 716, 721–722, 394 P. 2d 813, 817–818 (1964). As we noted in *Smith I*, the Oregon Supreme Court concluded that "the Native American Church is a recognized religion, that peyote is a sacrament of that church, and that respondent's beliefs were sincerely held." 485 U.S., at 667. Under Oregon law, as construed by that State's highest court, members of the Native American Church must choose between carrying out the ritual embodying their religious beliefs and avoidance of criminal prosecution. That choice is, in my view, more than sufficient to trigger First Amendment scrutiny.

There is also no dispute that Oregon has a significant interest in enforcing laws that control the possession and use of controlled substances by its citizens. See, *e.g.*, *Sherbert*, 374 U.S., at 403 (religiously motivated conduct may be regulated where such conduct "pose[s] some substantial threat to public safety, peace or order"); *Yoder*, 406 U.S., at 220 ("activities of individuals, even when religiously based, are often subject to regulation by the States in the exercise of their undoubted power to promote the health, safety and general welfare"). As we recently noted, drug abuse is "one of the greatest problems affecting the health and welfare of our population'' and thus ''one of the most serious problems confronting our society today.'' *Treasury Employees v. Von Raab,* 489 U.S.——, —— (1989) (slip op., at 10, 15). Indeed, under federal law (incorporated by Oregon law in relevant part, see Ore. Rev. Stat. § 475.005(6) (1989)), peyote is specifically regulated as a Schedule I controlled substance, which means that Congress has found that it has a high potential for abuse, that there is no currently accepted medical use, and that there is a lack of accepted safety for use of the drug under medical supervision. See 21 U.S.C. § 812(b)(1). See generally R. Julien, A Primer of Drug Action 149 (3d ed. 1981). In light of our recent decisions holding that the government interests in the collection of income tax, *Hernandez,* 490 U.S., at ——, a comprehensive social security system, see *Lee,* 455 U.S., at 258–259, and military conscription, see *Gillette,* 401 U.S., at 460, are compelling, respondents do not seriously dispute that Oregon has a compelling interest in prohibiting the possession of peyote by its citizens.

B

Thus, the critical question in this case is whether exempting respondents from the State's general criminal prohibition ''will unduly interfere with fulfillment of the governmental interest.'' *Lee, supra,* at 259; see also *Roy,* 476 U.S., at 727 (''[T]he Government must accommodate a legitimate free exercise claim unless pursuing an especially important interest by narrowly tailored means''); *Yoder,* 406 U.S., at 221; *Braunfield,* 366 U.S., at 605–607. Although the question is close, I would conclude that uniform application or Oregon's criminal prohibition is ''essential to accomplish,'' *Lee, supra,* at 257, its overriding interest in preventing the physical harm caused by the use of a Schedule I controlled substance. Oregon's criminal prohibition represents that State's judgment that the possession and use of controlled substances, even by only one person, is inherently harmful and dangerous. Because the health effects caused by the use of controlled substances exist regardless of the motivation of the user, the use of such substances, even for religious purposes, violates the very purpose of the laws that prohibit them. Cf. *State v. Massey,* 229 N. C. 734, 51 S. E. 2d 179 (denying religious exemption to municipal ordinance prohibiting handling of poisonous reptiles), appeal dism'd *sub nom. Bunn v. North Carolina,* 336 U.S. 942 (1949). Moreover, in view of the societal interest in preventing trafficking in controlled substances, uniform application of the criminal prohibition at issue is essential to the effectiveness of Oregon's stated interest in preventing any possession of peyote. Cf. *Jacobson v. Massachusetts,* 197 U.S. 11 (1905) (denying exemption from small pox vaccination requirement).

For these reasons, I believe that granting a selective exemption in this case would seriously impair Oregon's compelling interest in prohibiting possession of peyote by its citizens. Under such circumstances, the Free Exercise Clause does not require the State to accommodate respondents' religiously motivated conduct. See, *e. g., Thomas,* 450 U.S., at 719. Unlike in *Yoder,* where we noted that ''[t]he record strongly indicates that accommodating the religious objections of the Amish by forgoing one, or at most two, additional years of compulsory education will not impair the physical or mental health of the child, or result in an inability to be self-supporting or to discharge the duties and responsibilities of citizenship, or in any other way materially detract from the welfare of society,'' 406 U.S., at 234; see also *id.,* at 238–240 (WHITE, J., concurring), a religious exemption in this case would be incompatible with the State's interest in controlling use and possession of illegal drugs.

Respondents contend that any incompatibility is belied by the fact that the Federal Government and several States provide exemptions for the religious use of peyote, see 21 CFR § 1307.31 (1989); 307 Ore., at 73, n. 2 763 P. 2d, at 148, n. 2 (citing 11 state statutes that expressly exempt sacramental peyote use from criminal proscription). But other governments may surely choose to grant an exemption without Oregon, with its specific asserted interest in uniform application of its drug laws, being *required* to do so by the First Amendment. Respondents also note that the sacramental use of peyote is central to the tenets of the Native American Church, but I agree with the Court, *ante,* at 13–14, that because "[i]t is not within the judicial ken to question the centrality of particular beliefs or practices to a faith," *Hernandez, supra,* at ——— (slip op., at 17), our determination of the constitutionality of Oregon's general criminal prohibition cannot, and should not, turn on the centrality of the particular religious practice at issue. This does not mean, of course, that courts may not make factual findings as to whether a claimant holds a sincerely held religious belief that conflicts with, and thus is burdened by, the challenged law. The distinction between questions of centrality and questions of sincerity and burden is admittedly fine, but it is one that is an established part of our free exercise doctrine, see *Ballard,* 322 U.S., at 85–88, and one that courts are capable of making. See *Tony and Susan Alamo Foundation v. Secretary of Labor,* 471 U.S. 290, 303–305 (1985).

I would therefore adhere to our established free exercise jurisprudence and hold that the State in this case has a compelling interest in regulating peyote use by its citizens and that accommodating respondents' religiously motivated conduct "will unduly interfere with fulfillment of the governmental interest." *Lee,* 455 U.S., at 259. Accordingly, I concur in the judgment of the Court.

JUSTICE BLACKMUN, with whom JUSTICE BRENNAN and JUSTICE MARSHALL join, dissenting.

This Court over the years painstakingly has developed a consistent and exacting standard to test the constitutionality of a state statute that burdens the free exercise of religion. Such a statute may stand only if the law in general, and the State's refusal to allow a religious exemption in particular, are justified by a compelling interest that cannot be served by less restrictive means.[1]

Until today, I thought this was a settled and inviolate principle of this Court's First Amendment jurisprudence. The majority, however, perfunctorily dismisses it as a "constitutional anomaly." *Ante,* at 13. As carefully detailed in JUSTICE O'CONNOR's concurring opinion, *ante,* the majority is able to arrive at this view only by mischaracterizing this Court's precedents. The Court discards leading free exercise cases such as *Cantwell v. Connecticut,* 310 U.S. 296 (1940), and *Wisconsin v. Yoder,* 406 U.S. 205 (1972), as "hybrid." *Ante,* at 9. The Court views traditional free exercise analysis as

---

[1] See *Hernandez v. Commissioner,* 490 U.S. ——— (1989) ("The free exercise inquiry asks whether government has placed a substantial burden on the observation of a central religious belief or practice and, if so, whether a compelling governmental interest justifies the burden") (slip op. 17); *Hobbie v. Unemployment Appeals Comm'n of Fla.,* 480 U.S. 136, 141 (1987) (state laws burdening religions "must be subjected to strict scrutiny and could be justified only by proof by the State of a compelling interest"); *Bowen v. Roy,* 476 U.S. 693, 732 (1986) (O'CONNOR, J., concurring in part and dissenting in part) ("Our precedents have long required the Government to show that a compelling state interest is served by its refusal to grant a religious exemption"); *United States v. Lee,* 455 U.S. 252, 257–258 (1982) ("The state may justify a limitation on religious liberty by showing that it is essential to accomplish an overriding governmental interest"); *Thomas v. Review Bd. of Indiana Security Div.,* 450 U.S. 707, 718 (1981) ("The state may justify an inroad on religious liberty by showing that it is the least restrictive means of achieving some compelling state interest"); *Wisconsin v. Yoder,* 406 U.S. 205, 215 (1972) ("only those interests of the highest order and those not otherwise served can overbalance legitimate claims to the free exercise of religion"); *Sherbert v. Verner,* 374 U.S. 398, 406 (1963) (question is "whether some compelling state interest . . . justifies the substantial infringement of appellant's First Amendment right").

somehow inapplicable to criminal prohibitions (as opposed to conditions on the receipt of benefits), and to state laws of general applicability (as opposed, presumably, to laws that expressly single out religious practices). *Ante,* at 11–12. The Court cites cases in which, due to various exceptional circumstances, we found strict scrutiny inapposite, to hint that the Court has repudiated that standard altogether. *Ante,* at 10–11. In short, it effectuates a wholesale overturning of settled law concerning the Religion Clauses of our Constitution. One hopes that the Court is aware of the consequences, and that its result is not a product of overreaction to the serious problems the country's drug crisis has generated.

This distorted view of our precedents leads the majority to conclude that strict scrutiny of a state law burdening the free exercise of religion is a "luxury" that a well-ordered society cannot afford, *ante,* at 15, and that the repression of minority religions is an "unavoidable consequence of democratic government." *Ante,* at 17. I do not believe the Founders thought their dearly bought freedom from religious persecution a "luxury," but an essential element of liberty—and they could not have thought religious intolerance "unavoidable," for they drafted the Religion Clauses precisely in order to avoid that intolerance.

For these reasons, I agree with JUSTICE O'CONNOR's analysis of the applicable free exercise doctrine, and I join parts I and II of her opinion.[2] As she points out, "the critical question in this case is whether exempting respondents from the State's general criminal prohibition 'will unduly interfere with fulfillment of the governmental interest.' " *Ante,* at 15, quoting *United States v. Lee,* 455 U.S. 252, 259 (1982). I do disagree, however, with her specific answer to that question.

I

In weighing respondents' clear interest in the free exercise of their religion against Oregon's asserted interest in enforcing its drug laws, it is important to articulate in precise terms the state interest involved. It is not the State's broad interest in fighting the critical "war on drugs" that must be weighed against respondents' claim, but the State's narrow interest in refusing to make an exception for the religious, ceremonial use of peyote. See *Bowen v. Roy,* 476 U.S. 693, 728 (1986) (O'CONNOR, J., concurring in part and dissenting in part) ("This Court has consistently asked the Government to demonstrate that unbending application of its regulation to the religious objector 'is essential to accomplish an overriding governmental interest,' " quoting *Lee,* 455 U.S., at 257–258); *Thomas v. Review Bd. of Indiana Employment Security Div.,* 450 U.S. 707, 719 (1981) ("focus of the inquiry" concerning State's asserted interest must be "properly narrowed"); *Yoder,* 406 U.S., at 221 ("Where fundamental claims of religious freedom are at stake," the Court will not accept a State's "sweeping claim" that its interest in

---

[2] I reluctantly agree that, in light of this Court's decision in *Employment Division v. Smith,* 485 U.S. 660 (1988), the question on which certiorari was granted is properly presented in this case. I have grave doubts, however, as to the wisdom or propriety of deciding the constitutionality of a criminal prohibition which the State has not sought to enforce, which the State did not rely on in defending its denial of unemployment benefits before the state courts, and which the Oregon courts could, on remand, either invalidate on state constitutional grounds, or conclude that it remains irrelevant to Oregon's interest in administering its unemployment benefits program.

It is surprising, to say the least, that this Court which so often prides itself about principles of judicial restraint and reduction of federal control over matters of state law would stretch its jurisdiction to the limit in order to reach, in this abstract setting, the constitutionality of Oregon's criminal prohibition of peyote use.

compulsory education is compelling; despite the validity of this interest "in the generality of cases, we must searchingly examine the interests that the State seeks to promote . . . and the impediment to those objectives that would flow from recognizing the claimed Amish exception"). Failure to reduce the competing interests to the same plane of generality tends to distort the weighing process in the State's favor. See Clark, Guidelines for the Free Exercise Clause, 83 Harv. L. Rev. 327, 330–331 (1969) ("The purpose of almost any law can be traced back to one or another of the fundamental concerns of government: public health and safety, public peace and order, defense, revenue. To measure an individual interest directly against one of these rarified values inevitably makes the individual interest appear the less significant"); Pound, A Survey of Social Interests, 57 Harv. L. Rev. 1, 2 (1943) ("When it comes to weighing or valuing claims or demands with respect to other claims or demands, we must be careful to compare them on the same plane . . . [or else] we may decide the question in advance in our very way of putting it").

The State's interest in enforcing its prohibition, in order to be sufficiently compelling to outweigh a free exercise claim, cannot be merely abstract or symbolic. The State cannot plausibly assert that unbending application of a criminal prohibition is essential to fulfill any compelling interest, if it does not, in fact, attempt to enforce that prohibition. In this case, the State actually has not evinced any concrete interest in enforcing its drug laws against religious users of peyote. Oregon has never sought to prosecute respondents, and does not claim that it has made significant enforcement efforts against other religious users of peyote.[3] The State's asserted interest thus amounts only to the symbolic preservation of an unenforced prohibition. But a government interest in "symbolism, even symbolism for so worthy a cause as the abolition of unlawful drugs," *Treasury Employees v. Von Raab*, —— U.S. ——, —— (1989) (SCALIA, J., dissenting) (slip op. 8), cannot suffice to abrogate the constitutional rights of individuals.

Similarly, this Court's prior decisions have not allowed a government to rely on mere speculation about potential harms, but have demanded evidentiary support for a refusal to allow a religious exception. See *Thomas*, 450 U.S., at 719 (rejecting State's reasons for refusing religious exemption, for lack of "evidence in the record"); *Yoder*, 406 U.S., at 224–229 (rejecting State's argument concerning the dangers of a religious exemption as speculative, and unsupported by the record); *Sherbert v. Verner*, 374 U.S. 398, 407 (1963) ("there is no proof whatever to warrant such fears . . . as those which the [State] now advance[s]"). In this case, the State's justification for refusing to recognize an exception to its criminal laws for religious peyote use is entirely speculative.

The State proclaims an interest in protecting the health and safety of its citizens from the dangers of unlawful drugs. It offers, however, no evidence that the religious use of peyote has ever harmed anyone.[4] The factual findings of other courts cast doubt on the State's assumption that religious use of peyote is harmful. See *State v. Whittingham*, 19 Ariz. App. 27, 30, 504 P. 2d 950, 953 (1973) ("the State failed to prove that the quantities of peyote used in the sacraments of the Native American Church are sufficiently harmful to the health and welfare of the participants so as to permit a legitimate intrusion under the State's police power"); *People v. Woody*, 61 Cal. 2d 716, 722–723,

---

[3] The only reported case in which the State of Oregon has sought to prosecute a person for religious peyote use is *State v. Soto*, 21 Ore. App. 794, 537 P. 2d 142 (1975), cert. denied, 424 U.S. 955 (1976).
[4] This dearth of evidence is not surprising, since the State never asserted this health and safety interest before the Oregon courts; thus, there was no opportunity for factfinding concerning the alleged dangers of peyote use. What has now become the State's principal argument for its view that the criminal prohibition is enforceable against religious use of peyote rests on no evidentiary foundation at all.

394 P. 2d 813, 818 (1964) ("as the Attorney General . . . admits, the opinion of scientists and other experts is 'that peyote . . . works no permanent deleterious injury to the Indian' ").

The fact that peyote is classified as a Schedule I controlled substance does not, by itself, show that any and all uses of peyote, in any circumstance, are inherently harmful and dangerous. The Federal Government, which created the classifications of unlawful drugs from which Oregon's drug laws are derived, apparently does not find peyote so dangerous as to preclude an exemption for religious use.[5] Moreover, other Schedule I drugs have lawful uses. See *Olsen v. Drug Enforcement Admin.,* ——— U.S. App. D.C. ———, ———, n. 4, 878 F. 2d 1458, 1463, n. 4 (medical and research uses of marijuana).

The carefully circumscribed ritual context in which respondents used peyote is far removed from the irresponsible and unrestricted recreational use of unlawful drugs.[6] The Native American Church's internal restrictions on, and supervision of, its members' use of peyote substantially obviate the State's health and safety concerns. See *Olsen,* ———, U.S. App. D.C., at ———, 878 F. 2d, at 1467 ("The Administrator [of DEA] finds that . . . the Native American Church's use of peyote is isolated to specific ceremonial occasions," and so "an accommodation can be made for a religious organization which uses peyote in circumscribed ceremonies" (quoting DEA Final Order)); *id.,* at ———, 878 F. 2d, at 1464 ("for members of the Native American Church, use of peyote outside the ritual is sacrilegious"); *Woody,* 61 Cal. 2d, at 721, 394 P. 2d, at 817 ("to use peyote for nonreligious purposes is sacrilegious"); R. Julien, A Primer of Drug Action 148 (3d ed. 1981) ("peyote is seldom abused by members of the Native American Church"); J. Slotkin, The Peyote Way, in Teachings from the American Faith (D. Tedlock & B. Tedlock, eds., 1975) 96, 104 ("the Native American Church . . . refuses to permit the presence of curiosity seekers at its rites, and vigorously opposes the sale or use of Peyote for non-sacramental purposes"); R. Bergman, Navajo Peyote Use: Its Apparent Safety, 128 Am. J. Psychiatry 695 (1971) (Bergman).[7]

---

[5] See 21 CFR § 1307.31 (1989) ("The listing of peyote as a controlled substance in Schedule I does not apply to the nondrug use of peyote in bona fide religious ceremonies of the Native American Church, and members of the Native American Church so using peyote are exempt from registration. Any person who manufactures peyote for or distributes peyote to the Native American Church, however, is required to obtain registration annually and to comply with all other requirements of law"); see *Olsen v. Drug Enforcement Admin.,* ——— U.S. App. D.C. ———, ———, 878 F. 2d 1458, 1463–1464 (1989) (explaining DEA's rationale for the exception).

Moreover, 23 States, including many that have significant Native American populations, have statutory or judicially crafted exemptions in their drug laws for religious use of peyote. See *Smith v. Employment Division,* 307 Ore. 68, 73, n. 2, 763 P. 2d 146, 148, n. 2 (1988). Although this does not prove that Oregon must have such an exception too, it is significant that these States, and the Federal Government, all find their (presumably compelling) interests in controlling the use of dangerous drugs compatible with an exemption for religious use of peyote. Cf. *Boos v. Barry,* 485 U.S. 312, 329 (1988) (finding that an ordinance restricting picketing near a foreign embassy was not the least restrictive means of serving the asserted government interest; existence of an analogous, but more narrowly drawn, federal statute showed that "a less restrictive alternative is readily available").

[6] In this respect, respondents' use of peyote seems closely analogous to the sacramental use of wine by the Roman Catholic Church. During Prohibition, the Federal Government exempted such use of wine from its general ban on possession and use of alcohol. See National Prohibition Act, Title II, § 3, 41 Stat. 308. However compelling the Government's then general interest in prohibiting the use of alcohol may have been, it could not plausibly have asserted an interest sufficiently compelling to outweigh Catholics' right to take communion.

Moreover, just as in *Yoder,* the values and interests of those seeking a religious exemption in this case are congruent, to a great degree, with those the State seeks to promote through its drug laws. See *Yoder,* 406 U.S., at 224, 228–229 (since the Amish accept formal schooling up to 8th grade, and then provide "ideal" vocational education, State's interest in enforcing its law against the Amish is "less substantial than . . . for children generally"); *id.,* at 238 (WHITE, J., concurring opinion). Not only does the Church's doctrine forbid nonreligious use of peyote; it also generally advocates self-reliance, familial responsibility, and abstinence from alcohol. See Brief for Association on American Indian Affairs, et al., as *Amici Curiae* 3334 (the Church's "ethical code" has four parts: brotherly love, care of family, self-reliance, and avoidance of alcohol (quoting from the Church membership card)); *Olsen,* ——— U.S. App. D.C., at ———, 878 F. 2d, at 1464 (the Native American Church, "for all purposes other than the special, stylized ceremony, reinforced the state's prohibition"); *Woody,* 61 Cal. 2d, at 721–722, n. 3, 394 P. 2d, at 818, n. 3 ("most anthropological authorities hold Peyotism to be a positive, rather than negative, force in the lives of its adherents . . . the church forbids the use of alcohol . . ."). There is considerable evidence that the spiritual and social support provided by the Church has been effective in combatting the tragic effects of alcoholism on the Native American population. Two noted experts on peyotism, Dr. Omer C. Stewart and Dr. Robert Bergman, testified by affidavit to this effect on behalf of respondent Smith before the Employment Appeal Board. Smith Tr., Exh. 7; see also E. Anderson, Peyote: The Divine Cactus 165166 (1980) (research by Dr. Bergman suggests "that the religious use of peyote seemed to be directed in an ego-strengthening direction with an emphasis on interpersonal relationships where each individual is assured of his own significance as well as the support of the group;" many people have " 'come through difficult crises with the help of this religion. . . . It provides real help in seeing themselves not as people whose place and way in the world is gone, but as people whose way can be strong enough to change and meet new challenges' " (quoting Bergman, at 698)); P. Pascarosa and S. Futterman, Ethno-psychedelic Therapy for Alcoholics: Observations in the Peyote Ritual of the Native American Church, 8 (No. 3) J. of Psychedelic Drugs 215 (1976) (religious peyote use has been helpful in overcoming alcoholism); B. Albaugh and P. Anderson, Peyote in the Treatment of Alcoholism among American Indians, 131:11 Am. J. Psychiatry 1247, 1249 (1974) ("the philosophy, teachings, and format of the [Native American Church] can be of great benefit to the Indian alcoholic"); see generally O. Stewart, Peyote Religion 75 *et seq.* (1987) (noting frequent observations, across many tribes and periods in history, of correlation between peyotist religion and abstinence from alcohol). Far from promoting the lawless and irresponsible use of drugs, Native American Church members' spiritual code exemplifies values that Oregon's drug laws are presumably intended to foster.

The State also seeks to support its refusal to make an exception for religious use of peyote by invoking its interest in abolishing drug trafficking. There is, however,

---

[7] The use of peyote is, to some degree, self-limiting. The peyote plant is extremely bitter, and eating it is an unpleasant experience, which would tend to discourage casual or recreational use. See *State v. Whittingham,* 19 Ariz. App. 27, 30, 504 P. 2d 950, 953 (1973) ("peyote can cause vomiting by reason of its bitter taste"); E. Anderson, Peyote: The Divine Cactus 161 (1980) ("[T]he eating of peyote usually is a difficult ordeal in that nausea and other unpleasant physical manifestations occur regularly. Repeated use is likely, therefore, only if one is a serious researcher or is devoutly involved in taking peyote as part of a religious ceremony"); Slotkin, The Peyote Way, at 98 ("many find it bitter, inducing indigestion or nausea").

practically no illegal traffic in peyote. See *Olsen,* ——— U.S. App. D.C., at ———, ———, 878 F. 2d, at 1463, 1467 (quoting DEA Final Order to the effect that total amount of peyote seized and analyzed by federal authorities between 1980 and 1987 was 19.4 pounds; in contrast, total amount of marijuana seized during that period was over 15 million pounds). Also, the availability of peyote for religious use, even if Oregon were to allow an exemption from its criminal laws, would still be strictly controlled by federal regulations, see 21 U.S.C. §§ 821823 (registration requirements for distribution of controlled substances); 21 CFR § 1307.31 (1989) (distribution of peyote to Native American Church subject to registration requirements), and by the State of Texas, the only State in which peyote grows in significant quantities. See Texas Health & Safety Code, § 481.111 (1990); Texas Admin. Code, Tit. 37, pt. 1, ch. 13, Controlled Substances Regulations, §§ 13.3513.41 (1989); *Woody,* 61 Cal. 2d, at 720, 394 P. 2d, at 816 (peyote is "found in the Rio Grande Valley of Texas and northern Mexico"). Peyote simply is not a popular drug; its distribution for use in religious rituals has nothing to do with the vast and violent traffic in illegal narcotics that plagues this country.

Finally, the State argues that granting an exception for religious peyote use would erode its interest in the uniform, fair, and certain enforcement of its drug laws. The State fears that, if it grants an exemption for religious peyote use, a flood of other claims to religious exemptions will follow. It would then be placed in a dilemma, it says, between allowing a patchwork of exemptions that would hinder its law enforcement efforts, and risking a violation of the Establishment Clause by arbitrarily limiting its religious exemptions. This argument, however, could be made in almost any free exercise case. See Lupu, Where Rights Begin: The Problem of Burdens on the Free Exercise of Religion, 102 Harv. L. Rev. 933, 947 (1989) ("Behind every free exercise claim is a spectral march; grant this one, a voice whispers to each judge, and you will be confronted with an endless chain of exemption demands from religious deviants of every stripe"). This Court, however, consistently has rejected similar arguments in past free exercise cases, and it should do so here as well. See *Frazee v. Illinois Dept. of Employment Security,* ——— U.S. ———, ——— (1989) (slip op. 6) (rejecting State's speculation concerning cumulative effect of many similar claims); *Thomas,* 450 U.S., 719 (same); *Sherbert,* 374 U.S., at 407.

The State's apprehension of a flood of other religious claims is purely speculative. Almost half the States, and the Federal Government, have maintained an exemption for religious peyote use for many years, and apparently have not found themselves overwhelmed by claims to other religious exemptions.[8] Allowing an exemption for religious

---

[8] Over the years, various sects have raised free exercise claims regarding drug use. In no reported case, except those involving claims of religious peyote use, has the claimant prevailed. See, *e. g., Olsen v. Iowa,* 808 F. 2d 652 (CA8 1986) (marijuana use by Ethiopian Zion Coptic Church); *United States v. Rush,* 738 F. 2d 497 (CA1 1984), cert. denied, 470 U.S. 1004 (1985) (same); *United States v. Middleton,* 690 F. 2d 820 (CA11 1982), cert. denied, 460 U. S. 1051 (1983) (same); *United States v. Hudson,* 431 F. 2d 468 (CA5 1970), cert. denied, 400 U.S. 1011 (1971) (marijuana and heroin use by Moslems); *Leary v. United States,* 383 F. 2d 851 (CA5 1967), rev'd on other grounds, 395 U.S. 6 (1969) (marijuana use by Hindu); *Commonwealth v. Nissenbaum,* 404 Mass. 575, 536 N. E. 2d 592 (1989) (marijuana use by Ethiopian Zion Coptic Church); *State v. Blake,* ——— Haw. App. ———, 695 P. 2d 336 (1985) (marijuana use in practice of Hindu Tantrism); *Whyte v. United States,* 471 A. 2d 1018 (D.C. App. 1984) (marijuana use by Rastafarian); *State v. Rocheleau,* 142 Vt. 61, 451 A. 2d 1144 (1982) (marijuana use by Tantric Buddhist); *State v. Brashear,* 92 N. M. 622, 593 P. 2d 63 (1979) (marijuana use by nondenominational Christian); *State v. Randall,* 540 S. W. 2d 156 (Mo. App. 1976) (marijuana, LSD, and hashish use by Aquarian Brotherhood Church). See generally Annotation, Free Exercise of Religion as Defense to Prosecution for Narcotic or Psychedelic Drug Offense, 35 A. L. R. 3d 939 (1971 and Supp. 1989).

peyote use would not necessarily oblige the State to grant a similar exemption to other religious groups. The unusual circumstances that make the religious use of peyote compatible with the State's interests in health and safety and in preventing drug trafficking would not apply to other religious claims. Some religions, for example, might not restrict drug use to a limited ceremonial context, as does the Native American Church. See, *e. g., Olsen,* ——— U.S. App. D. C., at ———, 878 F. 2d, at 1464 ("the Ethiopian Zion Coptic Church . . . teaches that marijuana is properly smoked 'continually all day' "). Some religious claims, see n. 8, *supra,* involve drugs such as marijuana and heroin, in which there is significant illegal traffic, with its attendant greed and violence, so that it would be difficult to grant a religious exemption without seriously compromising law enforcement efforts.[9] That the State might grant an exemption for religious peyote use, but deny other religious claims arising in different circumstances, would not violate the Establishment Clause. Though the State must treat all religions equally, and not favor one over another, this obligation is fulfilled by the uniform application of the "compelling interest" *test* to all free exercise claims, not by reaching uniform *results* as to all claims. A showing that religious peyote use does not unduly interfere with the State's interests is "one that probably few other religious groups or sects could make," *Yoder,* 406 U.S., at 236; this does not mean that an exemption limited to peyote use is tantamount to an establishment of religion. See *Hobbie v. Unemployment Appeals Comm'n of Fla.,* 480 U.S. 136, 144–145 (1987) ("the government may (and sometimes must) accommodate religious practices and . . . may do so without violating the Establishment Clause"); *Yoder,* 406 U.S., at 220–221 ("Court must not ignore the danger that an exception from a general [law] . . . may run afoul of the Establishment Clause, but that danger cannot be allowed to prevent any exception no matter how vital it may be to the protection of values promoted by the right of free exercise"); *id.,* at 234, n. 22.

III

Finally, although I agree with JUSTICE O'CONNOR that courts should refrain from delving into questions of whether, as a matter of religious doctrine, a particular practice is "central" to the religion, *ante,* at 16, I do not think this means that the courts must turn a blind eye to the severe impact of a State's restrictions on the adherents of a minority religion. Cf. *Yoder,* 406 U.S., at 219 (since "education is inseparable from and part of the basic tenets of their religion . . . [just as] baptism, the confessional, or a sabbath may be for others," enforcement of State's compulsory education law would "gravely endanger if not destroy the free exercise of respondents' religious beliefs").

Respondents believe, and their sincerity has *never* been at issue, that the peyote plant embodies their deity, and eating it is an act of worship and communion. Without peyote, they could not enact the essential ritual of their religion. See Brief for Association on American Indian Affairs, et al., as *Amici Curiae* 5–6 ("To the members, peyote is consecrated with powers to heal body, mind and spirit. It is a teacher; it teaches the way to spiritual life through living in harmony and balance with the forces of the Creation. The rituals are an integral part of the life process. They embody a form of worship in which the sacrament Peyote is the means for communicating with the Great Spirit"). See also Stewart, Peyote Religion, at 327330 (description of peyote ritual); T. Hillerman, People of Darkness 153 (1980) (description of Navajo peyote ritual).

---

[9] Thus, this case is distinguishable from *United States v. Lee,* 455 U.S. 252 (1982), in which the Court concluded that there was "no principled way" to distinguish other exemption claims, and the "tax system could not function if denominations were allowed to challenge the tax system because tax payments were spent in a manner that violates their religious belief." 455 U.S., at 260.

If Oregon can constitutionally prosecute them for this act of worship, they, like the Amish, may be "forced to migrate to some other and more tolerant region." *Yoder*, 406 U.S., at 218. This potentially devastating impact must be viewed in light of the federal policy—reached in reaction to many years of religious persecution and intolerance—of protecting the religious freedom of Native Americans. See American Indian Religious Freedom Act, 92 Stat. 469, 42 U.S.C. § 1996 ("it shall be the policy of the United States to protect and preserve for American Indians their inherent right of freedom to believe, express, and exercise the traditional religions . . ., including but not limited to access to sites, use and possession of sacred objects, and the freedom to worship through ceremonials and traditional rites").[10] Congress recognized that certain substances, such as peyote, "have religious significance because they are sacred, they have power, they heal, they are necessary to the exercise of the rites of the religion, they are necessary to the cultural integrity of the tribe, and, therefore, religious survival." H. R. Rep. No. 95–1308, p. 2 (1978).

The American Indian Religious Freedom Act, in itself, may not create rights enforceable against government action restricting religious freedom, but this Court must scrupulously apply its free exercise analysis to the religious claims of Native Americans, however unorthodox they may be. Otherwise, both the First Amendment and the stated policy of Congress will offer to Native Americans merely an unfulfilled and hollow promise.

IV

For these reasons, I conclude that Oregon's interest in enforcing its drug laws against religious use of peyote is not sufficiently compelling to outweigh respondents' right to the free exercise of their religion. Since the State could not constitutionally enforce its criminal prohibition against respondents, the interests underlying the State's drug laws cannot justify its denial of unemployment benefits. Absent such justification, the State's regulatory interest in denying benefits for religiously motivated "misconduct," see *ante*, at 2, is indistinguishable from the state interests this Court has rejected in *Frazee, Hobbie, Thomas,* and *Sherbert*. The State of Oregon cannot, consistently with the Free Exercise Clause, deny respondents unemployment benefits.

I dissent.

---

[10] See Report to Congress on American Indian Religious Freedom Act of 1978, pp. 1–8 (1979) (history of religious persecution); Barsh, The Illusion of Religious Freedom for Indigenous Americans, 65 Ore. L. Rev. 363, 369–374 (1986).

Indeed Oregon's attitude toward respondents' religious peyote use harkens back to the repressive federal policies pursued a century ago:

"In the government's view, traditional practices were not only morally degrading, but unhealthy. 'Indians are fond of gatherings of every description,' a 1913 public health study complained, advocating the restriction of dances and 'sings' to stem contagious diseases. In 1921, the Commissioner of Indian Affairs Charles Burke reminded his staff to punish any Indian engaged in 'any dance which involves . . . the reckless giving away of property . . . frequent or prolonged periods of celebration . . . in fact, any disorderly or plainly excessive performance that promotes superstitious cruelty, licentiousness, idleness, danger to health, and shiftless indifference to family welfare.' Two years later, he forbid Indians under the age of 50 from participating in any dances of any kind, and directed federal employees 'to educate public opinion' against them." *Id.*, at 370–371 (footnotes omitted).

BIBLIOGRAPHIC NOTES

This chapter's first section hinted that western civilization is just now making a quantum change in its conception of politics and community. But if I am to practice what I preach, I should not pretend that I can prove that truth to you objectively. I can only make it easier for you to imagine what a less destructive politics could be. I can make that case only by putting many pieces of our experience together and suggesting that together they point strongly in that direction. I mentioned above that the environmental movement and the collapse of East–West ideological tensions point in this direction. To strengthen the case we might add these additional pieces of experience:

The feminist movement. See, for example, Marilyn French, *Beyond Power* (1985), which suggests that we should and can shift our conception of the moral basis of law and government from the morality of power to a morality of pleasure. The morality of pleasure is not a hedonistic call for partying on. Rather, it substitutes satisfying our deepest needs in place of complying with the law as the primary goal of collective action.

The Alternative Dispute Resolution movement in law itself. This movement's values draw on feminist theory. The works of Carrie Menkel-Meadow help link feminist literature and new ways of thinking about dispute resolution. See her "Portia in a Different Voice: Speculations on a Woman's Lawyering Process." (1985).

Persistently popular themes in the arts. As I complete this manuscript, American public television has just shown on four successive nights Richard Wagner's four-opera cycle, "Der Ring des Niebelungen." This magnificent work operates on many levels, but its political level unambiguously condemns all familiar, power-based theories of western politics and religion. At just the same time, the rap music of the group Public Enemy, whose political messages are as powerful for its audience as Wagner's are for his, penetrated mainstream consciousness. See Frank Owen, "Public Service" (1990).

The increasingly open criticisms of contemporary American politics from journalists of differing political colors. Compare, for example, George Will's "Come Home, America, Part 2" (1990) and Michael Kinsley's "Iranamok Finale" (1990). Kinsley reminds us that we hunger for examples of people who accept responsibility for their choices. Summarizing the John Poindexter trial, he wrote, "Responsibility is like a hot potato that gets passed around but is always magically in the hands of whoever isn't the focus of attention at the moment."

Finally, the broadening move in this direction in mainstream academic writing itself. In philosophy, compare Harold Bloom's *Ruin the Sacred Truths: Poetry and Belief from the Bible to the Present* (1989) with the growing popularity of the works of Georges Bataille summarized lucidly by Alexander Nehamas's "The Attraction of Repulsion" (1989). Or see Paul Feyerabend's *Farewell to Reason* (1988). In legal academic writing, the work of James Boyd White (1984 and 1985) is exceptionally suggestive. You might also want to consult my previous discussion of the academic schools of thought that support the position I have taken here. These include American pragmatism (particularly in the writings of Oliver Wendell Holmes, Jr., William James, and John Dewey), modern liberalism (particularly Owen Fiss and Ronald Dworkin), postmodern philosophies of Stanley Fish, Richard Rorty, and Richard Bernstein, and the recent works of Mark Tushnet, Duncan Kennedy, Robert Gordon, Paul Brest, and their fellow members of the critical legal studies movement. See my *Contemporary Constitutional Lawmaking: The Supreme Court and the Art of Politics* (1985). I wish I had known better then the work of Kenneth Burke, which extends Wittgenstein's perspective that language is itself action. See for starters Grieg Henderson, *Kenneth Burke: Literature and Language as Symbolic Action* (1988). Verbal expressions are actions. Their power as actions succeeds or fails in relation to the dramatic and poetic quality of language itself. This language saves us from the neutralizing and demoralizing effects of technology and bureaucracy. Two very recent works criticizing the rhetoric of rights and of adversariness in conventional American legal discourse are Neal Milner's "Rights Discourse and Policy Making: How Rights Talk Impoverishes and Enables" (1990) and Robert Kagan, "Adversarial Legalism and American Government" (1990). These essays have not yet been published, but they should be available by the time you read this book.

This chapter has also drawn upon:

Charles Norris Cochrane, *Christianity and Classical Culture* (1957) which explains how Augustine, by accepting his limitations and his sinfulness and by seeking a personal rule of life, helped overcome the classical impulse to look beyond individuals to nature's objective truths. Martha Nussbaum, *The Fragility of Goodness* (1986), a superb examination of the politics and arts in Greek culture. The quote is from her "Our Pasts, Our Selves" (1990). Rogers Smith, "The 'American Creed' and American Identity: The Limits of Liberal Citizenship in the United States" (1988). Philip Soper, *A Theory of Law* (1984). The Andrew Sullivan epigraph is from "Bookshelf" reviewing *The Voice of Liberal Learning: Michael Oakeshott on Education*, Timothy Fuller, ed., *The Wall Street Journal*, May 31, 1989, p.A-16. Charles Taylor, *Sources of the Self: The Making of the Modern Identity* (1989).

Bibliography

Alexander, Frank. (1986). "Beyond Positivism: A Theological Perspective," *Georgia Law Review* 20: 1089.

Alter, Robert. (1981). *The Art of Biblical Narrative* (New York: Basic Books).

Aquinas, Thomas. (1964). *Summa Theologiae* (New York: McGraw-Hill).

Arthur, John. (1989). *The Unfinished Constitution* (Belmont, CA: Wadsworth).

Ball, Milner. (1981). *The Promise of American Law* (Athens, GA: University of Georgia Press).

———— (1985). *Lying Down Together* (Madison, WI: University of Wisconsin Press).

Barber, Benjamin. (1989). "The Civic Mission of the University," *The Kettering Review*, (Fall 1989); 62.

Barber, Sotirios. (1984). *On What the Constitution Means* (Baltimore: Johns Hopkins University Press).

Berman, Harold. (1983). *Law and Revolution: The Formation of the Western Legal Tradition* (Cambridge, MA: Harvard University Press).

Bloom, Harold. (1989). *Ruin the Sacred Truths: Poetry and Belief from the Bible to the Present* (Cambridge, MA: Harvard University Press).

Bork, Robert. (1990). *The Tempting of America: The Political Seduction of the Law* (New York: Free Press).

Buber, Martin. (1960). *The Prophetic Faith* (New York: Harper & Row).

Buckley, Thomas, S.J. (1977). *Church and State in Revolutionary Virginia: 1776–1787* (Charlottesville: University Press of Virginia).

Carter, Lief. (1985). *Contemporary Constitutional Lawmaking: The Supreme Court and the Art of Politics* (Elmsford, NY: Pergamon).

Cochrane, Charles. (1957): *Christianity and Classical Culture* (Oxford: Oxford University Press).

Conrad, Stephen. (1988). "The Constitutionalism of the Common-Law Mind," *Law and Social Inquiry* 13: 619.

Costner, Herbert. (1989). *New Perspectives on Liberal Education* (Seattle: University of Washington Press).

Daube, David. (1969). *Studies in Biblical Law* (Hoboken, NJ: Ktav).

d'Errico, Peter. (1975). "The Law Is Terror Put Into Words," *Learning and the Law* (Fall 1975); 38.

Ehler, Sidney. (1957). *Twenty Centuries of Church and State: A Survey of Their Relations Past and Present* (Westminster, MD: Newman Press).

Feyerabend, Paul. (1987). *Farewell to Reason* (London: Verso).

Fish, Stanley. (1989). *Doing What Comes Naturally: Change, Rhetoric, and the Practice of Theory in Literary and Legal Studies* (Durham, NC: Duke University Press).

Fisher, Louis. (1990). *American Constitutional Law* (New York: McGraw-Hill).

French, Marilyn. (1985). *Beyond Power: On Women, Men, and Morals* (New York: Summit Books).

Fuller, Timothy, and Michael Oakeshott. (1989). *The Voice of Liberal Learning: Michael Oakeshott on Education* (New Haven: Yale University Press).

Geertz, Clifford. (1973). *Interpretation of Culture* (New York: Basic Books).

Gierke, Otto Friedrich von. (1900, 1968). *Political Theories of the Middle Ages*. Trans. Frederic Maitland (Cambridge: Cambridge University Press).

Hanson, Robert, ed. (1986). *Science and Creation* (New York: Macmillan).

Hawking, Stephen. (1988). *A Brief History of Time* (New York: Bantam Books).

Henderson, Greig. (1988). *Kenneth Burke: Literature and Language as Symbolic Action* (Athens, GA: University of Georgia Press).

Howe, Mark DeWolfe. (1965). *The Garden and the Wilderness: Religion and Government in American Constitutional History* (Chicago: University of Chicago Press).

Jacob, Margaret. (1988). *The Cultural Meaning of the Scientific Revolution* (Philadelphia: Temple University Press).

Jefferson, Thomas (1907 ed.). *Autobiography; Writings*. Ed. Albert Bergh. (Washington, DC: Jefferson Memorial Association).

Kagan, Robert. (1990). "Adversarial Legalism and American Government," unpublished paper delivered at 1990 Annual Meeting of the Law and Society Association, Berkeley, CA, May 31.

Keen, Maurice. (1989). "A Master of the Middle Ages," *New York Review of Books* (18 May 1989): 47–49.

Kinsley, Michael. (1990). "TRB from Washington: Iranamok Finale," *The New Republic* (9 April 1990): 4.

Kitcher, Philip. (1982). *Abusing Science* (Cambridge, MA: MIT Press).

Krauthammer, Charles. (1981). "Science ex Machina," *The New Republic* (6 June 1981): 19–25.

LaRue, L. H. (1988). *Political Discourse* (Athens, GA: University of Georgia Press).

Lecler, Joseph. (1960). *Toleration and the Reformation*. Trans T. L. Westow. (New York: Association Press).

Le Goff, Jacques. (1988). *The Medieval Imagination*. Trans. Arthur Goldhammer. (Chicago: University of Chicago Press).

Levinson, Sanford. (1988). *Constitutional Faith* (Princeton: Princeton University Press).

Levy, Leonard. (1986). *The Establishment Clause: Religion and the First Amendment* (New York: Macmillan).

———— (1988). *Original Intent and the Framers' Constitution* (New York: Macmillan).

Locke, John. (1968 ed.). *Epistola de Tolerantia; A Letter on Toleration*. Ed. Raymond Klibansky and John Gough. (Oxford: Clarendon Press).

Mackenzie, Ross, ed. (1988). *Education for Ministry: Year One, Hebrew Scriptures*, vol. 1. (Sewanee, TN: University of the South).

Madison, James. (1962 ed.). *Papers*. Eds. William Hutchison and William Rachal (Chicago): University of Chicago Press.

Malbin, Michael. (1978). *Religion and Politics: The Intentions of the Authors of the First Amendment* (Washington, DC: American Enterprise Institute).

Marcus, Jacob. (1938). *The Jew in the Medieval World: A Source Book* (Cincinnati: Union of American Hebrew Congregations).

McCoy, Drew. (1989). *The Last of the Fathers: James Madison and the Republican Legacy* (Cambridge, England: Cambridge University Press).

McLoughlin, William. (1971). *New England Dissent, 1630–1833: The Baptists and Separation of Church and State* (Cambridge, MA: Harvard University Press).

Menkel-Meadow, Carrie. (1985). "Portia in a Different Voice," *Berkeley Women's Law Journal* 1: 39.

Miller, Perry. (1967). *Nature's Nation* (Cambridge, MA: Harvard University Press).

Milner, Neal. (1990). "Rights Discourse and Policy Making: How Rights Talk Impoverishes and Enables," unpublished paper presented at 1990 Annual Meeting of the Law and Society Association, Berkeley, CA, May 31.

Moore, Michael. (1987). "Precedent, Induction, and Ethical Generalization," in Laurence Goldstein, ed., *Precedent in Law* (Oxford: Clarendon Press).

Murphy, Walter, James Fleming, and William Harris (1986). *American Constitutional Interpretation* (Mineola, NY: Foundation Press).

Nehamas, Alexander. (1989). "The Attraction of Repulsion," *The New Republic* (23 October 1989): 31–36.

Neuhaus, Richard John. (1984). *The Naked Public Square* (Grand Rapids, MI: Eerdmans).

Noonan, John. (1987). *The Believer and the Powers That Are* (New York: Macmillan).

Nussbaum, Martha. (1990). "Our Past, Ourselves," *The New Republic* (9 April 1990): 27–34.

Owen, Frank. (1990). "Public Service," *Spin* (March 1990): 57–61, 86.

Pelikan, Jaroslav. (1968). *Spirit Versus Structure: Luther and the Institutions of the Church* (New York: Harper & Row).

———— (1984). *The Vindication of Tradition* (New Haven: Yale University Press).

Perry, Michael. (1988). *Morality, Politics and Law* (New York: Oxford University Press).

Pfeffer, Leo. (1975). *God, Caesar, and the Constitution* (Boston: Beacon Press).

Powell, H. Jefferson. (1985). "The Original Understanding of Original Intent," *Harvard Law Review* 98: 885.

———— (1987). "Rules for Originalists," *Virginia Law Review* 73: 659.

Rodell, Fred. (1939). *Woe Unto You Lawyers!* (New York: Reynal and Hitchcock).

Rorty, Richard. (1979). *Philosophy and the Mirror of Nature* (Princeton: Princeton University Press).

———— (1988). "That Old-Time Philosophy," *The New Republic* (4 April 1988): 28–33.

Sanford, John. (1987). *The Kingdom Within* (New York: Harper & Row).

Sherry, Suzanna. (1987). "The Founders' Unwritten Constitution," *University of Chicago Law Review* 54: 1127.

Smith, Michael. (1983). "The Special Place of Religion in the Constitution," *Supreme Court Review 1983*: 83.

Smith, Rogers. (1988). "The 'American Creed' and American Identity: The Limits of Liberal Citizenship in the United States," *Western Political Quarterly* 41: 225.

Soper, Philip. (1984). *A Theory of Law* (Cambridge, MA: Harvard University Press).

Stephenson, Carl, and Frederick Marcham, eds. (1937). *Sources of English Constitutional History* (New York: Harper & Row).

Stone, Christopher. (1985). "Introduction: Interpreting the Symposium," *Southern California Law Review* 58: 1.

Sullivan, Andrew. (1989). "Bookshelf," *The Wall Street Journal* (31 May 1989): A16.

Taylor, Charles. (1989). *Sources of the Self* (Cambridge, MA: Harvard University Press).

Tocqueville, Alexis de. (1875 ed.). *Democracy in America*. Trans. Henry Reeve (London: Longman, Green, Longman, and Roberts).

Tuchman, Barbara. (1978). *A Distant Mirror: The Calamitous Fourteenth Century* (New York: Ballantine Books).

——— (1987). "A Nation in Decline?" *New York Times Magazine* (20 September 1987): 52.

Tushnet, Mark. (1988). *Red, White, and Blue* (Cambridge, MA: Harvard University Press).

Updike, John. (1986). *Roger's Version* (New York: Knopf).

White, James Boyd. (1984). *When Words Lose Their Meaning* (Chicago: University of Chicago Press).

——— (1985). *Heracles' Bow* (Madison, WI: University of Wisconsin Press).

Will, George. (1990). "Come Home, America, Part 2," *Newsweek* (15 January 1990): 72.

Index

This index references all cases, sources, concepts, and other materials presented in the text proper, which includes the hypothetical conversations and lectures. This index does not reference cases, sources, concepts, and other materials contained either in the bibliographic notes or in the judicial opinions reprinted in the three major cases, *Edwards*, *Goldman*, and *Smith*.

Abington School District v. *Schempp*, 40
Act of Toleration of 1689, 82
Aesthetics. *See* Constitutional
   interpretation
Alexander, Frank, xiv, 112
Alter, Robert, 111
American Constitutional Interpretation
   (Murphy, Fleming, and Harris), xii
Amish. *See Wisconsin* v. *Yoder*
Anderson v. *Laird*, 26
Anti-Semitism. *See* Jews, Religious
   persecution
Aquinas, Thomas, 95–96
Aristotle, 95–96, 105–106, 123
Augustine, 96, 121

"Balanced Treatment" act, 5, 36,
   40–41
  history, 68–69

Ball, Milner, xiv, 113
Barber, Benjamin, xi
Barber, Sotirios, xii
Becket, Thomas, 77–78
Berman, Harold, 86
Bible. *See* Holy Bible
Biblical interpretation, 3–4, 109–113.
   See also Constitutional
   interpretation, Religion
Black, Charles, xii
Black, Hugo, 39–41
Board of Education v. *Mergens*, 4
Bob Jones University v. *United States*, 29
Bork, Robert, 2, 29, 85–86
Braunfield v. *Brown*, 29
Brennan, William, 8, 35, 40, 75, 103,
   122–123
Brown v. *Glines*, 29
Bubonic plague, 78

Cantwell v. *Connecticut*, 26, 30
Chappell v. *Wallace*, 29
Charlemagne, Emperor, 76
Christianity. *See also* Holy Bible,
    Religion
    and development of modern science,
    94–99
    early history, 75–82
    foundation for U.S. constitution,
    88–92
    fundamentalism in, 68–69, 99–102
Cochrane, Charles, 121
Coherence, xiii, 98–102. *See also*
    Constitutional interpretation,
    Political virtue
Communication. *See* Political virtue
Community. *See also* Political virtue
    constituted discursively, 73, 103–106
    constituted upon shared values, 86
Congress
    and overturning of *Goldman* ruling,
    24–25
Conrad, Stephen, 90
Constantine, Emperor, 75
Constitutional interpretation. *See also*
    Interpretation
    and aesthetics, xii
    and biblical interpretation compared,
    108–113
    coherence theories, 98–99, 119–124
    conventional theories, xi, xii, 2–3
    historical method of, 74
    literal method of, 26, 73
    and narrativity, 117–120
    and natural law, 94–96
    role of precedents in, 26–34
Constitutional law
    applicability to military affairs, 29–30,
    121
    study by laity, xi–xiv, 6–8
Constitutional rights, 116–117
Copernicus, Nicholas, 79, 97
Creationism
    and Christian fundamentalism, 84
    litigation prior to *Edwards*, 40, 68–69.
    See also Scopes trial
    scientific evidence for and against,
    99–102
Crusades, 78

Dark Ages, 76
Darrow, Clarence, 84
Davis v. *Beason*, 28, 30
Declaration of Independence, 88
Diocletian, Emperor, 75
Douglas, William O., 37

Edwards v. *Aguillard*, xii, 5, 8, 26,
    35–72, 74, 84, 91, 122–123
Einstein, Albert, 102
Electoral representation
    and failure to limit oppression through
    law, 116–117
Elizabeth I, 80–81
Elwanger, Paul, 68–69, 72
Emerson, Ralph Waldo, 91
Employment Division v. *Smith*, 27, 117,
    124–148
Engel v. *Vitale*, 39–40
Epperson v. *Arkansas*, 40
d'Errico, Peter, 116
Establishment clause, 5, 8. *See also*
    First Amendment
    case law, 36–42
    consistent with government support of
    religion, 36–38
    history, 35
    modern interpretation of, 91
    and "wall of separation," 39
Estate of Thornton v. *Caldor*, 42
Everson v. *Board of Education*, 39

Faith
    same in science as in religion, 99–102
First Amendment, 5, 35–36. *See also*
    Establishment clause, Free exercise
    clause
    historical meaning of, 74, 87–90
    modern doctrine of, 90–91
Fish, Stanley, xi, xii
Flag Protection Act of 1989, 1
Flag Salute cases. *See Minersville* and
    West Virginia Board
Fortas, Abe, 40
Frankfurter, Felix, xiii, 91
Free exercise clause, 5, 8. *See also* First
    Amendment
    case law, 27–34

"compelling state interest" test, 31,
121
Fundamentalism. *See* Christianity

Galileo, 97–98
Geertz, Clifford, 102, 108
Gierke, Otto von, 77
Gillette v. *United States*, 29
Goldman v. *Weinberger*, xii, 5, 8, 34,
36, 42, 74–75, 84, 90–92, 120–123
Gorbachev, Mikhail, 92
Gregory the Great, 77

Hand, Learned, 109
Hawking, Stephen, 106
Heffron v. *International Society for
Krishna Consciousness*, 29
Hegel, Georg W. F., 6
Henry VIII, 79–81
Hitler, Adolph, 119
Hobbie v. *Unemployment Appeals
Commission*, 34
Holy Bible, 3–4, 95. *See also*
Christianity, Religion
contradictions within, 110–111
interpretation of, 96, 99–103, 105,
108–113
as narrative, 110–113, 120
political philosophy in, 91–92
Holy Trinity Church v. *United States*,
37, 40
Hundred Years' War, 78, 95
Hutchinson, Anne, 82

Intentions of Framers, 85. *See also*
Constitutional interpretation
Interpretation. *See also* Constitutional
interpretation
as form of political power, 3–5

Jackson, Robert, 31, 91, 120
Jacob, Margaret, 97
Japanese Americans
World War II internment of, 33
Jefferson, Thomas, 27, 88–89, 92
Letter to Danbury Baptists, 39
Jews. *See also* Religious persecution
persecution of, 36, 76, 78–79, 96;
endorsed by Martin Luther, 80–81

Joan of Arc, 78
Judicial review
constitutional authority for, 1–2
political significance of, 2
Justice. *See* Law, Political virtue

Katcoff v. *Marsh*, 38
Keen, Maurice, 76
Khomeini, the Ayatollah, 4
Kitcher, Philip, 105
Krauthammer, Charles, 102

Law. *See also* Constitutional law,
Religion, Political virtue
as communal language, xii, xiii,
117–120
as political oppression, 116–117,
123–124
theory and practice contrasted,
xii
Lecker, Joseph, 79
Lecler, Joseph, 81
LeGoff, Jacques, 76–77
Lemon v. *Kurtzman*, 41, 73
"*Lemon*" test, 41–42, 70, 91, 122
Levinson, Sanford, xiv, 8
Liberalism, 103, 116–117
history of, 82–85
Christian foundations of, 86–88
Locke, John, 83, 85, 96, 116, 119, 121
Christianity's influence upon, 87,
111–112
influence on Madison, 88
Lovejoy, Arthur, 1, 5
Luther, Martin, 79–81, 87, 96
Lynch v. *Donnelly*, 38, 40, 90

McCollum v. *Board of Education*, 39
McGowen v. *Maryland*, 37
Machiavelli, Nicolo, 79
McLean v. *Arkansas Board of
Education*, 68–69, 72, 123
Madison, James, 27, 82–83, 85
Christian beliefs of, 88–90
Memorial and Remonstrance, 88
Marbury v. *Madison*, 1–2
Marsh v. *Chambers*, 38
Mary Tudor (Bloody Mary), 80–81
Menno Simons, 81, 87

Michelangelo, 79
Middle Ages, 77–79
Minersville School District v. *Gobitis*,
    31
Moral philosophy, 102–106, 108
More, Thomas, 81
Moyers, Bill, 85
Mueller v. *Allen*, 38
Murphy, Walter
    Murphy, Fleming, and Harris,
    *American Constitutional
    Interpretation*, xii

Narrativity. *See* Constitutional
    interpretation, Holy Bible, Political
    virtue
Natural law. *See* Constitutional
    interpretation, Philosophy
Nero, Emperor, 75
Neuhaus, Richard John, 110
Nietzsche, Friedrich, 3
Noonan, John, xiv, 8
Nussbaum, Martha, 117, 124

Oakeshott, Michael, 123
Old Testament. *See also* Holy Bible
    and American constitutional narrative,
    112–113
Orloff v. *Willoughby*, 29

Papal revolution, 79–80
Peace of Augsburg, 80
Pelikan, Jaroslav, 91
People against Ruggles, 36, 89
People v. *Woody*, 31
Perry, Michael, 8, 104–105
Peyote case. *See Employment Division*
Philosophy
    natural, 94–106
    Greek, 95
    medieval, 95–96
    of science, 96–102
    moral, 102–106, 108
Picasso, Pablo, xii, xiii
Pierce v. *Society of Sisters*, 30–31
Pluralism, 102–103
Political power
    three basic forms, 4–5, 120

Political virtue, 6, 84–92, 101–106,
    117–124
Powell, H. Jefferson, 85
Powell, Lewis, 123
Polygamy
    legal response to Mormon practice of,
    27–28, 30
Precedents. *See* Constitutional
    interpretation
Protestant Reformation, 7, 79
    impact on science, 97–98
Puritan movement, 81–82

Quakers, 89

Raphael, 79
Rawls, John, 106
Reagan, Ronald, 2, 119
Reformation. *See* Protestant Reformation
Rehnquist, William, 8, 10, 103,
    120–123
Religion, 6. *See also* Christianity, Holy
    Bible
    in American political history, 88–90
    and constitutional interpretation,
    108–113
    political role in general, 86–87
    and science, 94–102
    sectarianism within, 109
    similarities to law, xiii, 6,
    115–119
Religious persecution, 75–84, 119–120
Reynolds v. *United States*, 27–28, 30,
    33. *See also* Polygamy
Rodell, Fred, 108
Roe v. *Wade*, 4
Roman Empire, 75–76, 86
Romney v. *United States*, 28
Rorty, Richard, xi, xii
Rostker v. *Goldberg*, 29
Rushdie, Salman, 4

Sale, Roger, xiv
Sanford, John, 113
Scalia, Antonin, 8, 70–71, 73, 84,
    122–123
School Prayer cases. *See Abington* and
    Engel

Science
  philosophy of, 94–102
  and religion, 97–98, 108
  skepticism in, 98–102
Scopes trial ("monkey trial"), 40, 84, 100
Separation of church and state. *See also* Establishment clause, Religion
  at founding, 85
  scientific impetus for, 97–98
  Tocqueville's analysis of, 88
Shaw, George Bernard, 115–116
Sherbert v. *Verner*, 31–32, 34
Smith, Rogers, 116–117
Snake handling, 30
Soper, Philip, 118
Sullivan, Andrew, 115
Stone, Christopher, 8
Stone v. *Graham*, 41
Sunday closing laws, 37, 70–71

Taylor, Charles, 117
Texas v. *Johnson*, 1–2
Tocqueville, Alexis de, 88–90
Toleration Act of 1689, 83
Trial procedures, 42, 118
Tuchman, Barbara, 78
Tucker Act of 1887, 28

Tushnet, Mark, xi, 8, 123
"Two Swords" theory of medieval authority, 77

United States v. *Eichman*, 1–2
United States v. *Lee*, 29
United States v. *Macintosh*, 28
Updike, John, 3–4

Virginia statute on religious freedom, 27

Wallace v. *Jaffree*, 42
Walz v. *Tax Commission*, 37–38
West Virginia State Board of Education v. *Barnette*, 31, 33
White, James Boyd, xii
Williams, Roger, 83, 87
  letter to Town of Providence quoted, 83
Wisconsin v. *Yoder*, 28, 32
Witte, John, xiv
Wittgenstein, Ludwig von, 94

Zorach v. *Clauson*, 37
Zumwalt, Elmo, 24
Zwingli, Huldryk, 82